CONTENTS

OSBORNE REVISE!

ACCA

ACCA F1 Accountant in Business

NOTES

Published by Osborne Books Limited

Unit 2
The Business Centre
Molly Millars Lane
Wokingham
Berkshire RG41 2QZ

Tel 01905 748071

Email books@osbornebooks.co.uk

Website www.osbornebooks.co.uk

Printed and bound in Great Britain.

British Library Cataloguing in Publication Data

A catalogue record for this book is available from the British Library

ISBN: 978-1-911198-21-5

HOW TO USE THESE *ACCA Notes*

These *ACCA Notes* have been designed to help you to:

- **Renew** your approach to syllabus areas that might not have been clear first time around. Use them to supplement your learning and to help you to clarify details of the syllabus of which you are unsure. It is easy to look things up using the detailed index and contents page and find quickly the topic you need help with

- **Refresh** topics you have covered before but may have forgotten. If it is a while since you studied a topic which underpins a higher level subject that you now need to study, for example, use them as a refresher tool to remind yourself of what you have already learnt

- **Revise** and make the best use of your time before your examinations. Take advantage of the summarised topics, learning summaries, summary diagrams, key points, definitions and exam tips to support your revision in the critical period leading up to your real exam.

PREPARING FOR THE EXAM

To pass your exam you need an understanding of the syllabus and exam technique is vital. These *ACCA Notes* follow the syllabus with succinct coverage, offering tips on how to get the best results in the exam.

ACCA Notes – ICONS

LEARNING SUMMARY

The 'learning summary' provides details of the key learning objectives of each section of content.

DEFINITION

The 'definition' boxes highlight and explain key terms.

KEY POINT

The 'key point' boxes emphasise key points which are fundamental to your understanding of the syllabus.

Do you understand?
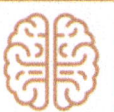

The 'do you understand' boxes contain short form questions which are not necessarily exam style, but which test that you have understood the core syllabus content before you progress onto exam style questions.

PAPER INFORMATION

The aim of ACCA Paper F1, Accountant in Business/FIA Diploma in Accounting and Business, Accountant in Business is to introduce knowledge and understanding of the business and its environment and the influence this has on how organisations are structured and on the role of the accounting and other key business functions in contributing to the efficient, effective and ethical management and development of an organisation and its people and systems.

SYLLABUS

A   THE BUSINESS ORGANISATION, ITS STAKEHOLDERS AND THE EXTERNAL ENVIRONMENT

(1)   The purpose and types of business organisation   Ch1

(a)   Define business organisations and explain why they are formed.

(b)   Describe common features of business organisations.

(c)   Outline how business organisations differ.

(d)   List the industrial and commercial sectors in which business organisations operate.

(e)   Identify the different types of business organisation and their main characteristics

    (i)   Commercial

    (ii)   Not-for-profit and cooperatives

    (iii)   Public sector

    (iv)   Non-governmental organisations and cooperatives.

(2)   Stakeholders in business organisations   Ch5

(a)   Define stakeholders and explain the agency relationship in business and how it may vary in different types of business organisation.   **Ch11**

(b)   Define internal, connected and external stakeholders and explain their impact on the organisation.

(c)   Identify the main stakeholder groups and the objectives of each group.

(d)   Explain how the different stakeholder groups interact with each other and how their objectives may conflict with each other.

(e)   Compare the power and influence of various stakeholder groups and how their needs should be accounted for, such as under the Mendelow framework.

(3)   Political and legal factors affecting business   Ch6

(a)   Explain how the political system and government policy affects the organisation.

(b)   Describe the sources of legal authority, including supra-national bodies, national and regional governments.

(c)   Explain how the law protects the employee and the implications of employment legislation for the manager and the organisation.

(d)   Identify the principles of data protection and security.

(e)   Explain how the law promotes and protects health and safety in the workplace.

(f)   Recognise the responsibility of the individual and organisation for compliance with laws on data protection, security and health and safety.

(g)   Outline principles of consumer protection such as sale of goods and simple contract.

(4) Macro-economic factors   **Ch7**

(a) Define macro-economic policy and explain its objectives.

(b) Explain the main determinants of the level of business activity in the economy and how variations in the level of business activity affect individuals, households and businesses.

(c) Explain the impact of economic issues on the individual, the household and the business:

    (i)   inflation

    (ii) unemployment

    (iii) stagnation

    (iv) international payments disequilibrium.

(d) Describe the main types of economic policy that may be implemented by government and supra-national bodies to maximise economic welfare.

(e) Recognise the impact of fiscal and monetary policy measures on the individual, the household and businesses.

(5) Micro economic factors   **Ch7**

(a) Define the concept of demand and supply for goods and services.

(b) Explain elasticity of demand and the impact of substitute and complementary goods.

(c) Explain the economic behaviour of costs in the short and long term.

(d) Define perfect competition, oligopoly, monopolistic competition and monopoly.

(6) Social and demographic factors   **Ch8**

(a) Explain the medium and long-term effects of social and demographic trends on business outcomes and the economy.

(b) Describe the impact of changes in social structure, values, attitudes and tastes on the organisation.

(c) Identify and explain the measures that governments may take in response to the medium and long-term impact of demographic change.

(7) Technological factors   **Ch8**

(a) Explain the effects of technological change on the organisation structure and strategy

(i) Downsizing

(ii) Delayering

(iii) Outsourcing.

(b) Describe the impact of information technology and information systems development on business processes.

(8) Environmental factors   **Ch8**

(a) List ways in which the business can affect or be affected by its physical environment.

(b) Describe ways in which businesses can operate more efficiently and effectively to limit damage to the environment.

(c) Identify the benefits of economic sustainability to a range of stakeholders.

(9)   Competitive factors   **Ch9**

(a)   Identify a business's strengths, weaknesses, opportunities and threats (SWOT) in a market and the main sources of competitive advantage.

(b)   Describe the activities of an organisation that affect its competitiveness: purchasing, production, marketing and service.

(c)   Explain the factors or forces that influence the level of competitiveness in an industry or sector using Porter's five forces model.

(d)   Identify the main elements within Porter's value chain and explain the meaning of a value network.

B   BUSINESS ORGANISATION STRUCTURE, FUNCTIONS AND GOVERNANCE

(1)   The formal and informal business   **Ch 3**

(a)   Explain the informal organisation and its relationship

       with the formal organisation.

(b)   Describe the impact of the formal organisation on the business.

(2)   Business organisation, structure and design   **Ch2**

(a)   Describe Mintzberg's components of the organisation and explain the different ways in which formal organisations may be structured: entrepreneurial, functional, matrix, divisional (geographical, by product, or by customer type), boundaryless (virtual, hollow or modular).

(b)   Explain basic organisational structure concepts:

       (i)   separation of ownership and management

       (ii)   separation of direction and management

       (iii)   span of control and scalar chain

       (iv)   tall and flat organisations

       (v)   outsourcing and offshoring

       (vi)   shared services approach.

(c)   Explain the characteristics of the strategic, tactical and operational levels in the organisation in the context of the Anthony hierarchy.

(d)   Explain centralisation and decentralisation and list their advantages and disadvantages.

(e)   Describe the roles and functions of the main departments in a business organisation:

       (i)   research and development

       (ii)   purchasing

       (iii)   production and direct service provision

       (iv)   marketing

       (v)   administration

       (vi)   finance.

(f)   Explain the role of marketing in an organisation

       (i)   the definition of marketing

       (ii)   the marketing mix

       (iii)   the relationship of the marketing plan to the strategic plan.

(3)   **Organisational culture in business**   Ch3

(a)   Define organisational culture.

(b)   Describe the factors that shape the culture of the organisation.

(c)   Explain the contribution made by writers on culture: Schein, Handy and Hofstede.

(4)   **Committees in business organisations**   Ch11

(a)   Explain the purposes of committees.

(b)   Describe the types of committee used by business organisations.

(c)   List the advantages and disadvantages of committees.

(d)   Explain the role of the Chair and Secretary of a committee.

(5)   **Governance and social responsibility in business**   Ch11

(a)   Explain the agency concept in relation to corporate governance.

(b)   Define corporate governance and social responsibility and explain their importance in contemporary organisations.

(c)   Explain the responsibility of organisations to maintain appropriate standards of corporate governance and corporate social responsibility.

(d)   Briefly explain the main recommendations of best practice in effective corporate governance: executive and non-executive directors, remuneration committees, audit committees and public oversight.

(e)   Explain how organisations take account of their social responsibility objectives through analysis of the needs of internal, connected and external stakeholders.

(f)   Identify the social and environmental responsibilities of business organisations to internal, external and connected stakeholders.

C   **ACCOUNTING AND REPORTING SYSTEMS, CONTROLS AND COMPLIANCE**

(1)   **The relationship between accounting and other business functions**   Ch15

(a)   Explain the relationship between accounting and other key functions within the business such as procurement, production and marketing.

(b)   Explain financial considerations in production and production planning.

(c)   Identify the financial issues associated with marketing.

(d)   Identify the financial costs and benefits of effective service provision.

(2)   **Accounting and finance functions within business**   Ch13

(a)   Explain the contribution of the accounting function to the formulation, implementation and control of the organisation's policies, procedures and performance.

(b)   Identify and describe the main financial accounting functions in business: recording financial information, codifying and processing financial information and preparing financial statements.

(c)   Identify and describe the main management accounting and performance management functions in business: recording and analysing costs and revenues, providing management accounting information for decision-making and planning and preparing budgets and exercising budgetary control.

(d)   Identify and describe the main finance and treasury functions: calculating and mitigating business tax liabilities, evaluating and obtaining finance, managing working capital and treasury and risk management.

(e)   Identify and describe the main audit and assurance roles in business: internal and external audit.   **Ch16**

(f)   Explain the main functions of the internal auditor and the external auditor and how they differ.   **Ch16**

(3)   Principles of law and regulation governing accounting and audit   **Ch12**

(a)   Explain basic legal requirements in relation to retaining and submitting proper records and preparing and auditing financial statements.

(b)   Explain the broad consequences of failing to comply with the legal requirements for maintaining and filing accounting records.

(c)   Explain how the international accountancy profession regulates itself through the establishment of reporting standards and their monitoring.

(4)   The sources and purpose of internal and external financial information, provided by business   **Ch13**

(a)   Explain the various business purposes for which the following financial information is required: the income statement, the statement of cash flows and the statement of financial position.

(b)   Describe the main purposes of the following types of management accounting reports:

    (i)   Cost schedules

    (ii)   Budgets

    (iii)   Variance reports.

(5)   Financial systems, procedures and related IT applications   Ch14

(a)   Identify an organisation's system requirements in relation to the objectives and policies of the organisation.

(b)   Describe the main financial systems used within an organisation:

    (i)   purchases and sales invoicing

    (ii)   payroll and credit control

    (iii)   cash and working capital management.

(c)   Explain why it is important to adhere to policies and procedures for handling clients' money.

(d)   Identify weaknesses, potential for error and inefficiencies in accounting systems.

(e)   Recommend improvements to accounting systems to prevent error and fraud and to improve overall efficiency.

(f)   Explain why appropriate controls are necessary in relation to business and IT systems and procedures.

(g)   Identify business uses of computers and IT software applications: spreadsheet applications, database systems and accounting packages. Describe the relative benefits and limitations of manual and automated financial systems that may be used within an organisation.

(6) **Internal controls, authorisation, security and compliance within business** Ch16

(a) Explain internal control and internal check.

(b) Explain the importance of internal financial controls in an organisation.

(c) Describe the responsibilities of management for internal financial control.

(d) Describe the features of effective internal financial control procedures in an organisation, including authorisation.

(e) Identify and describe the types of information technology and information systems used by the business organisation for internal control.

(f) Identify and describe features for protecting the security of IT systems and software within businesses.

(g) Describe general and application systems controls in business.

(7) **Fraud and fraudulent behaviour and their prevention in business** Ch17

(a) Explain the circumstances under which fraud is likely to arise.

(b) Identify different types of fraud in the organisation.

(c) Explain the implications of fraud for the organisation.

(d) Explain the role and duties of individual managers in the fraud detection and prevention process.

(e) Define the term 'money laundering'.

(f) Give examples of recognised offences under typical money laundering regulation.

(g) Identify methods for detecting and preventing money laundering and explain how suspicions of money laundering should be reported to the appropriate authorities.

D **LEADING AND MANAGING INDIVIDUALS AND TEAMS**

(1) **Leadership, management and supervision** Ch18

(a) Define leadership, management and supervision and explain the distinction between these terms.

(b) Explain the nature of management:

    (i) scientific/classical theories of management – Fayol, Taylor

    (ii) the human relations school – Mayo

    (iii) the functions of a manager – Mintzberg, Drucker.

(c) Explain the areas of managerial authority and responsibility.

(d) Explain the situational, functional and contingency approaches to leadership with reference to the theories of Adair, Fiedler, Bennis, Kotter and Heifetz.

(e) Describe leadership styles and contexts: using the models of Ashridge and Blake and Mouton.

(2) **Recruitment and selection of employees** Ch19

(a) Explain the importance of effective recruitment and selection to the organisation.

(b) Describe the recruitment and selection process and explain the stages in this process.

(c) Describe the roles of those involved in the recruitment and selection processes.

(d) Describe the methods through which organisations seek to meet their recruitment needs.

(e) Explain the advantages and disadvantages of different recruitment and selection methods.

(f) Explain the purposes of a diversity policy within the human resources plan.

(g) Explain the purposes and benefits of an equal opportunities policy within human resource planning and the practical steps that an organisation may take to ensure the effectiveness of its diversity and equal opportunities policy.

(3)   Individual and group behaviour in business organisations   Ch20

(a) Describe the main characteristics of individual and group behaviour.

(b) Outline the contributions of individuals and teams to organisational success.

(c) Identify individual and team approaches to work.

(4)   Team formation, development and management   Ch20

(a) Explain the differences between a group and a team.

(b) Define the purposes of a team.

(c) Explain the role of the manager in building the team and developing individuals within the team. Belbin's team role theories and Tuckman's theory of team development.

(d) List the characteristics of effective and ineffective teams.

(e) Describe tools and techniques that can be used to build the team and improve team effectiveness.

(5)   Motivating teams and individuals   Ch21

(a) Define motivation and explain its importance to the organisation, teams and individuals.

(b) Explain content and process theories of motivation: Maslow, Herzberg, McGregor and Vroom.

(c) Explain and identify types of intrinsic and extrinsic rewards.

(d) Explain how reward systems can be designed and implemented to motivate teams and individuals.

(6)   Learning and training at work   Ch22

(a) Explain the importance of learning and development in the workplace.

(b) Describe the learning process: Honey and Mumford, Kolb.

(c) Describe the role of the human resources department and individual managers in the learning process.

(d) Describe the training and development process: identifying needs, setting objectives, programme design, delivery and validation.

(e) Explain the terms 'training', 'development' and 'education' and the characteristics of each.

(f) List the benefits of effective training and development in the workplace.

(7) **Review and appraisal of individual performance**   **Ch23**

(a)   Explain the importance of performance assessment.

(b)   Explain how organisations assess the performance of human resources.

(c)   Define performance appraisal and describe its purposes.

(d)   Describe the performance appraisal process.

(e)   Explain the benefits of effective appraisal.

(f)   Identify the barriers to effective appraisal and how these may be overcome.

(g)   Explain how the effectiveness of performance appraisal may be evaluated.

E   **PERSONAL EFFECTIVENESS AND COMMUNICATION IN BUSINESS**

(1) **Personal effectiveness techniques**   **Ch24**

(a)   Explain the importance of time management.

(b)   Describe the barriers to effective time management and how they may be overcome.

(c)   Describe the role of information technology in improving personal effectiveness.

(2) **Consequences of ineffectiveness at work**   **Ch24**

(a)   Identify the main ways in which people and teams can be ineffective at work.

(b)   Explain how individual or team ineffectiveness can affect organisational performance.

(3) **Competence frameworks and personal development**   **Ch24**

(a)   Describe the features of a competence framework.

(b)   Explain how a competence framework underpins professional development needs.

(c)   Explain how personal and continuous professional development can increase personal effectiveness at work.

(d)   Explain the purpose and benefits of coaching, mentoring and counselling in promoting employee effectiveness.

(e)   Describe how a personal development plan should be formulated, implemented, monitored and reviewed by the individual.

(4) **Sources of conflict and techniques for conflict resolution and referral**   **Ch24**

(a)   Identify situations where conflict at work can arise.

(b)   Describe how conflict can affect personal and organisational performance.

(c)   Explain how conflict can be avoided.

(d)   Identify ways in which conflict can be resolved or referred.

| (5) | **Communicating in business** | **Ch25** |

(5)   **Communicating in business**   **Ch25**

(a)   Define communications and identify methods of communication used in the organisation and how they are used.

(b)   Explain how the type of information differs and the purposes for which it is applied at different levels of the organisation: strategic, tactical and operational.

(c)   List the attributes of good quality information.   **Ch4**

(d)   Explain a simple communication model: sender, message, receiver, feedback, noise.   **Ch25**

(e)   Explain formal and informal communication and their importance in the workplace and identify the consequences of ineffective communication.

(f)   Describe the attributes of effective communication, the barriers to effective communication and identify practical steps that may be taken to overcome them.

(g)   Describe the main methods and patterns of communication.

F   **PROFESSIONAL ETHICS IN ACCOUNTING AND BUSINESS**

(1)   **Fundamental principles of ethical behaviour**   **Ch10**

(a)   Define business ethics and explain the importance of ethics to the organisation and to the individual.

(b)   Describe and demonstrate the following principles from the IFAC code of ethics, using examples: Integrity, Objectivity, Professional competence, Confidentiality and Professional behaviour.

(c)   Describe organisational values which promote ethical behaviour using examples: Openness, Trust, Honesty, Respect, Empowerment and Accountability.

(d)   Explain the concept of acting in the public interest.

(2)   **The role of regulatory and professional bodies in promoting ethical and professional standards in the accountancy profession**   **Ch10**

(a)   Recognise the purpose of international and organisational codes of ethics and codes of conduct, IFAC, ACCA, etc.

(b)   Describe how professional bodies and regulators promote ethical awareness and prevent or punish illegal or unethical behaviour.

(c)   Identify the factors that distinguish a profession from other types of occupation.

(d)   Explain the role of the accountant in promoting ethical behaviour.

(e)   Recognise when and to whom illegal, or unethical conduct by anyone within the organisation should be reported.

(3)   **Corporate codes of ethics**   **Ch10**

(a)   Define corporate codes of ethics.

(b)   Describe the typical contents of a corporate code of ethics.

(c)   Explain the benefits of a corporate code of ethics to the organisation and its employees.

(4)   **Ethical conflicts and dilemmas**   **Ch10**

(a)   Describe situations where ethical conflicts can arise.

(b)   Identify the main threats to ethical behaviour.

(c)   Outline situations at work where ethical dilemmas may be faced.

(d)   List the main safeguards against ethical threats and dilemmas.

TOP 10 TIPS TO IMPROVE YOUR RESULT

Be organised and plan your study time – there are more tips on how to do this below.

'Mens sana in corpore sano' – prepare your body; sleep well and eat right as a healthy body leads to a healthy mind!

Study according to your learning style – different people have different learning styles. Some people are visual learners, some people prefer sound, some need physical motion – try out different methods to see what works best for you.

Try using a study buddy – this could be someone taking the same exam, or a friend or family member.

Revise knowledge efficiently – stay focused, stop procrastinating and don't let your mind wander.

Read questions very carefully – many students fail to answer the actual question set. Read the question once right through and then again more slowly. Make note of key words in the question when you read through it.

Ensure you know the structure of the exam – how many questions (and of what type) you will be expected to answer. During your revision, attempt all the different styles of questions you may be asked.

Be a good test-taker. Get lots of practice – the ACCA release sample assessments and practice CBE mock exams are available.

Read good newspapers and professional journals, especially ACCA's *Student Accountant* – this can give you a distinct advantage in the exam.

Adopt a positive mental attitude. You may have nerves and feel anxious but with the correct preparation and practice you can have confidence in your ability to succeed.

PLAN YOUR STUDY TIME

Decide which times of the week you will devote to revising.

Put the times you plan to revise onto a study plan for the weeks from now until the exam and set yourself targets for each period of revision, ensuring that you cover the whole syllabus.

If you are studying for more than one paper at a time, try to mix and match your subjects as this can help you to keep motivated and see each subject in its broader context.

When working through your course, compare your progress with your plan and, if you fall behind, re-plan your work (perhaps including extra sessions). If you are ahead, do some extra revision/practice questions.

EXTRA QUESTIONS

Practising exam standard questions is a critical part of your revision.

Specimen Exams and Practice Tests are available from
http://www.accaglobal.com/gb/en/student/exam-support-resources.html

and Exam Kits and Mock Exams in the style of the real exam can be obtained from

http://kaplan-publishing.kaplan.co.uk/acca-books/pages/acca-books.aspx.

1 The business organisation

The following topics are covered in this chapter:

- Business organisations and the reason they are formed
- Different types of organisation
- Sectors in which organisations operate

1.1 BUSINESS ORGANISATIONS

LEARNING SUMMARY

After studying this section you should be able to:

- define 'business organisations' and explain why they are formed
- describe common features of business organisations.

What is a business organisation?

Defining an organisation is difficult as there are many types of organisations set up to meet a variety of needs, such as clubs, schools, companies, charities and hospitals. What they have in common is summarised in the definition produced by Buchanan and Hczynski.

DEFINITION 'Organisations are social arrangements for the controlled performance of collective goals'.

Collective goals	e.g. a school will be organised differently to a company that aims to make profits.
Social arrangements	Someone working alone is not an organisation.
Controlled performance	An organisation will have systems and procedures in place to ensure group goals are achieved.

Note the three key aspects of this definition:
- Collective goals
- Social arrangements
- Controlled performance

Why do we need organisations?

KEY POINT 'Organisations enable people to share skills and knowledge, specialise and pool resources. This results in synergy where organisations can achieve more than individuals on their own.'

Questions testing this syllabus area often present a scenario which focusses on the benefits of forming an organisation in the context of the situation.

1.2 DIFFERENT TYPES OF ORGANISATION

LEARNING SUMMARY

After studying this section you should be able to:

- outline how business organisations differ.

Commercial organisations

KEY POINT Commercial (or profit-seeking) organisations see their main objective as maximising the wealth of their shareholders.

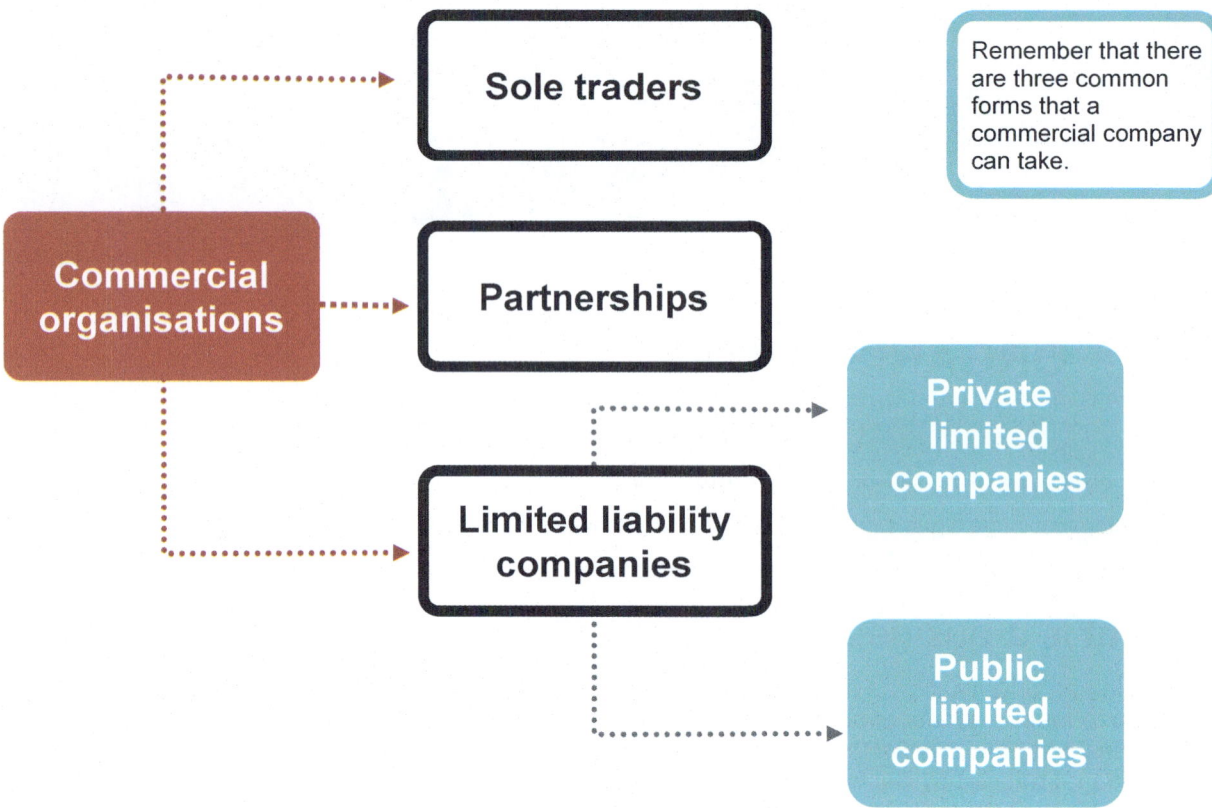

Remember that there are three common forms that a commercial company can take.

KEY POINT Sole traders and partnerships - the owners are not legally separate from the business itself. If the business is sued by a customer, the customer is actually suing the owner themselves.

Take note that alternative partnership structures also exist, such as Limited Liability Partnerships (LLPS) in the UK, where the business exists as a separate legal entity and the owners' liability is limited to the amount they have invested.

- **Sole traders** – the organisation is owned and run by one person.

- **Partnerships** – the organisation is owned and run by two or more individuals.

- **Limited liability companies** – a company has a separate legal identity to its owners (shareholders). The owners' liability is limited to the amount of money they have invested into the company.

  In the UK there are two types of limited company:

  – **Private limited companies** (with 'Ltd' after their name). Shares cannot be offered to the general public.

  – **Public limited companies** (with 'plc' after their name). These can be much larger businesses. Shares can be offered to the general public.

Not for profit organisations

DEFINITION   Not-for-profit organisations (NFPs or NPOs) do not see profitability as their main objective. Instead, they seem to satisfy the particular needs of their members or the sectors of society that they have been set up to benefit.

The objectives of different NFPs will vary significantly:

Hospitals – treat patients.	**Government organisations** – implement government policies.
Councils – care for their communities.	**A charity** – may have 'provision of relief to victims of disasters' as its objective.

Public versus private sector organisations

The **public sector** is the part of the economy that provides basic government services

Normally include:
- police
- military
- public transport
- primary education
- healthcare for the poor

The **private sector** consists of organisations that are run by private individuals and groups rather than government

Normally include:
- businesses
- charities
- clubs

A **non-governmental organisation** (NGO) is one which does not have profit as its primary goal and is not directly linked to national government

Examples:
- The Red Cross
- Greenpeace
- Amnesty International

Co-operatives

DEFINITION Co-operatives are organisations that are owned and democratically controlled by their members – the people who buy their goods and services.

Remember the key differences between the various types of organisation in terms of ownership.

Co-operatives are organised solely to meet the needs of the member-owners, who usually share any profit.

Each member of the co-operative usually gets a single vote on key decisions – unlike companies where shareholders get one vote for each share that they own.

1.3 MARKET SECTORS

LEARNING SUMMARY

After studying this section you should be able to:

- list the industrial and commercial sectors in which business organisations operate.

Sectors in which organisations operate

KEY POINT A further difference between organisations is the market in which they operate.

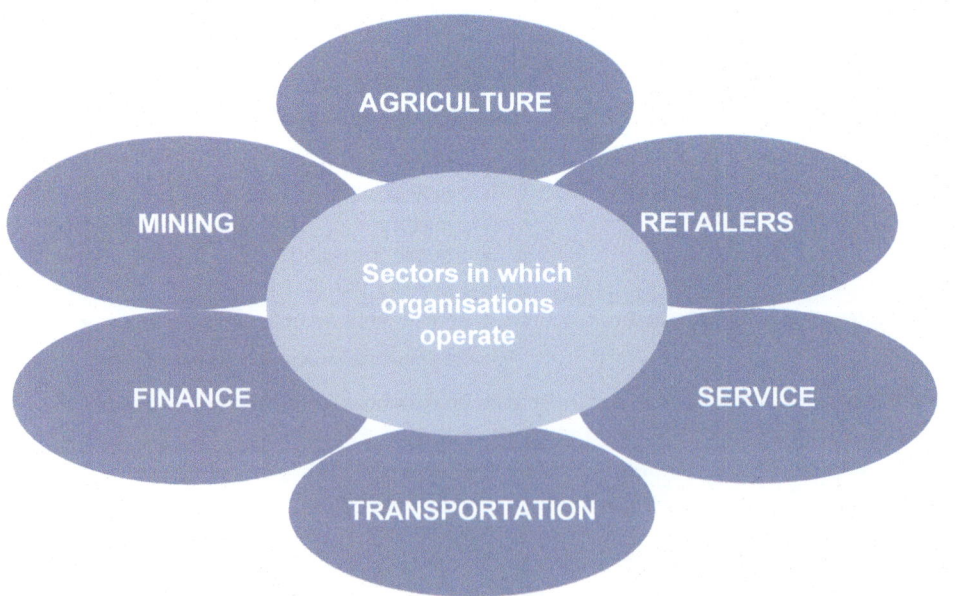

Take note that this is not an exhaustive list and different examples of market sectors may be presented in the exam.

Do you understand?

1   Which of the following would be considered to be an organisation according to the definition produced by Buchanan and Huczynski?

   (i) a sole trader (ii) a golf club (iii) the police force

2   Many schools run fund-raising events, such as fetes, where the intention is to make a profit. This makes them profit-seeking.

   True or false?

3   Which of the following are usually seen as the primary objectives of companies?

   (i)   To maximise the wealth of shareholders

   (ii)   To protect the environment

   (iii) To make a profit

4   Which of the following organisations is most likely to be classified as part of the public sector?

   (i) a charity (ii) a social club (iii) public transport (iv) a public limited company

1 **Which of the following is NOT a key feature of an organisation?**

    A   Controlled performance company

    B   Collective goals

    C   Social arrangements

    D   Marketing of a product or service

2 Consider the following list of different organisations:

    (i)   Government departments

    (ii)   Partnerships

    (iii)   Charities

    (iv)   Companies

    Which of these organisations would normally be classified as BOTH a not-for-profit organisation AND a private sector organisation?

    A   (i) and (iii) only

    B   (iii) only

    C   (i) only

    D   (ii) and (iii) only

3 Consider the following statements:

    (i)   Public limited companies have access to a wider pool of finance than partnerships or sole traders.

    (ii)   A co-operative is an organisation that is owned and democratically controlled by its members.

    Which of these statements is/are correct?

    A   (i) only

    B   (ii) only

    C   Both

    D   Neither

4 Perimax is an organisation which manufactures garden furniture and sells its products to the public in order to make a profit. It is owned by ten individual investors, each of whom owns an equal number of shares in the company. They are looking to expand the range to include storage solutions for garden furniture during the winter months. Perimax is not a public limited company.

    Which of the following is likely to be the most appropriate source of finance for Perimax?

    A   Central government funding

    B   The existing owners of Perimax

    C   Issue of shares to the public

    D   Donations from the public

2 Business organisation and structure

The following topics are covered in this chapter:

- Organisational structure
- Other basic organisational concepts
- Centralisation and decentralisation
- Levels of strategy
- Roles and functions of the main departments
- Marketing

2.1 ORGANISATIONAL STRUCTURE

LEARNING SUMMARY

After studying this section you should be able to:

- describe ways in which formal organisations may be structured.

What is organisational structure?

DEFINITION **Organisational structure** is concerned with the way in which work is divided up and allocated.

It outlines the roles and responsibilities of individuals and groups within the organisation.

KEY POINT The structure of most organisations will change over time as the company grows.

> There are several different ways an organisation can be structured. For this exam you need to be familiar with each of them, as well as being able to weigh up their advantages and disadvantages.

Entrepreneurial structure

DEFINITION **Entrepreneurial structure** is built around the owner.

```
        Entrepreneur
             |
         Employees
```

ADVANTAGES		DISADVANTAGES	
Fast decision-making	Good control	Lack of career structure	Cannot cope with growth
Responsive to market	Goal congruence	Dependent on capabilities of owner/ manager	
Close bond to workforce			

> If a question presents you with a scenario of a small business in the early stages of development or where the entrepreneur has specialist knowledge of the product or service, a likely choice of structure would be entrepreneurial.

Functional/ departmental structure

DEFINITION **Functional organisations** group together employees that undertake similar tasks into departments.

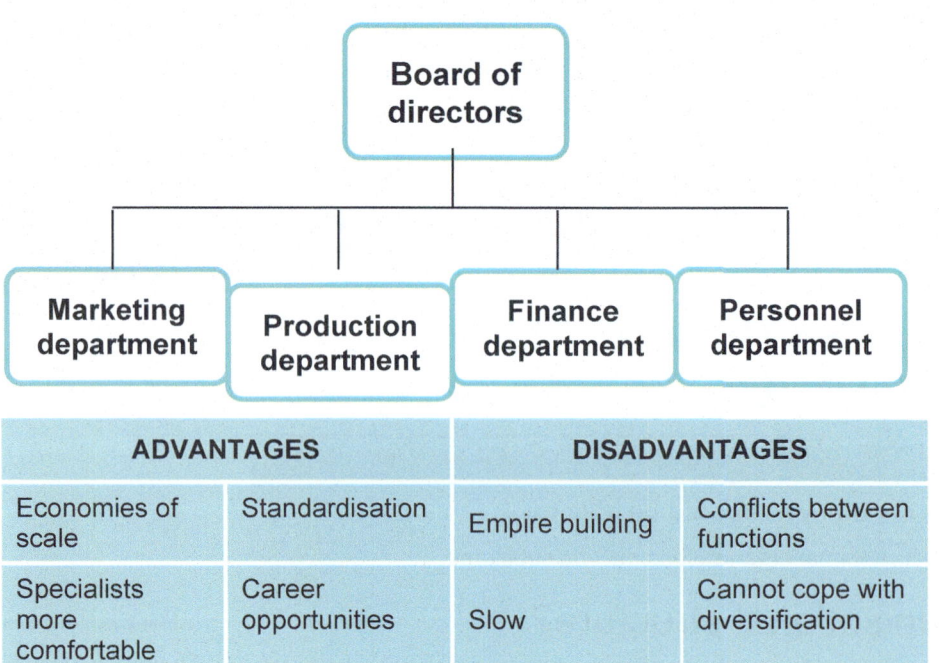

ADVANTAGES		DISADVANTAGES	
Economies of scale	Standardisation	Empire building	Conflicts between functions
Specialists more comfortable	Career opportunities	Slow	Cannot cope with diversification

If a question presents you with a scenario of a business that has outgrown the entrepreneurial structure or has relatively few products/ locations which exist in a relatively stable environment, a likely choice of structure would be functional.

Divisional/ product structure

DEFINITION **Divisional structure** occurs where an organisation is split into several divisions – each one autonomously overseeing a product, a geographic section or even by customer.

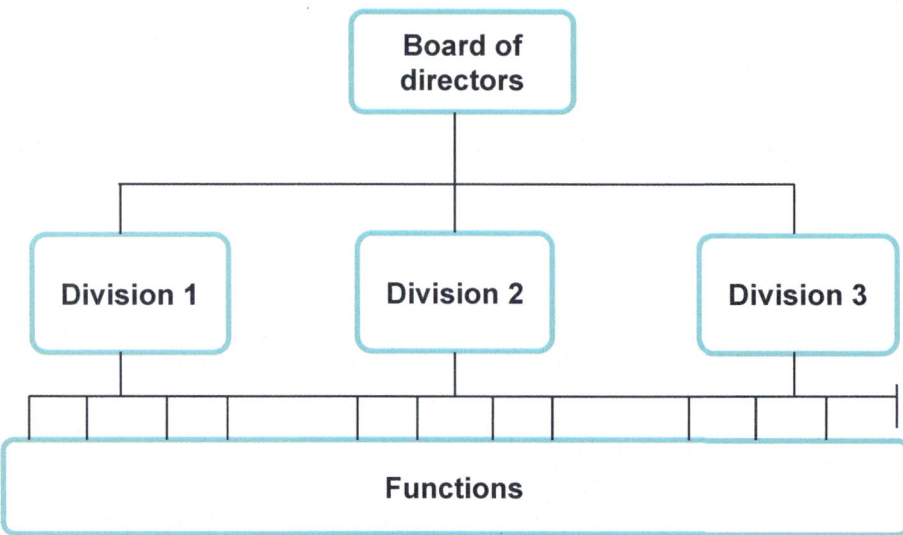

ADVANTAGES		DISADVANTAGES	
Enables growth	Adaptable for diversification	Potential loss of control	Specialists may feel isolated
Clear responsibility for divisions	Top management free to concentrate on strategic matters	Lack of goal congruence	Allocation of central costs can be a problem
Training of managers		Duplication	

If a question presents you with a scenario of an organisation with separate divisions e.g. for motor cars and bikes, or for US and Europe or perhaps that separately look after corporate clients and private clients, a likely choice of structure would be divisional.

KEY POINT Geographically structure is similar to divisional structure, but involves each decision covering a specific location.

Matrix structure

The matrix requires dual reporting to two different managers.

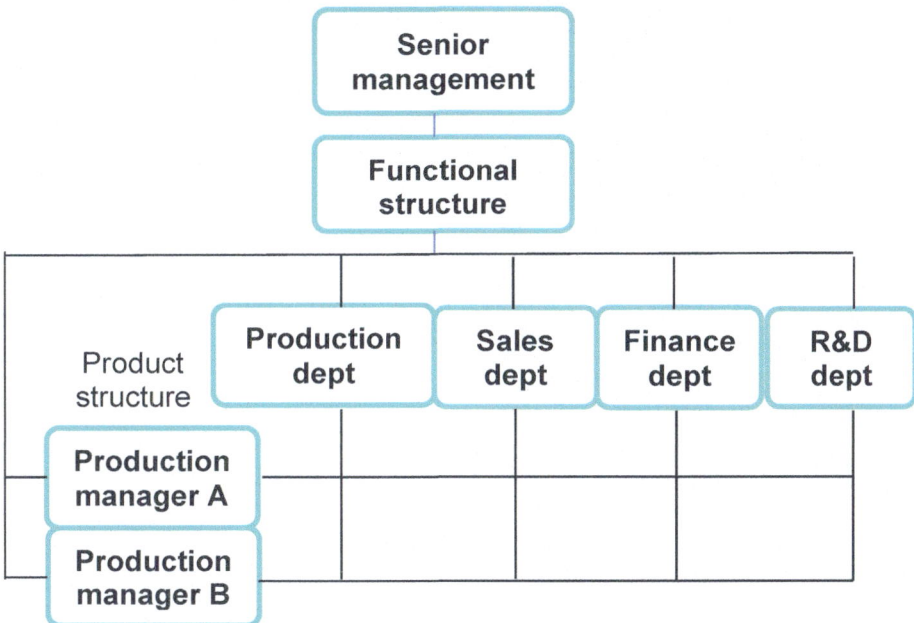

ADVANTAGES		DISADVANTAGES	
Flexibility	Encourage teamwork and the exchange of opinions and expertise	Dual command and conflict	Time-consuming meetings
Customer orientation		Higher admin costs	Dilution of functional authority
Advantages of both functional and divisional structures			

If a question presents you with a scenario of an individual being required to report to two different managers, a likely choice of structure would be matrix

Boundaryless structure

Boundaryless organisations

Hollow organisations – split into functions into core and non-core activities (these are outsourced)

Modular organisations – they break the manufacturing process down into modules

Virtual organisations – outsources many of its functions and simply exists as a network of contracts

For your exam, there are a number of boundaryless structures you need to be aware of.

Mintzberg's Organisational Configurations

Management theorist Henry Mintzberg argued that organisations are made up of five key 'building blocks'.

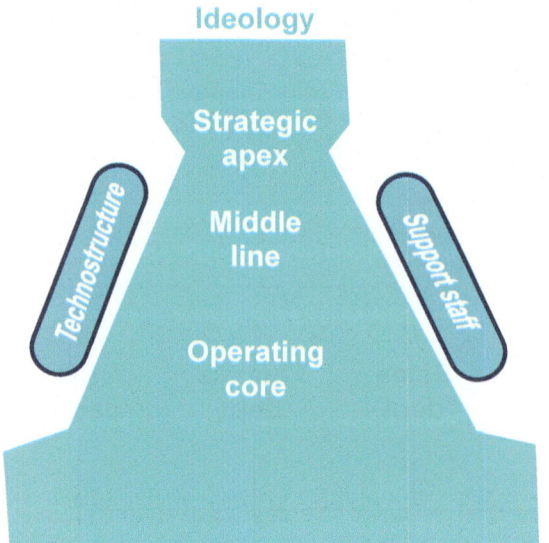

A question may give details of a specific person within the organisation and ask you to choose which organisational building block they should be included within.

- **Strategic apex** – senior levels of management.

- **Middle line** – middle management.

- **Operating core** – workers involved in producing the core product/ service offered by the organisation.

- **Technostructure** – provide technical input that is not part of the core activities. They are analysts who plan and control the work of others.

- **Support staff** – administrative support and indirect services.

A sixth block was later added to Mintzberg's model:

- **Ideology** – the organisation's beliefs and values.

KEY POINT Mintzberg argued that any one of these building blocks could dominate within the organisation, leading to a variety of possible structures.

- **Simple structure** – strategic apex dominates.

- **Machine bureaucracy** – technostructure dominates.

- **Professional bureaucracy** – operating core dominates

- **Divisionalised** – middle line dominates.

- **Adhocracy** – support staff/ operating core dominates.

- **Missionary** – ideology dominates.

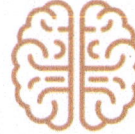

Do you understand?

1   The entrepreneurial structure will enable rapid decision-making within the organisation.

   True or false?

2   Allocation of central costs can be a problem within a divisional structure.

   True or false?

3   Q Co runs five factories that assemble children's toys. According to Mintzberg's organisational configurations model, which building block would assembly staff be included within?

   (i) support staff (ii) operating core (iii) strategic apex (iv) technostructure

3   (iii) Operating core. These staff are involved in the actual production of Q's product.
2   True
1   True

2.2 OTHER BASIC ORGANISATIONAL CONCEPTS

LEARNING SUMMARY

After studying this section you should be able to:

- explain basic organisational structure concepts.

Separation of direction and management

Ownership and management of larger organisations are often separated. The owners (shareholders) elect directors to run the company on their behalf.

Offshoring

Offshoring refers to the process of outsourcing or relocating some of an organisation's functions from one country to another, usually to reduce costs.

While cost savings can be significant, offshoring can create additional problems for the organisation, including problems with cultural differences and language barriers.

Scalar chain

DEFINITION **Scalar chain** is the line of authority which can be traced up or down the chain of command, from the most senior member of staff to the most junior. It relates to the number of levels of management within an organisation.

> As well as the different types of organisation structure, you need to be aware of four other key structural concepts.

Span of control

Tall and flat organisations

Shared services approach

A shared services approach involves restructuring the provision of certain services within the organisation so that the service is centralised into one specific part of the organisation.

2.3 CENTRALISATION AND DECENTRALISATION

The advantages and disadvantages of decentralisation are:

ADVANTAGES	DISADVANTAGES
Senior management free to concentrate on strategy	Loss of control by senior management and duplication of roles
Better local decisions due to local expertise	Dysfunctional decision due to lack of goal congruence
Better motivation due to increased training and career path	Poor decisions made by inexperienced managers and training costs
Quicker responses/ flexibility due to smaller chain of command	Extra costs in obtaining information

The advantages and disadvantages of centralisation can also of course be deduced from this table.

The factors that will affect the amount of decentralisation are:

- management style.
- ability of management.
- geographic spread.
- size of organisation/ scale of activities.

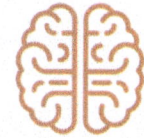

Do you understand?

1   Harry works for F Co, a manufacturing company. The work undertaken is simple, meaning that each manager looks after a large number of employees. Because of this, there are relatively few levels of management within the company. With regards to F Co's structure, the company was a narrow span of control and a short scalar chain.

True or false?

2   Which of the following would be a typical feature of a flat organisation?

(i) easy career progression for employees (ii) faster decision-making

3   Which of the following is an advantage of centralised decision-making?

(i) Improved local decisions (ii) Avoidance of dysfunctional decision-making

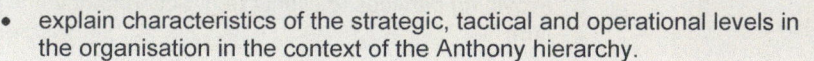

1   False. B Co has a wide span or control and a short scalar chain. The fact that each manager has a large number of subordinates would indicate a wide span of control. There are few levels of management, meaning the scalar chain is short.

2   (ii) flat organisations have wide spans of control and a short scalar chain. This means that there will be relatively few management positions for staff to be promoted to. However, fewer managers tend to mean faster decisions can be made.

3   (ii) Centralisation ensures that decisions are made by the same team of managers, improving goal congruence.

2.4   LEVELS OF STRATEGY

LEARNING SUMMARY

After studying this section you should be able to:

- explain characteristics of the strategic, tactical and operational levels in the organisation in the context of the Anthony hierarchy.

Within an organisation, each level of management will have different roles and responsibilities. This is especially the case when it comes to developing a strategy/ plan for the future, for the organisation.

KEY POINT The Anthony Triangle is a model that can be used to illustrate the types of strategic planning that will be made at each level of the organisation's hierarchy.

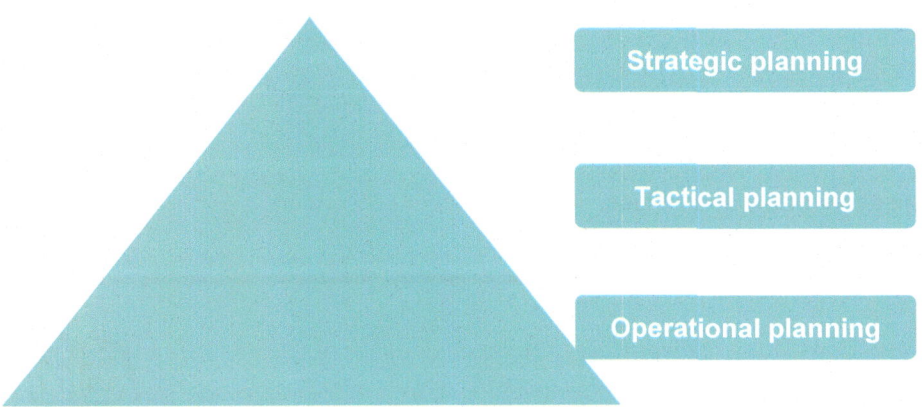

Different levels of planning:

- **Strategic planning** is undertaken by senior managers. It involves making long-term decisions for the entire organisation.

- **Tactical planning** is undertaken by middle management. It tends to look at plans for specific divisions or departments and specifies how to use resources.

- **Operational planning** is undertaken by junior managers and supervisors. It is short-term, detailed and practical.

A question may describe one of the levels of planning and ask you to label it as one of the three levels.

2.5   THE ROLES AND FUNCTIONS OF MAIN DEPARTMENTS IN A BUSINESS ORGANISATION

LEARNING SUMMARY

After studying this section you should be able to:

- describe the roles and functions of the main departments.

Department	Function
Research and development	Improving existing products and developing new products
Purchasing	Acquiring the goods and services necessary for business
Production	Converting raw materials into finished goods
Direct service provision	Providing services to clients (e.g. accountancy firm)
Marketing	Identifying customer needs, market research, product design, price, promotion and distribution
Administration	Converting raw materials into finished goods
Finance	Improving existing products and developing new products

2.6 MARKETING

What is meant by 'marketing'?

DEFINITION **Marketing** is the management process that identifies, anticipates and supplies customer needs efficiently and profitably.

KEY POINT Marketing involves much more than just advertising!

The marketing mix

DEFINITION **The marketing mix** is the set of controllable variables that a firm blends to produce desired results from its chosen target market.

> A question can focus on the marketing mix in general or it can seek greater depth of knowledge in terms of the specifics of each element of the 4Ps.

KEY POINT There are four basic elements (the '4Ps') which must be managed to satisfy customers' needs at a profit.

The traditional 4Ps of the marketing mix:

Price	Promotion	Place	Product

Product issues:

Product definition
– what exactly the product should be

Product positioning
– how does our product compare with the offerings of our competitors?

Place (distribution) issues:

Key decision is whether to sell direct to the ultimate consumer without using middlemen or use the channel strategy which comprises a mixture of retailer, distributors, wholesalers etc.

Pricing issues:

- cost
- customers
- competition
- corporate objectives

These issues can be blended to give a range of pricing tactics:

- Cost plus pricing
- Penetration pricing
- Perceived quality pricing
- Price discrimination
- Going rate pricing
- Price skimming
- Loss leaders
- Captive product pricing

Promotional issues:

Promotion is essentially about market communication. The primary aim is to encourage customers to buy the products by moving along the AIDA timeline:
- Awareness
- Interest
- Desire
- Action

Promotional techniques include:
- Advertising
- Sales promotion techniques
- Personal selling
- Public relations

Additional 3Ps for the service industry:

People – this relates to both staff and the need to understand customer needs.

Processes – these are the systems through which the service is delivered.

Physical evidence – testimonials and references regarding proposed service.

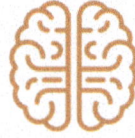

Do you understand?

1   A supermarket is planning to hire twenty new checkout operators within the next five weeks to help reduce customer queue times. Using the Anthony triangle model, what would this strategy be classed as?

(i) strategic (ii) tactical (iii) operational

2   Promotion involves the use of the AIDA sequence, which stands for Advertise, Interest, Desire and Action.

True or false?

3   M Co has created a new type of printer. It took a number of years of research and development and the company is about to start selling its new product. M Co has decided on a price that is significantly lower than its competitors to encourage customers to try the product. What type of pricing strategy is M Co using?

(i) Price skimming (ii) Penetration pricing

1   (iii) Operational. This strategy is short term.
2   False. The 'A' in AIDA stands for awareness, not advertise.
3   (ii) This is a classic example of penetration pricing – a low price is set to gain market share.

1   K Co is a medical company that relies heavily on highly skilled members of staff. There are a large number of rules and procedures, but decision-making is decentralised, with each individual staff member having significant independence and power.

    Which one of the following structural configurations (as popularised by Mintzberg) K Co does K Co most closely conform to.

    A   Professional bureaucracy

    B   Divisional

    C   Machine bureaucracy

    D   Simple

2   Rex Co makes a variety of unrelated products, including books, electronics and animal houses. It is aware that each of these products requires very different strategies and functions. Rex Co wishes to use a structure that will allow for each product to be managed separately, but wishes to minimise its overall administrative costs.

    Which of the following organisational structures would be most appropriate for Rex Co to adopt?

    A   Divisional

    B   Entrepreneurial

    C   Functional

    D   Matrix

3   Pocta Co is planning to outsource all of its functions to third party suppliers – even those that it feels are core activities which give the company competitive advantage in the market place.

    Which boundaryless structure is Pocta Co planning to adopt?

    A   Virtual

    B   Hollow

4   Consider the following statements:

    (i)   Offshoring refers to the transfer of existing staff members to other countries with lower wage rates.

    (ii) Adopting a shared services approach refers to the centralisation of an internal service within the organisation. The operations of the internal service will be unaffected.

    Which of these statements is/are correct?

    A   (i) only

    B   (ii) only

    C   Both

    D   Neither

5 **A company with a marketing orientation believes that:**

A products should be sold actively and aggressively

B meeting customer needs better than competitors is the key to corporate success

C the level of sales, advertising and sales promotion is key to corporate success

D producing goods and services of optimum quality is the key to corporate success

6 Halo Co manufactures and sells board games. It is currently considering the packaging, quality and design of the board games as part of a strategic review.

What element of the marketing mix is Halo Co reviewing?

A Product

B Place

C Price

D Promotion

3 Organisational culture in business

The following topics are covered in this chapter:

- Defining organisational culture
- Factors that shape organisational culture
- Writers on culture
- The informal organisation and its relationship with the formal organisation

3.1 DEFINING ORGANISATIONAL CULTURE

LEARNING SUMMARY

After studying this section you should be able to:

- define organisational culture.

Definition

DEFINITION Ultimately, **culture** means the sum total of all the beliefs, attitudes, norms and customs that prevail within an organisation.

KEY POINT Each organisation will have its own distinctive culture and behaviour acceptable in one organisational culture may be inappropriate in another.

Components of culture

```
              ┌─────────────────────┐
              │   Organisational     │
              │      culture         │
              └─────────────────────┘
             /            |            \
┌──────────────────┐ ┌──────────────┐ ┌──────────────────┐
│ A set of norms of│ │              │ │   Symbols and    │
│    behaviour     │ │              │ │ symbolic actions │
└──────────────────┘ │              │ └──────────────────┘
              ┌─────────────────────┐
              │  A set of shared     │
              │  values and beliefs  │
              └─────────────────────┘
```

3.2 FACTORS THAT SHAPE THE CULTURE OF THE ORGANISATION

LEARNING SUMMARY

After studying this section you should be able to:

- describe the factors that shape the culture of the organisation.

Factors that shape organisational culture

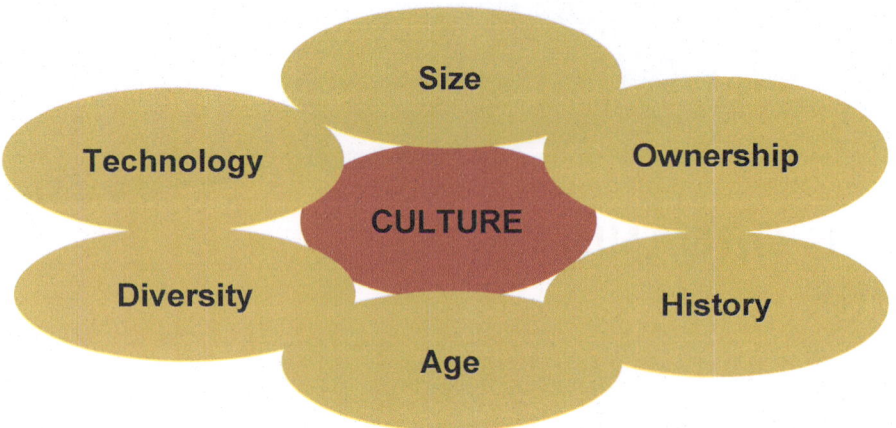

3.3   WRITERS ON CULTURE

Schein

Schein argues that the first leaders of a company create its culture. Future leaders will only be selected if they support this organisational culture.

Schein further commented that if leaders are to lead, it is essential that they understand the culture of the organisation. In order to try and define culture, Schein described three levels:

* **Artefacts** – these are the aspects of culture that can be easily seen, e.g. the way people dress.

* **Espoused values** – these are the strategies and goals of an organisation, including company slogans etc.

* **Basic assumptions and values** – these are difficult to identify as they are unseen, and exist mainly at the unconscious level.

> There are three writers you need to have knowledge of.

Handy

Handy popularised four culture types:

* **Power** – here there is one major source of power and influence e.g. in a small owner-managed business the owner may strive to maintain absolute control over subordinates.

* **Role** – people describe their job by its duties, not by its purpose, so job descriptions dictate 'the way we do things around here'.

* **Task** – emphasis here is on achieving the particular task at hand and staff may need to be flexible to ensure deadlines are met.

* **Person** – this is characterised by the fact it exists to satisfy the requirements of the particular individual(s) involved in the organisation.

> A question may give details of an organisation and ask you to choose which one of Handy's four cultural types fits best with the scenario.

Hofstede

Hofstede looked for national differences between over 100,000 of IBM's employees in different parts of the world, in an attempt to find aspects of culture that might influence business behaviour.

He found four traits or 'cultural dimensions'.

- **Individualism (vs collectivism)** – looks at the extent to which people are integrated into groups. Some cultures are more cohesive than others. High individualism indicates that staff expect to be assessed on their own achievements and performance.

- **Uncertainty avoidance (UA) index** – deals with a society's tolerance for uncertainty and ambiguity. High UA cultures will not like to act outside their normal job descriptions or roles. They prefer to be directed by management and like formal rules.

- **Power distance (PD) index** – the extent to which the less powerful members of organisations and institutions accept and expect that power is distributed unequally. High PD cultures expect to answer to powerful managers and do not expect to have any democratic input into decisions that are made. Low PD cultures expect to be involved with the decision-making process and want less direct supervision by managers.

- **Masculinity (vs femininity)** - a masculine culture is one where the distinction between the roles and values of the genders is large and the males focus on work, power and success whereas in feminine cultures the differences between the gender roles is much smaller.

More recently, two additional dimensions have been added to Hofstede's model.

- **Long-term orientation (vs short-term orientation)** – societies with a long-term orientation focus on future rewards, with particular focus on saving, persistence and the ability to adapt to changing circumstances.

- **Indulgence (vs restraint)** – indulgent societies allow relatively free gratification of basic and natural human drives related to enjoying life and having fun.

> A question may give details of an organisation and ask you to choose which one of Hofstede's four traits fits best with the scenario.

3.4 THE INFORMAL ORGANISATION AND ITS RELATIONSHIP WITH THE FORMAL ORGANISATION

LEARNING SUMMARY

After studying this section you should be able to:

- explain the informal organisation and its relationship with the formal organisation.

DEFINITION The **informal organisation** is the network of relationships that exist within an organisation.

This network evolves over time and tends to arise through common interests and friendships between staff members.

KEY POINT An informal organisation will be present to some degree within all formal organisations.

Advantages and disadvantages of informal organisation are:

ADVANTAGES	DISADVANTAGES
Better motivation	Inefficient organisations
Better communication	Opposition to change can be intensified
Provision of social control	The 'grapevine effect', where potentially inaccurate information or rumours spread through the informal organisation
	Conformity

A question could ask you to state whether various advantages or disadvantages are true or false.

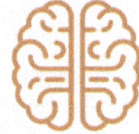

Do you understand?

1   According to Schein, there is a strong link between culture and _____.

      (i) Management style (ii) Leadership (iii) The size of the organisation

2   Staff in country F dislike their managers interfering in their work. According to Hofstede, this means that the culture is:

      (i) Low power-distance (ii) Masculine

3   Informal relationships are shown on organisational charts.

      True or false?

4   Informal relationships within an organisation can be across divisions.

      True or false?

1   (ii) Leadership. While the others are factors that may affect culture, Schein believed in a strong link between leadership and culture.
2   (i) By definition.
3   False.
4   True.

1   Consider the following two statements:

    (1)   The informal organisation can either enhance or hold the
          business back.

    (2)   According to Handy's theory, in the person culture, status
          symbols are there to remind staff of their place.

    Which of the above statements is/are correct?

    A   (1) only

    B   (2) only

    C   Both

    D   Neither

2   **Which of the following is one of the three levels of culture
    described by Schein?**

    A   Things that are short term only, such as staffing levels

    B   Things that are difficult to identify as they are unseen and often
          unconscious

    C   Things that endure, such as organisational hierarchy

    D   Things that initially appear superficial, such as timekeeping
          rules

3   Research has indicated that workers in country A display
    characteristics such as the desire for material wealth and
    possessions, while workers in country B value personal relationships,
    belonging and the quality of life.

    **According to Hofstede's theory, these distinctions relate to
    which of the following cultural dimensions?**

    A   Masculinity-femininity

    B   Power-distance

    C   Indulgence-restraint

    D   Uncertainty avoidance

4   'The _____ is the network of relationships that exist within
    an organisation and arises through common interests and friendships
    between members of staff.'

    Which word fits the gap in the above definition?

    A   Grapevine

    B   Organisational culture

    C   Scalar chain

    D   Informal organisation

4

Information technology and information systems

The following topics are covered in this chapter:

- Data and information
- Information technology and information systems
- Types of information system
- Software applications
- The advantages of computerisation

4.1 DATA AND INFORMATION

LEARNING SUMMARY

After studying this section you should be able to:

- define data and information
- identify attributes of good information.

Data and information

> **DEFINITION** **Data** consists of numbers, letters, symbols, raw facts, events and transactions which have been recorded but not yet processed into a form suitable for use.

> **DEFINITION** **Information** is data that has been processed in such a way that someone can use it in order to make decisions.

Data and information are terms which need to be distinguished. Although some may use these terms interchangeably they have distinct differences.

Information is vital to an organisation and is required both internally and externally. Management requires information:

- to provide records, both current and historical
- to analyse what is happening in the business
- to provide the basis for decision-making in the short and long-term
- to monitor the performance of the business by comparing actual results with plans and forecasts.

This information will be used by various third parties, including:

- the shareholders or owners
- customers and suppliers
- employees
- government agencies

Attributes of good information

Management use information to be able to plan, control and make decisions. A high quality of information improves management's decision making. Good information has to be:

Accurate	The degree of accuracy depends on the reason why the information is needed.
Complete	Information should be sufficient and not excessive.
Cost effective	The value of information should exceed the cost of producing it.

Understandable	Use of technical language or jargon must be limited.
Relevant	The information should be relevant to its purpose.
Accessible	Information should be accessible via the appropriate channels of communication to the appropriate persons.
Timely	Information should be provided to a manager in time for decisions to be made based on that information.
Easy to use	Information should be easy to use for the purposes intended.

> You can remember these characteristics using the acronym **ACCURATE**.

4.2 INFORMATION TECHNOLOGY AND INFORMATION SYSTEMS

LEARNING SUMMARY

After studying this section you should be able to:

- define information systems (IS) and information technology (IT).

Definitions

DEFINITION **Information systems (IS)** refer to the management and provision of information to support the running of the organisation.

> There are five types of information system that you need to be aware of for your exam, which we will examine in detail shortly.

DEFINITION **Information technology (IT)** describes any equipment concerned with the capture, storage, transmission or presentation of data.

4.3 TYPES OF INFORMATION SYSTEM

LEARNING SUMMARY

After studying this section you should be able to:

- explain how types of information differ and the purposes for which it is applied at different levels of the organisation: strategic, tactical and operational

- identify an organisation's system requirements in relation to the objectives and policies of the organisation.

Management structure and information requirements

As outlined in Chapter 2, there are three levels of management – strategic, tactical and operational.

Each level creates different types of strategy within the organisation and therefore needs different types of information, as outlined by the following chart:

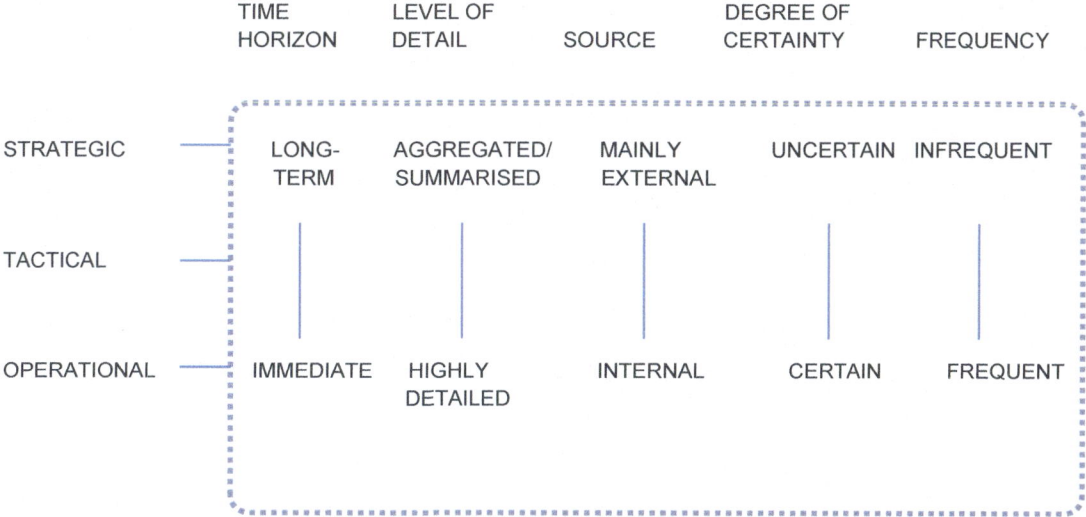

	TIME HORIZON	LEVEL OF DETAIL	SOURCE	DEGREE OF CERTAINTY	FREQUENCY
STRATEGIC	LONG-TERM	AGGREGATED/ SUMMARISED	MAINLY EXTERNAL	UNCERTAIN	INFREQUENT
TACTICAL					
OPERATIONAL	IMMEDIATE	HIGHLY DETAILED	INTERNAL	CERTAIN	FREQUENT

- The **strategic level of management** requires information from internal and external sources in order to plan the long-term strategies of the organisation. Internal information – both quantitative and qualitative – is usually supplied in a summarised form.

- The **tactical level of management** requires information and instructions from the strategic level of management, together with routine and regular quantitative information from the operational level of management. The information could be in summarised form, but detailed enough to allow tactical planning of resources and manpower.

- The **operational level of management** requires information and instructions from the tactical level of management. The operational level is primarily concerned with the day-to-day performance of tasks and most of the information is obtained from internal sources. The information must be detailed and precise.

Operational
Programmable decisions with specific inputs and outputs.
Transaction processing system (TPS) used.

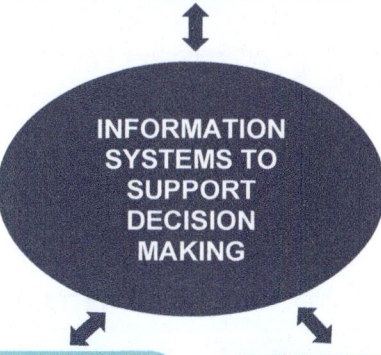

INFORMATION SYSTEMS TO SUPPORT DECISION MAKING

Tactical
Use variety of data from different sources – emphasis on exception reporting.
Management information system (MIS) used.

Strategic
Varied information needs – sometimes difficult to predict.
MIS and Executive information system (EIS) used.

System definitions

DEFINITION **A Transaction processing system (TPS)** records the daily transactions of the organisation and summarises them so they can be reported on a routine basis.

Your knowledge of these five definitions can be directly tested in the exam.

DEFINITION **Management information systems (MIS)** convert data into information for tactical managers. This information will be designed to help them monitor performance, maintain co-ordination and provide background information about the organisation's operations.

DEFINITION **A Decision Support System (DSS)** is a computer system that helps decision-makers deal with semi-structured or unstructured decisions, where there is a high degree of uncertainty, or unknown factors that may affect the decision.

DEFINITION **Executive Information Systems (EIS)** provide strategic managers with flexible access to information from the entire business, as well as relevant information from the external environment.

The EIS enables senior management to easily model the entire business by turning its data into useful, summarised reports. This information can then easily be distributed to key staff members.

DEFINITION **Expert Systems (ES)** hold specialist knowledge and allow non-experts to interrogate the system for information, advice and recommended decisions.

4.4 SOFTWARE APPLICATIONS

LEARNING SUMMARY

After studying this section you should be able to:

- identify business uses of computers and IT software applications: spreadsheets, databases and accounting packages.

KEY POINT Software applications are computer programmes that are designed to help users with certain tasks.

For your exam, you need to be able to discuss three specific software applications.

Spreadsheets

Spreadsheets are designed to analyse data and sort lists of items, not for long-term storage of raw data.

ADVANTAGES	DISADVANTAGES
Relatively easy to use.	Data must be re-copied over and over again to maintain it in separate data files.
Require little training to get started.	They are unable to efficiently identify data errors.

Most data managers are familiar with them.	Lack of detailed sorting and querying abilities.
	There can be sharing violations among users wishing to view or change data at the same time.
	They are often restricted to a finite number of records, and can require a large amount of hard-drive space for data storage.

Databases

To store large amounts of raw data, it is best to use a database. This is especially true in circumstances where two or more users share the information.

ADVANTAGES	DISADVANTAGES
The most important benefit gained by using a database is the ease of reporting and sharing data.	Requires the user to learn a new system.
Databases require little or no duplication of data between information tables.	Requires a greater investment in training and software.
Changes made to the data do not corrupt the programming (e.g. at the cell level of a spreadsheet where calculations are running).	The initial time and cost of migrating all of the data into a new database is significant.
Databases offer better security to restrict users from accessing privileged information, and from changing coded information in the programming.	

Accountancy packages

Many businesses choose to utilise specialised software packages that record and process the individual transactions within the business, rather than relying on manual records.

These accountancy packages are often designed to automatically produce year-end accounts and management reports when requested.

ADVANTAGES	DISADVANTAGES
Rapid recording of transactions, when compared with manual systems.	Usually requires training before use.
Lower likelihood of mistakes.	Packages can be expensive to purchase and install.
Rapid production of reports and financial statements.	May be unnecessary for a small business with low numbers of transactions.

4.5 THE ADVANTAGES OF COMPUTERISATION

LEARNING SUMMARY

After studying this section you should be able to:

- describe and compare the relative benefits of manual and automated financial systems that may be used in an organisation.

Advantages

Most aspects of the economy, from the music industry to manufacturing, banking, retail and defence, are now totally dependent on modern information processing systems.

Computers have revolutionised information systems for the following reasons:

- **Speed** – computers are ideal for dealing with repetitive processes.

- **Accuracy** – in general, computers do not suffer from errors, or lapses in concentration but process data perfectly.

- **Volume** – not only do computers work fast, but they do not need to rest. They are therefore able to handle vast volumes of data.

- **Complexity** – once subsystems are computerised they can generally function more reliably than human beings. This makes it easier to integrate various subsystems. Computers are therefore able to handle complex information systems efficiently.

- **Cost** – all the above advantages mean that computers have become highly cost-effective providers of information.

- **Presentation** – more recently, emphasis has been placed on displaying information in as 'user-friendly' a way as possible.

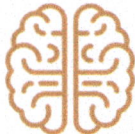

Do you understand?

1   A transaction processing system (TPS) would normally be used by operational-level managers.

     True or false?

2   Michael has to analyse the historic results for his business over the last ten years. He wishes to represent the information using a series of graphs that he can show to potential investors. Which software application would be most appropriate for Michael to use?

     (i) Spreadsheet (ii) Database (iii) Accountancy package

3   Data is facts and figures that have been processed in such a way that it has meaning to the user.

     True or false?

1   True. A TPS is a low-level system that summarises internal information, such as transactions. This would be used by either junior or operational level managers.

2   (i) spreadsheet. This would be a typical use of a spreadsheet application, which is designed for number-crunching and graphical analysis of information.

3   False. This definition given for data is actually that of information.

1   Consider the following two statements:

(1)   Strategic level decisions will usually need to be supported with highly detailed, mainly internal information.

(2)   Spreadsheet packages are primarily used to analyse and sort data.

Which of these statements is/are correct?

A   (1) only

B   (2) only

C   Both

D   Neither

2   **Which of the following is an advantage of using an accounting package over a manual accounting system?**

A   Set-up costs tend to be lower

B   Recording transactions is usually faster

C   Little training is usually required

D   Better for small businesses with low volumes of transactions

3   **Which of the following converts data from a transaction processing system into information for monitoring performance and maintaining co-ordination?**

A   Expert systems

B   Decision support systems

C   Executive information systems

D   Management information systems

4   Abacus Co, an indoor furniture manufacturer has recently commissioned a report into the potential sales of an outdoor furniture range. The report is extremely detailed and filled with jargon. The management of Abacus are finding it difficult to follow the report's findings.

Which of the following criteria of good quality information is NOT being met by this report?

A   Relevant

B   Complete

C   Accurate

D   Understandable

5

Stakeholders in business organisations

The following topics are covered in this chapter:
- Definition of stakeholders
- Types of stakeholder
- Stakeholder conflict

5.1 WHAT ARE STAKEHOLDERS?

LEARNING SUMMARY

After studying this section you should be able to:

- define stakeholders.

Definition

> **DEFINITION** A **stakeholder** is an individual or group who has an interest in what the organisation does, or who affects, or can be affected by, the organisation's actions.

5.2 TYPES OF STAKEHOLDER

LEARNING SUMMARY

After studying this section you should be able to:

- define internal, external and connected stakeholders and explain their impact on the organisation

- identify the main stakeholder groups and the objectives of each group.

Internal stakeholders

> **DEFINITION** **Internal stakeholders** are any stakeholders that are within the organisation itself. Their objectives are likely to have a strong influence on how it is run.

Familiarise yourself with the different types of stakeholders and their needs/ expectations.

STAKEHOLDER	NEED/ EXPECTATION
Employees	Pay, working conditions and job security.
Managers/ directors	Status, pay, bonus, job security.

Connected stakeholders

> **DEFINITION** **Connected stakeholders** either invest in or have dealings with the organisation.

STAKEHOLDER	NEED/ EXPECTATION
Shareholders	Steady flow of income, possible capital growth and the continuation of the business.
Customers	Satisfaction of customers' needs will be achieved through providing value-for-money products and services.

Suppliers	Paid promptly.
Finance providers	Ability to repay the finance including interest, security of investment.

External stakeholders

DEFINITION **External stakeholders** tend to not have a direct link to the organisation, but can influence or be influenced by its activities.

STAKEHOLDER	NEED/ EXPECTATION
Community at large	The general public can be a stakeholder, especially if their lives are affected by an organisation's decisions.
Environmental pressure groups	The organisation does not harm the external environment.
Government	Company activities are central to the success of the economy (providing jobs and taxes). Legislation (e.g. health and safety) must be met by the company.
Trade unions	Taking an active part in the decision-making process.

Primary and secondary stakeholders

This is a different method of categorising stakeholders, which is based on whether or not they have a contractual relationship with the organisation.

DEFINITION **Primary stakeholders** are those that have a contractual relationship, for instance employees, directors and shareholders.

DEFINITION **Secondary stakeholders** are parties that have an interest in the organisation, but have no contractual link, such as the public.

> **Learning tip:** you can think of primary stakeholders as those which fall into the 'connected' or 'internal' categories above.

> Any stakeholders in the 'external' category would fall into the secondary stakeholders group.

5.3 STAKEHOLDER CONFLICT

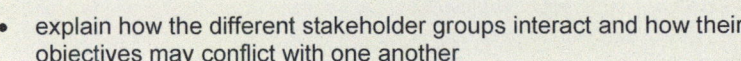

LEARNING SUMMARY

After studying this section you should be able to:

- explain how the different stakeholder groups interact and how their objectives may conflict with one another

- compare the power and influence of various stakeholder groups and how their needs should be accounted for, such as under the Mendelow framework.

Stakeholder conflict

An organisation can have many different stakeholders, all with different needs. Inevitably, the needs of some stakeholders will come into conflict with the needs of others.

Some of the most common conflicts include:

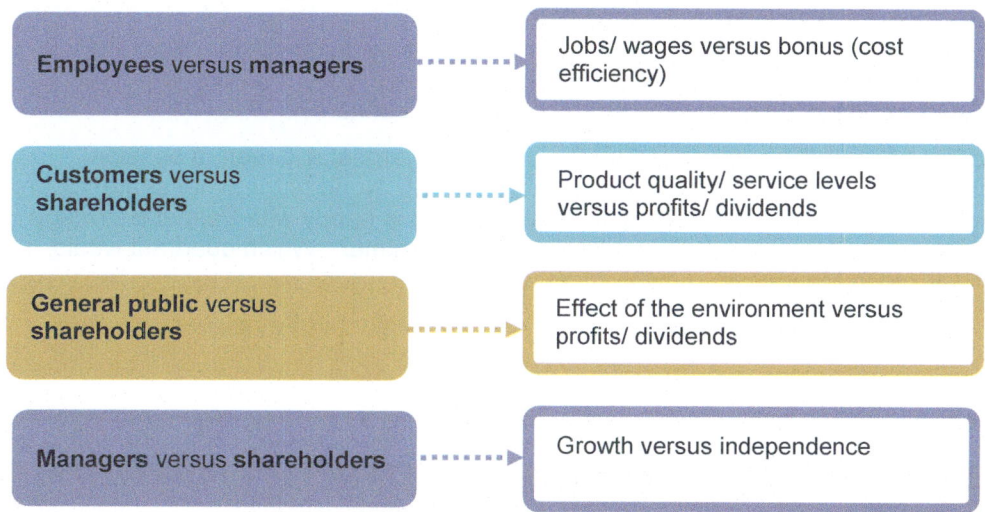

Employees versus **managers**	Jobs/ wages versus bonus (cost efficiency)
Customers versus **shareholders**	Product quality/ service levels versus profits/ dividends
General public versus **shareholders**	Effect of the environment versus profits/ dividends
Managers versus **shareholders**	Growth versus independence

Mendelow's power-interest matrix

If an organisation is having difficulty deciding who the dominant stakeholder is, they can use **Mendelow's power-interest matrix**.

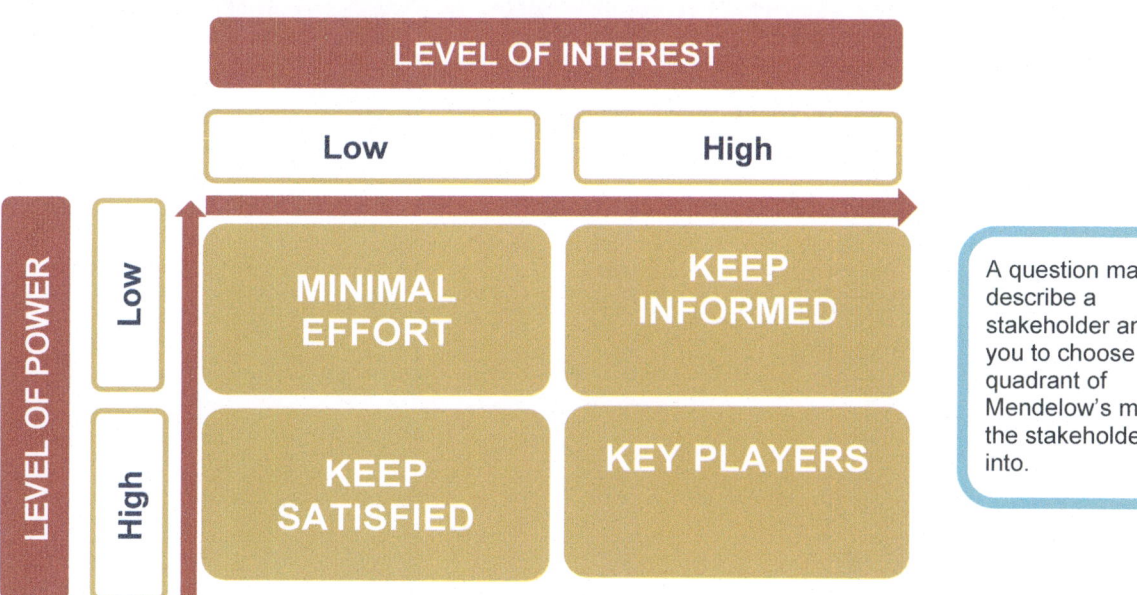

A question may describe a stakeholder and ask you to choose which quadrant of Mendelow's matrix the stakeholder falls into.

KEY POINT It should be noted that, in reality, managers need to consider the needs of as many stakeholders as possible. This means that nearly every decision becomes a compromise.

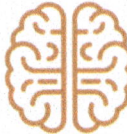

Do you understand?

1   The needs and expectations of managers and employees will always tend to be the same as they are both internal stakeholders.

   True or false?

2   How could a conflict arise between shareholders and bankers?

3   Palmer Co has a large number of shareholders. The largest is Green, a pension company. Green owns 40% of Palmer's share capital. None of the other shareholders own more than 10% of the share capital each. Green is happy with Palmer's strategy and dividends and has no intention of intervening in Palmer. Which quadrant would Green fall into in Mendelow's power-interest matrix?

   (i)   Minimal effort (ii) Keep informed (iii) Keep satisfied (iv) Key player

1   False. Just because managers and employees are in the same category of stakeholder does not mean that managers and employees have the same goals. E.g. managers will want to keep profits high to ensure they maximise their bonuses. This may encourage them to keep staff wages low, which is clearly not in the interests of employees.

2   The shareholders may be willing to take more risks in return for higher profits/ returns, whereas the bankers will be more concerned with low risk/ security.

3   (iii)   Keep satisfied. Green has comparatively high power due to its large number of shares. However, it has expressed a low level of interest in the running of Palmer. This means that Palmer's directors should work to keep Green from taking an active interest in the future.

1   (a)   M Co is attempting to classify its stakeholders. It wishes to analyse them into one of the following two categories:

         A   Internal

         B   Connected

         Required:

         Classify the following stakeholders as either A (internal) or B (connected):

         (i)   Employees

         (ii)   Shareholders

         (iii)   Customers

         (iv)   Directors

       (b)   M Co wishes to use Mendelow's matrix to decide on what approach to take to each stakeholder. The matrix suggests four possible approaches:

         A   Keep informed

         B   Key players

         C   Keep satisfied

         D   Minimal effort

         The following sentences contain gaps which specify which approach to stakeholder management should be taken.

         M Co is partly owned by J, who is considered to have high power and low interest in M Co and has therefore decided to use a _1_ strategy to manage this stakeholder.

         Required:

         (i)   Select the type of organisation that appropriately fills gap 1 above; i.e. select A, B, C or D.

         M Co is aware that its actions are regularly commented on by ZZ, which would be classified by Mendelow as _2_. ZZ has a high level of interest, but low power.

         Required:

         (ii)   Select the type of approach that appropriately fills gap 2 above; i.e. select A, B, C or D.

2   Marsh Co is a large national manufacturer of animal feed based in country T. Marsh sells dried food – primarily for chickens and sheep. This is not a competitive market and Marsh's large number of small farmer customers have little alternative but to purchase Marsh's products for their animals. The farming industry is struggling in country T with farmers earning very low margins and many being forced out of business.

The Government of country T has publically expressed concerns about the state of the national farming industry and has vowed to do whatever is necessary to protect farmers from what one minister has referred to as 'money-making corporations that are making excessive profits from farmers.'

Marsh's shares are mainly held by individual investors – many of whom have invested a significant amount of money into Marsh. No one shareholder in Marsh has more than 4% of the total share capital of the company.

Marsh's employees are largely unskilled and are not members of any union.

Marsh is currently considering raising its prices by around 15% to improve its margins. It has identified four main stakeholder groups who may be affected by the decision. These have been allocated to the quadrants in the matrix shown below.

		Stakeholder interest	
		High	Low
Stakeholder power	**High**	A	B
	Low	C	D

Required:

Indicate which quadrant of the matrix each stakeholder group has been allocated to by writing the appropriate letter (A, B, C or D) against the name of the group.

(i)   Customers

(ii)   Government

(iii)   Shareholders

(iv)   Employees

6

External analysis – political and legal factors

The following topics are covered in this chapter:

- Political systems and government policy
- Employee protection
- The principles of data protection
- Data security
- Health and safety in the workplace
- Consumer protection

6.1 INTRODUCTION

LEARNING SUMMARY

After studying this section you should be able to:

- recognise the elements of PEST analysis.

PEST analysis

In order to fully understand an organisation, we need to fully examine the environment that it operates in.

This analysis should include the following factors:

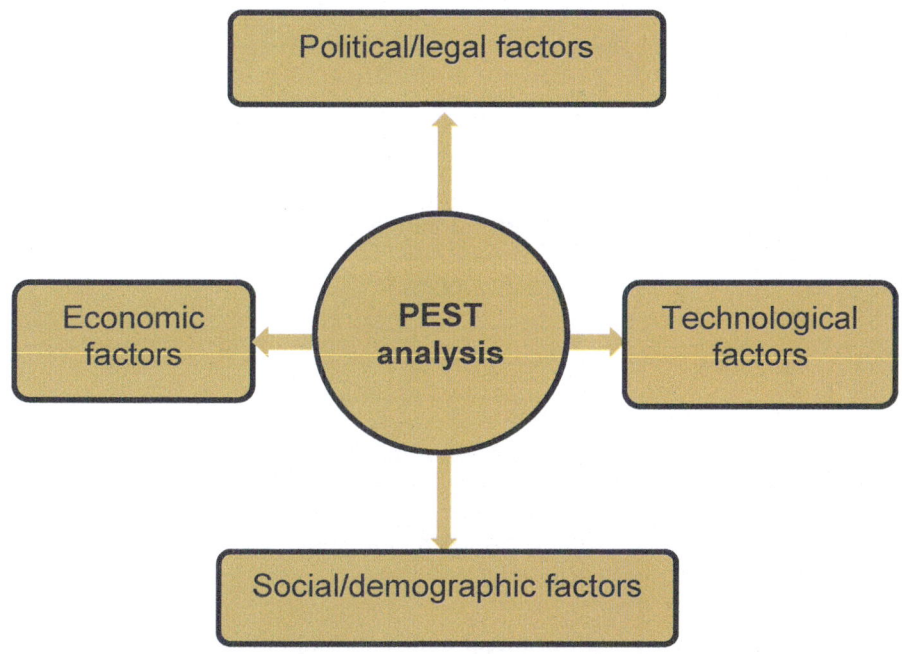

> Make sure you know what each element of the PESTLE acronym stands for.

KEY POINT The same categorisation of environmental factors is sometimes referred to as PESTLE analysis – political, economic, social, technical, legal and ecological environmental.

6.2 POLITICAL SYSTEMS AND GOVERNMENT POLICY

LEARNING SUMMARY

After studying this section you should be able to:

- explain how the political system and government policy affect the organisation

- describe the sources of legal authority, including supra-national bodies, national bodies and regional governments.

A political system

A political system is:

- a set of institutions, political organisations and interest groups (such as lobby groups); and

- the relationship between the; and

- the rules and norms that govern their functions (such as constitutions and election law).

Sources of legal authority

Sources of legal authority include the following:

Supra-national	UN resolutions
	International Court of Justice
	European Parliament
	European Courts

National	National Governments through Acts of Parliament
	Senior Courts (such as the Supreme Court in the UK and USA)
	Other major courts through the principles of case law and the setting of precedents

Regional	Regional/Federal Government (e.g. Welsh Assembly in the UK, State Government in the USA)
	Local councils through the use of bye-laws

How the government can affect an organisation

Governments can affect organisations in two major ways.

The first is government policy.

- **Housing** – new housing developments can give opportunities to house building firms and will create new communities that will demand shops, leisure facilities etc.

- **Crime** – crime policy affects firms that specialise in security.

- **Education** – education policy can affect the availability of suitable potential employees for firms.

- **Defence** – defence policy will primarily affect arms manufacturers. Closure of a military base could have serious implications for local suppliers.

- **Healthcare** – healthcare policy has obvious implications for drugs and equipment manufacturers and private hospitals.

- **Energy** – Policy regarding choice of energy sources (e.g. nuclear) will be critical to power generators.

- **Environmental** – Targets on greenhouse gas emissions will affect major manufacturers.

- **Farming** – government support through subsidies is critical for many farmers.

- **Town planning** – national plans to build new roads could influence business location.

- **Domestic** – a government may use regional development grants to attract new employers to areas of high unemployment.

- **Foreign** – protectionism and trade relations with other countries e.g. a ban on the sale of arm to Iran.

The other way that governments can affect organisations is by direct legislation.

Most industries have specific legislation that they have to comply with e.g. food labelling in the food industry. However, there are a number of pieces of **legislation that apply to most of all organisations**.

These include:

- employee protection

- data protection

- health and safety

- consumer protection

These are covered in detail below.

KEY POINT Organisations must comply with appropriate legislation. Failure to do so could result in fines, closure, bad publicity and/or loss of customers.

6.3 EMPLOYEE PROTECTION

LEARNING SUMMARY

After studying this section you should be able to:

- explain how the law protects the employee and the implications of employment legislation for the manager and the organisation.

Dismissal

KEY POINT Within many countries, the national governments have passed legislation which protects employees from unfair treatment by their employers.

Sometimes employees may resign because their employer has breached the terms of their contract of employment. This is known as constructive dismissal. Examples of constructive dismissal include employees resigning due to their employer:

- reducing their wages without agreement.

- allowing them to be bullied or harassed in the workplace.

Under the **Employment Rights Act** in the UK, to be 'fair', an employee must have been dismissed for one of the following reasons:

- they lacked the capability or qualifications for the job.

- they were guilty of misconduct (such as dishonesty or theft).

- the job was redundant.

- they were dismissed for legal reasons e.g. some jobs require employees to have no criminal record.

If an organisation is unable to prove that a dismissal was fair, they may be accused of unfair dismissal.

KEY POINT Unfair dismissal occurs when an employee has been dismissed for an 'unfair' reason (i.e. one that is not on the above list of 'fair' reasons).

In the UK, unfair reasons could include:

- pregnancy or parental leave.

- joining a trade union.

- discrimination over an employee's religion, ethnicity gender or sexuality.

> Note that unfair dismissal is not the same as wrongful dismissal.

KEY POINT Wrongful dismissal occurs with an employer breaks the terms of the employee's contract during the dismissal – for instance by not giving a proper notice period for dismissal.

Redundancy

DEFINITION **Redundancy** is a form of dismissal which occurs when an employer needs to reduce the size of their workforce.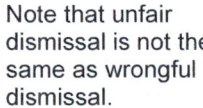

Legislation in this area gives several rights to the employee being made redundant, including:

- the right to consultation.

- the right to a fair notice period.

- the right to redundancy pay (will vary according to circumstances).

- the right for redundancy selection to be carried out fairly.

6.4 THE PRINCIPLES OF DATA PROTECTION

LEARNING SUMMARY

After studying this section you should be able to:

- identify the principles of data protection and security.

Data protection

DEFINITION   Data protection is concerned with protecting individuals against the misuse of information about them.

Under the **UK Data Protection Act 1998**, the main principles of data protection are:

- Personal data should be obtained and processed fairly and lawfully.

- Personal data should be held for one or more specified and lawful purposes, and should not be further processed in any manner incompatible with those purposes.

- Personal data should be adequate, relevant and not excessive in relation to the purposes for which it is processed.

- Personal data should be accurate and kept up-to-date.

- Personal data should not be kept for longer than as it necessary.

- Personal data shall be processed in accordance with the rights of data subjects.

- A data user is responsible for the security and protection of data against unauthorised access, alteration, destruction, disclosure or accidental loss.

- Personal data should not be transferred to another country outside the European Economic Area unless that country ensures an adequate level of protection for the rights and freedoms of data subjects in relation to the processing of personal data.

- Town planning – national plans to build new roads could influence business location.

- Domestic – a government may use regional development grants to attract new employers to areas of high unemployment.

- Foreign – protectionism and trade relations with other countries e.g. a ban on the sale of arms to Iran.

> A question can focus on your awareness of any one or more of these principles.

6.5   DATA SECURITY

LEARNING SUMMARY

After studying this section you should be able to:

- recognise the responsibility of the individual and the organisation for compliance with laws on data protection and security.

Data security

KEY POINT Data security is concerned with keeping data safe from various hazards that could destroy or compromise it.

Data security includes:

Physical risks – impact on the physical environment in which the system exists (e.g. fire or flood).

Human risks – access is gained to the system by an unauthorised user, either physically or remotely (e.g. hacking, virus infection or fraud).

Main risks to computer systems

The main risks to computer systems and the data they contain include the following:

POTENTIAL THREATS	COUNTER MEASURES
Physical damage, due to:	Well documented fire procedures.
	Staff training.
Fire.	Provide fire extinguishers and smoke/heat detectors, fire doors.
Flooding.	
Terrorist activities.	Computer equipment might be located in a segregated area in which air conditioning and dust controls operate.
Power failures.	Back-up generators.
Other environmental – heat, cold, humidity, dust.	Off-site facilities to cater for the possibility of total destruction of the in-house computer equipment.
	Off-site back-up copies of data files.

POTENTIAL THREATS	COUNTER MEASURES
Human damage, due to:	
Human interference, such as unauthorised access resulting in theft, piracy.	Restricted access to the computer room. Closed circuit TV and security guards. Hardware can be locked down.
Operational problems, such as program bugs and user operational errors.	Thorough testing of new programmes. Strict operating procedures. Adequate training of all staff members.
Data corruption e.g. viruses, hackers.	Anti-virus, firewall software and passwords. Off-site back-up copies of data files.
Data theft e.g. fraud, industrial espionage, loss of confidentiality.	Data encryption techniques and passwords. Physical access controls.

6.6 HEALTH AND SAFETY IN THE WORKPLACE

LEARNING SUMMARY

After studying this section you should be able to:

- recognise the responsibility of the individual and the organisation for compliance with laws on health and safety.

Health and safety

There are a number of potential hazards in any workplace.

Some examples include unsafe electrics, torn carpets, poor lighting, wet floors and top-heavy filing cabinets.

KEY POINT The law typically puts the responsibility for health and safety on both the employer and the employee.

EMPLOYER'S RESPONSIBILITIES (duties, amongst other things)

- provide a safe working environment
- prevent risks to health
- ensure that plant and machinery is safe
- inform staff of any potential hazards
- set up emergency plans
- provide adequate first aid facilities
- check that the right equipment is used and that it is regularly maintained

EMPLOYEE'S RESPONSIBILITIES (duties, amongst other things)

- take reasonable care of their own health and safety
- take reasonable care not to put other people at risk
- co-operate with their employer to ensure they have adequate training and are familiar with their employer's health and safety policies
- report any injuries suffered as a result of performing their job
- inform their employer if anything affects their ability to work safely
- check that the right equipment is used and that it is regularly maintained

Breaches of health and safety

If employers fail to provide a safe and healthy working environment, they may be in breach of common law, enabling employees to make a civil claim against them. In addition, they may be guilty of a criminal offence and be open to prosecution.

6.7 CONSUMER PROTECTION

LEARNING SUMMARY

After studying this section you should be able to:

- outline principles of consumer protection such as sale of goods and simple contracts.

Legislation

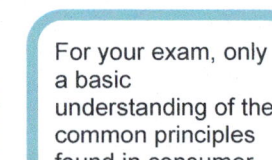

> **KEY POINT** Many countries have legislation which attempts to protect consumers from falling victim to unscrupulous or unethical business.

For your exam, only a basic understanding of the common principles found in consumer protection legislation is required.

Sale of goods

In the UK, there is a **Sale of Goods Act (1979)**. This has many features, but there are several key principles built into the Act. These include:

- The seller must have legal title to, or ownership of, the item they are selling.

- The goods sold must be of satisfactory quality and fit for their intended purpose.

- When a buyer makes a purpose based on the description of an item, the goods must correspond with the description.

In addition, legislation also often extends to the provision of services – not just goods. In the UK this is covered by the **Supply of Goods and Services Act (1982)**.

This requires services provided to be:

- Carried out with reasonable skill and care.

- Completed within a reasonable length of time.

- Completed at a reasonable price.

Simple contracts

> **DEFINITION** A contract is a legally enforceable agreement between two or more parties. Such a contract is known as a **'simple contract'** if it is not required to be in any particular form.

Remember, it is a common misconception that all contracts must be written in order to be legally binding. Many contracts can be in other forms, such as verbal contracts.

Features of a simple contract

Simple contracts must have the following features in order to be valid:

AGREEMENT – the parties must have agreed on the terms of the contract.

CONSIDERATION – in many countries, both parties usually have to get some value from the contract. Each party must offer some consideration to the other.

INTENTION TO CREATE LEGAL RELATIONS – both parties must clearly intend their relationships to be legally binding.

CAPACITY AND LEGALITY – each party to the contract must have the capability to enter to contract. In many countries, individuals under the ae of 16 cannot enter a legally binding contract. In addition, contracts cannot be formed for the purposes of an illegal act.

Do you understand?

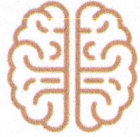

1   Senior courts are a source of supra-national authority.

    True or false?

2   Jeremy has found that an online retailer has sold information about him to a market research company. Is this an example of data protection or data security?

3   Campa Co holds data about many of its customers. It has recently set up an off-site back-up of this data to improve its security. Which potential data security threat will this measure most likely reduce?

    (i)   Data theft (ii) Viruses (iii) Fire or flood

4   While Jim was running down a staircase at work, he tripped and injured himself. Who is responsible for this accident?

    (i)   Jim (ii) His employer

5   Alison is a manager at D Co. As part of her contract with D, she is not supposed to hire any employees who are male or over the age of forty five. This contract is subsequently found to be unenforceable. Which of the features of a simple contract is missing from this agreement?

    (i)   Agreement (ii) Legality (iii) Consideration

1   False. Courts are a source of national authority.
2   Data protection.
3   (iii) Fire or flood. Off-site back-ups will not help prevent the theft of data.
4   (i) Jim. Jim's employer is responsible for ensuring that there are safe ways in and out of the place of work and that Jim has a safe working environment. Unless there was a problem with the staircase (e.g. poorly lit, uneven steps), which is not indicated, then it would appear that the employer has fulfilled their responsibility.
5   (ii) Legality. This contract involves discriminating against some potential employees, which is illegal in most jurisdictions. Remember that a contract is not valid if it requires one or more parties to break the law.

1   **Which of the following would a transport company monitor under the Technological heading as part of a PEST analysis?**

   A   Tracking systems to monitor driver hours/anti-theft devices/developments in tyre technology

   B   State of the economy/oil price movements/a rise in interest rates

   C   Fuel tax/congestion charges in cities/plans to build new roads

   D   Predicted car numbers and usage/public concerns over safety

2   Constructive dismissal occurs when an organisation no longer needs an employee and therefore terminates their contract.

   Is this statement TRUE or FALSE?

   A   True

   B   False

3   **Which of the following are typical rights of individuals with respect to data stored about them in data protection legislation?**

   (i)   Right of subject access – individuals are entitled to be told whether the data controller holds personal data about them

   (ii)   Right to prevent processing for the purposes of direct marketing

   (iii)   Right to take action to rectify, block or erase personal data through application to the courts

   (iv)   Right to require the data controller to reconsider a decision made on a purely automated basis

   A   (i) and (ii) only

   B   (ii), (iii) and (iv) only

   C   (i), (ii) and (iii) only

   D   (i), (ii), (iii) and (iv)

4   Consider the following statements:

   (1)   All contracts must be signed by all relevant parties in order to be binding.

   (2)   Consumer legislation typically only covers purchases of goods.

   Which of these statements is/are correct?

   A   (1) only

   B   (2) only

   C   Both

   D   Neither

5   To be valid, a simple contract must clearly indicate that both parties intended to create a legally binding relationship.

   Is this statement TRUE or FALSE?

   A   True

   B   False

7 **External analysis – economic factors**

The following topics are covered in this chapter:

- Introduction to economics
- Microeconomics
- Macroeconomics
- Economic policy options

7.1 INTRODUCTION TO ECONOMICS

LEARNING SUMMARY

After studying this section you should be able to:

- define economics and distinguish between microeconomics and macroeconomics.

Economics

Part of an organisation's external PEST analysis will involve assessing the economic factors which will affect its industry. The key issue is to identify potential opportunities and threats.

DEFINITION **Economics** can be defined in various ways, including:

'The study of how society allocates scarce resources, which have alternative uses, between competing ends'.

'The study of wealth creation'.

KEY POINT It is useful to distinguish between two aspects of economics:

Microeconomics – the study of the economic behaviour of individual consumers, firms and industries.

Macroeconomics – considers aggregate behaviour, and the study of the sum of individual economic decisions – in other words, the workings of the economy as a whole.

7.2 MICROECONOMICS

LEARNING SUMMARY

After studying this section you should be able to:

- define the concept of demand and supply for goods and services
- explain elasticity of demand and the impact of substitute and complementary goods
- explain the economic behaviour of costs in the short and long term
- define perfect competition, oligopoly, monopolistic competition and monopoly.

Demand

Substitution effect and income effect

For most goods, the lower the price, the higher its demand will be. This is the result of two processes:

- There is a **substitution effect**. This is where a consumer buys more of one good and less of another because of the relative price changes. Thus if two goods are substitutes, a fall in price of the first will lead consumers to switch some demand to the lower-priced good.

- There is an **income effect**. This is where a change in the price of a good affects the purchasing power of the consumers' income (a change in their real income). If the price of a good falls, the consumer experiences a rise in their real income and, as a result, tends to buy more of all normal goods and services.

Factors affecting demand for a good

FACTORS	
The price (P) of the good	For most goods as P↑, demand ↓ due to substitution and income effects
Prices of other goods	Substitutes v complementary goods
Income	Compare normal goods v inferior goods
Taste/ fashion	Could be influenced by advertising
Other factors	Population size, credit terms etc.

> Make sure you are happy with the distinction between instances that would cause a movement along the demand curve (either upwards or downwards) and instances which would cause a shift in the demand curve itself (either to the left or right).

Changes in the factors affecting demand

Changes in price

Leads to movements **along** the curve

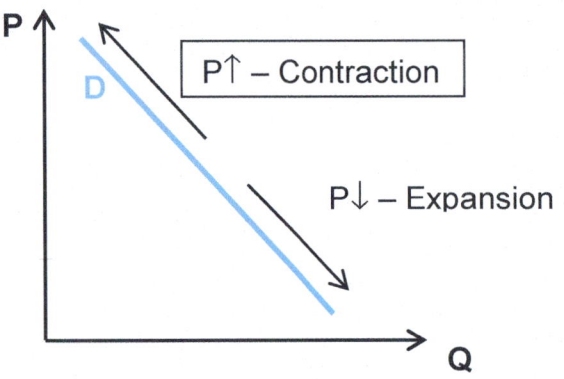

Changes in the conditions of demand

Leads to movements of the curve

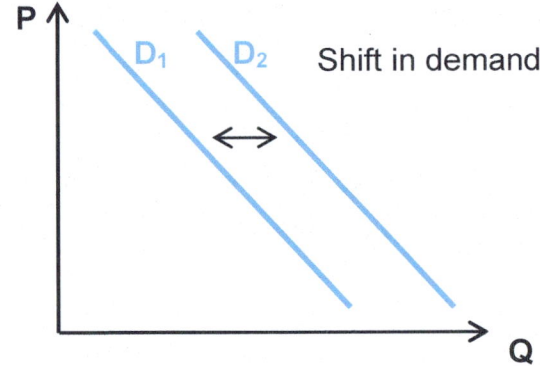

Price elasticity of demand (PED)

PED explains the responsiveness of demand to changes in price.

$$\text{PED} = \frac{\%\ \text{change in demand}}{\%\ \text{change in price}}$$

> Make sure you are comfortable working with this formula. Questions can be numerical in nature.

- Usually negative – assume this in questions unless otherwise indicated.

- Different methods of calculation:

  Arc method – non-average and average methods

  Point method

- >1 is 'elastic'. A price drop should increase revenue.

  ($\%\Delta Q > \%\Delta P$)

- <1 is 'inelastic'. A price increase should increase revenue.

  ($\%\Delta Q < \%\Delta P$)

Factors affecting elasticity of demand

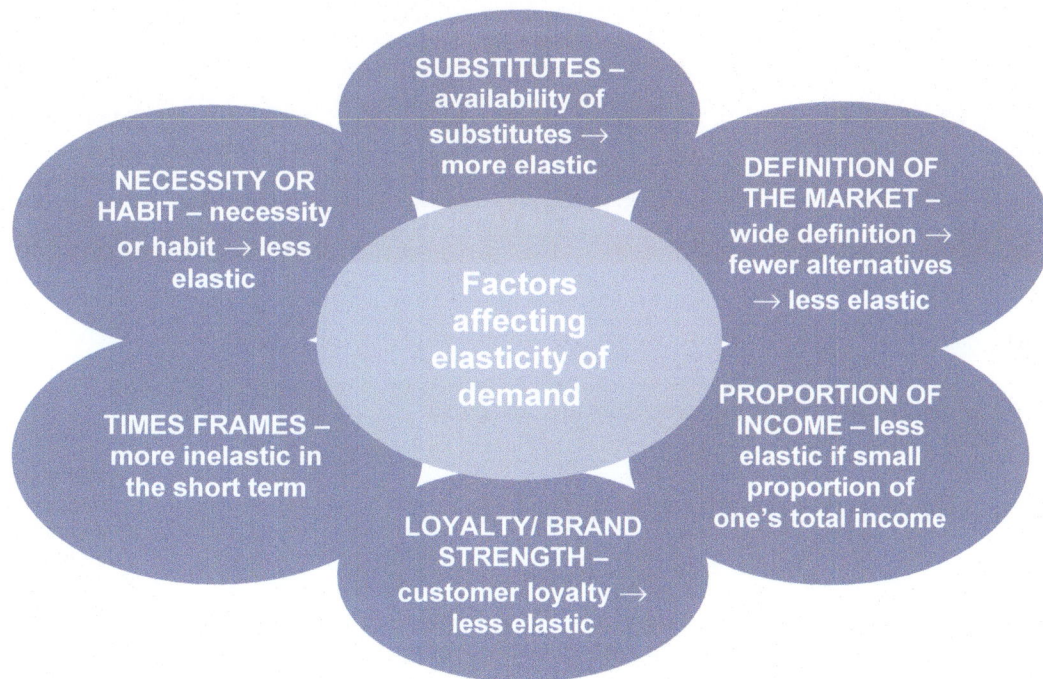

SUBSTITUTES – availability of substitutes → more elastic

NECESSITY OR HABIT – necessity or habit → less elastic

DEFINITION OF THE MARKET – wide definition → fewer alternatives → less elastic

Factors affecting elasticity of demand

TIMES FRAMES – more inelastic in the short term

PROPORTION OF INCOME – less elastic if small proportion of one's total income

LOYALTY/ BRAND STRENGTH – customer loyalty → less elastic

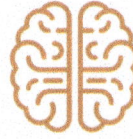

Do you understand?

1. A rise in the exchange rate for the domestic currency would NOT lead to a shift in the demand curve for overseas holidays.

   True or false?

2. Kitch Co are currently selling a product at a price of $20 with a resulting demand of 400,000 units her annum. They are considering reducing the price to $19 and expect demand will rise to 450,000 units.

   Calculate the PED.

3. The government of country X provides free healthcare to all its citizens. However, for more affluent citizens, a small charge is made if they need medication. The government has recently decided to increase this charge by a moderate amount to reflect the increasing cost of the medicines.

   What effect is this likely to have on the demand for medicine within country X?

Supply

> **DEFINITION** **Supply** is the amount that producers are willing and able to produce at a given price.

Factors affecting supply for a good

FACTORS	
Price	As P↑, supply ↑ due to cost considerations
Prices of other goods	Better to make them instead?
Cost changes	e.g. new technology, greater efficiency, VAT
Success of harvests	Especially agricultural goods

Make sure you are happy with the distinction between instances that would cause a movement along the supply curve (either upwards or downwards) and instances which would cause a shift in the supply curve itself (either to the left or right).

Changes in the factors affecting supply

Changes in price

Leads to movements **along** the curve

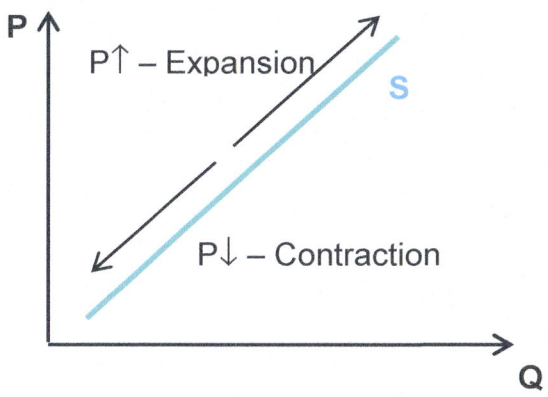

Changes in the conditions of supply

Leads to **movements of the curve**

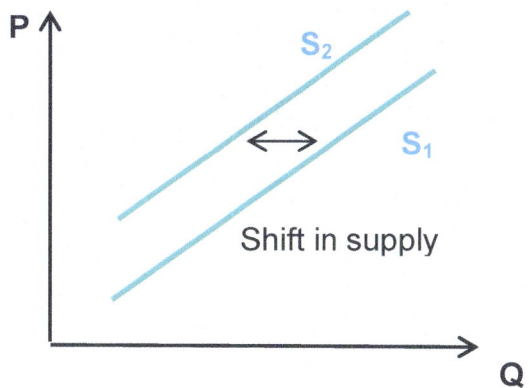

Price elasticity of supply

$$\text{Price elasticity of supply} = \frac{\% \text{ change in demand}}{\% \text{ change in price}}$$

- Always positive

- >1 is 'elastic'

- <1 is 'inelastic'

Make sure you are comfortable working with this formula. Questions can be numerical in nature.

Factors affecting elasticity of supply

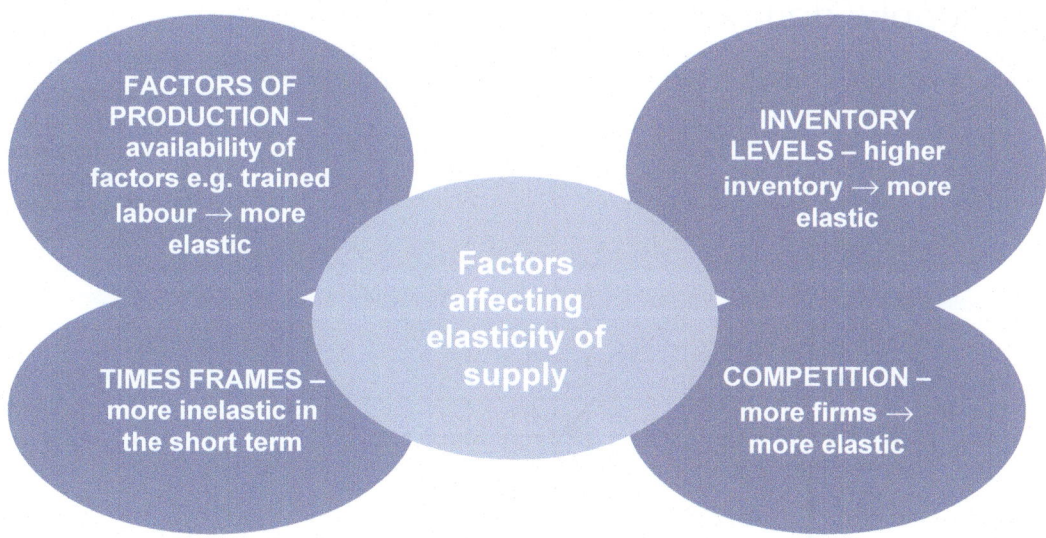

The price mechanism

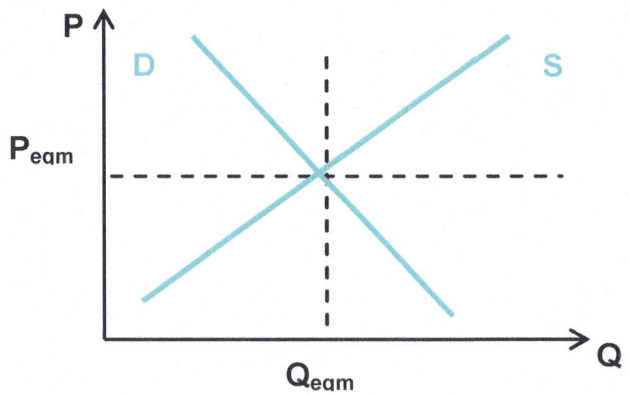

Price higher than equilibrium

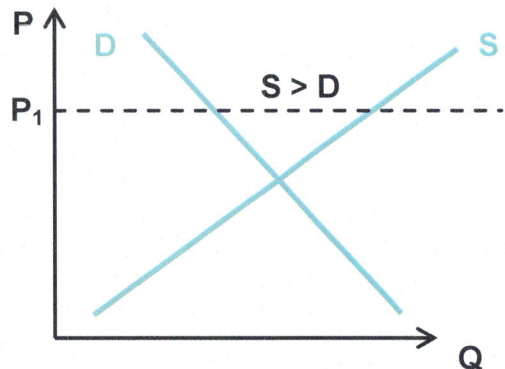

Excess supply – producers drop prices to clear surplus

Price lower than equilibrium

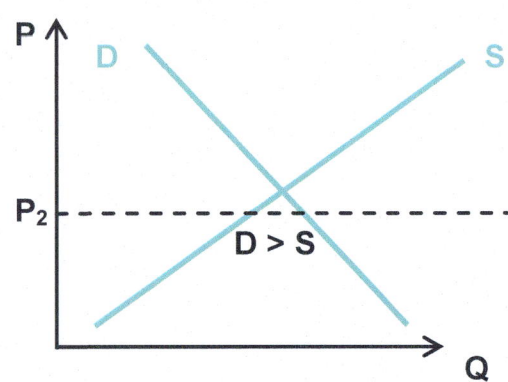

Excess demand – shortages force prices up

Shifts in supply/ demand

Changes in supply/ demand result in new equilibrium price e.g. a good tea harvest will result in lower prices.

In exam questions, consider whether it is the supply curve or the demand curve that is moving and in which direction.

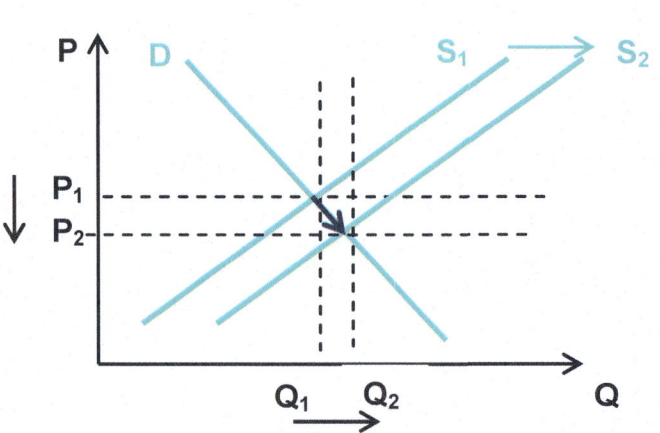

Interference with market prices

A government sets minimum prices typically to protect suppliers/ producers.

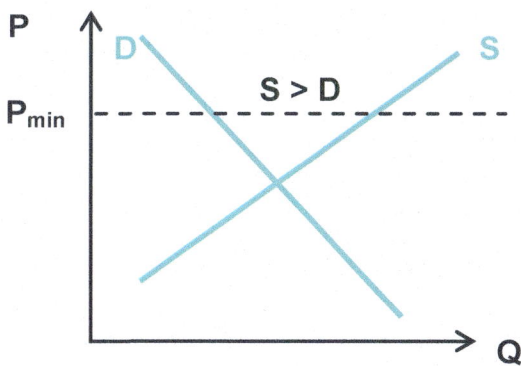

A government sets maximum prices typically to protect consumers and/ or control inflation.

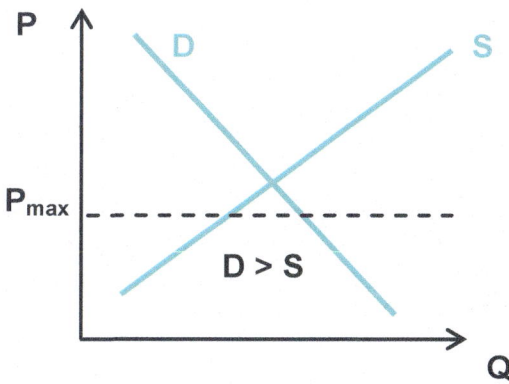

The economic behaviour of costs

KEY POINT The relationship between selling process and the quantity supplied or demanded is not the only relationship explored by microeconomics. It also examines how costs tend to vary over time.

Short term cost behaviour – in the short term, micro economists believe that costs follow the law of diminishing returns.

As equal quantities of one variable factor of input (such as labour or materials) are added to a fixed factor, output initially increases by a greater proportion, increasing returns and causing the average cost per unit to fall.

However, beyond a certain point, the addition to output will begin to decrease and the average cost per unit will start to rise again.

The short-run average total cost curve (SRATC) tends to therefore be 'U' shaped.

Long term cost behaviour – in the long term, all costs tend to be variable in nature. This is because it is now possible to vary the quantities of any factors that were fixed in the short term.

Eventually, however, as the business expands, it will tend to become less efficient controlling costs due to poor management and pressure on supplies. This effect is sometimes referred to as **diseconomies of scale** and results in the average cost of production increasing.

This gives rise to a long-run average total cost curve (LRATC) which is broadly similar to the SRATC.

Types of market

A **perfect market** exists when the following criteria are met:

- **Large numbers of customers and suppliers** – none of whom have the power to dominate the market.

- The **products or services** sold by all suppliers **are identical** (homogenous).

- There is **perfect information** – all customers and suppliers have complete information on the prices that goods and services are being sold at elsewhere in the market.

- **No barriers to entry to, or exit from, the market** – that is, competitors can easily enter and exit the market.

> **KEY POINT** A perfect market is seen as being the 'ideal' market position. If any of the factors above do not hold true, the market is described as imperfect. In the real world, most markets are imperfect.

Each of these forms depend on how organisations compete within the market.

Monopoly

Occurs when one company controls all or nearly all of the market for a particular product or service with no major competitors.

Often caused by high barriers to entry for the market, or due to government legislation.

Monopolistic competition

Occurs when a business has many different competitors, but each offers a somewhat differentiated product.

Typically there are no barriers to entering or leaving the market and there is significant advertising expenditure due to the large amount of competition.

As products are differentiated, businesses can charge more or less than their competitors.

Oligopoly

Market is dominated typically by between two and six different organisations.

If only two firms dominate the market it is referred to as a duopoly.

It is difficult for new firms to enter the market and the dominant businesses have significant influence over the prices of the goods and services they sell.

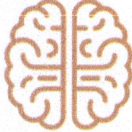

Do you understand?

1   When the price of a good is held above the equilibrium price, the result will be a shortage of the good.

   True or false?

2   The government of country Y has decided to impose a minimum wage for all workers, which is above the current average market labour rate. Which of the following is a potential consequence of this?

   (i)   Surplus labour created in country Y (ii) Rising employment in country Y

3   Not all items being bought and sold in a market have to be identical for it to be perfect.

   True or false?

7.3   MACROECONOMICS

LEARNING SUMMARY

After studying this section you should be able to:

- define macroeconomic policy and explain its objectives

- explain the main determinants of the level of business activity in the economy and how variations in the level of business affect individuals, households and businesses

- explain the impact of economic issues on the individual, the household and businesses.

Policy objectives

KEY POINT While some economists advocate a free market (one without government interference), in reality most governments intervene through various macroeconomic policies in an attempt to improve the performance of the economy.

Typically, governments will have four macroeconomic policy objectives:

- **Economic growth** – how can productive capacity be increased?

- **Inflation** – how can we ensure that general price levels do not increase?

- **Unemployment** – how can we ensure that everyone who wants a job has one?

- **Balance of payments** – how should we manage our financial relationships and trade with other countries?

Economic growth

WHY WE WANT GROWTH	COUNTER ARGUMENT
More goods produced for people to buy.	Need growth > inflation, i.e. real growth.
Lower unemployment.	Market failure issues – e.g. growth may be in demerit goods, may produce more pollution, may be due to exploiting the poor, etc.
People earn more so can afford these extra goods.	Need growth per head.
The above should result in an improved standard of living for citizens.	Measurement of growth is difficult given 'black markets' and non-marketed goods.

Inflation

WHY WE WANT LOW INFLATION	COUNTER ARGUMENT
Inflation causes uncertainty and stifles investment.	If inflation is uniform and predictable, then not a problem.
The poor and those on fixed incomes suffer.	Those on index linked pay may benefit.
Inflation discourages savings.	Companies can see their profits↑.
In extreme cases the function of money may break down.	
Inflation distorts the working of the price mechanism.	

Unemployment

WHY WE WANT LOW UNEMPLOYMENT	COUNTER ARGUMENT
The Government has to pay out benefits rather than collect taxes.	Some unemployment will arise even in a healthy economy as people have the confidence to change jobs.
Unemployment has been linked to rising crime, poor health and the breakdown of the family.	
Unemployment can damage peoples' self-esteem.	
The long-term unemployed may become deskilled/ unemployable.	
Unemployment is a wasted resource.	

Managing the balance of trade

WHY WE WANT TO AVOID A LONG TERM DEFICIT	WHY WE WANT TO AVOID A LONG TERM SURPLUS
It will have to borrow money to fund the deficit, resulting in extra interest payments.	A long-term trade surplus can cause significant inflationary pressures.
The alternative is to sell assets.	A long term surplus is presumably at the expense of other countries' deficits.
There will be pressure on the country's currency to depreciate.	

Aggregate demand (AD)

While the level of activity within a particular industry will depend on specific PEST issues, the overall level of activity in an economy (and therefore its growth) can be predicted by reference to several key factors.

KEY POINT

AD = total demand for goods and services in the economy.

AD = C + I + G + (X – M)

Key definitions:

- **C = Consumption.** Goods produced and sold to customers

- **S = Savings.** Income not spent

- **I = Investment.** Production of, or expenditure on, non-consumption goods. Carried out by firms

- **G = Government expenditure**

- **X = Exports**

- **M = Imports**

The economy can be measured in 3 ways, each of which gives the same answer:

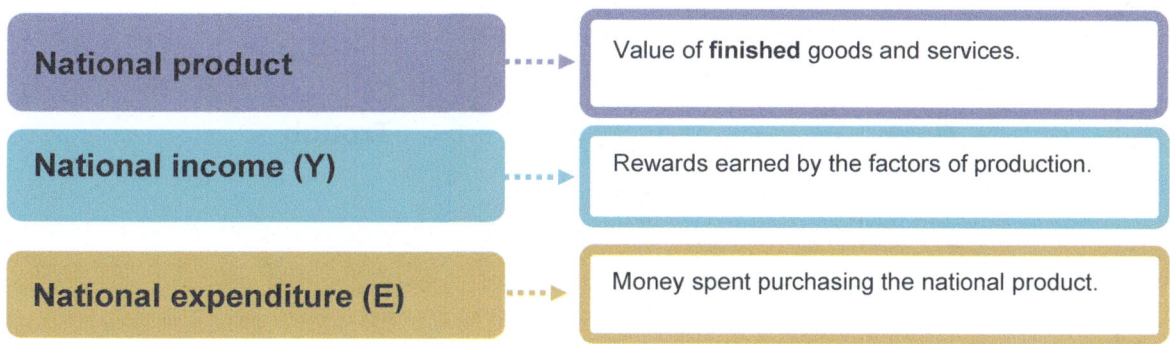

National product ····▶ Value of **finished** goods and services.

National income (Y) ····▶ Rewards earned by the factors of production.

National expenditure (E) ····▶ Money spent purchasing the national product.

AD is inversely related to prices since a price fall would raise everyone's real wealth and thus tends to raise spending.

AD may shift if any one component (e.g. investment or exports) changes.

Thus the AD curve slopes down from left to right but may shift.

Movements in aggregate demand

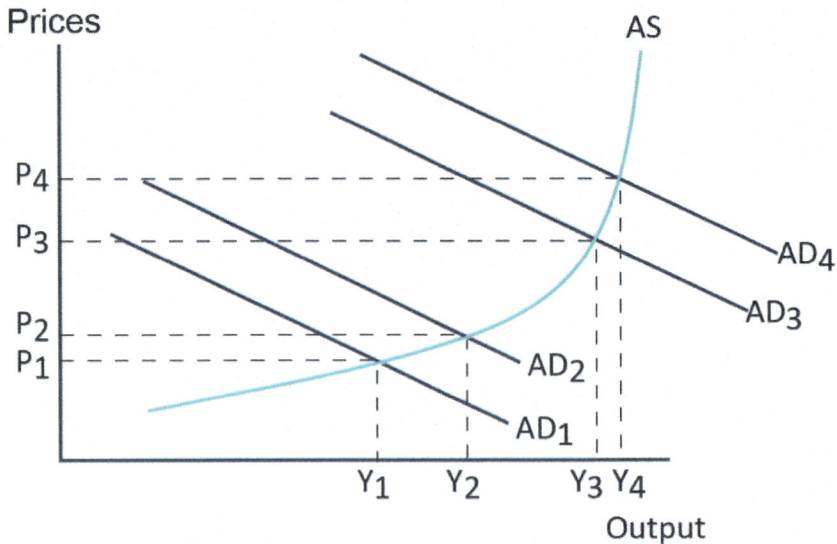

- If demand increases from AD_1 to AD_2, then this should give significant growth (Y_1 to Y_2) – with reduced unemployment – but without significant increases in inflation (P_1 to P_2).

- However, attempts to move AD from AD_3 to AD_4 will result in a smaller impact on unemployment and output (Y_3 to Y_4) but a much larger increase in inflation (P_3 to P_4).

- The impact of moving AD thus depends on where you are on the AS curve.

Trade cycles

KEY POINT Some economists argue that another objective of governments should be to smooth out trade cycles to avoid 'boom and bust' years.

7.4 ECONOMIC POLICY OPTIONS

LEARNING SUMMARY

After studying this section you should be able to:

- describe the main types of economic policy that may be implemented by government and supra-national bodies to maximise economic welfare

- recognise the impact of fiscal and monetary policy measures on the individual, the household and businesses.

Introduction

KEY POINT Governments have two main ways of affecting the economy.

Fiscal policy – refers to the government's taxation and spending plans.

Monetary policy – refers to the management of the money supply in the economy.

Fiscal policy options

The two key elements that government must plan for each year are:

Income – this is primarily the money the government raises from direct and indirect taxes on individuals and businesses.

Expenditure – this is the total amount the government will need to spend to provide services for the population.

In the medium- to long-term, most governments would prefer to run a balanced budget. This occurs when government income and expenditure are exactly matched.

Budget deficit/ surplus

A **budget deficit** occurs when government spending > government income.

To fund a budget deficit, the governments will need to borrow money, referred to as the **Public Sector Net Cash Requirement (PSNCR).**

Government is injecting more money into the economy than it is taking out. An **expansionary strategy.**

Often used when a **deflationary gap** exists in the economy. This occurs when the level of aggregate demand is insufficient to lead to full employment.

A **budget surplus** occurs when government spending < government income.

By running a surplus, the government is taking money out of the economy, reducing aggregate demand. **A contractionary policy.**

Often used when an **inflationary gap** exists in the economy. This occurs when aggregate demand is higher than the country can supply – leading to high inflation.

Monetary policy

Monetary policy refers to the management of the **money supply**, via:

- Changing interest rates (in some countries,, such as the UK, interest rates are set by the central bank (i.e. the Bank of England in the UK). In other countries, rates are directly set by the government.

- Directly affecting the money supply using open market operations.

- Indirectly affecting the money supply using banks' reserve requirements.

KEY POINT Monetary policy (like fiscal policy) can be expansionary or contractionary.

An **expansionary policy** increases the money supply in the economy, helping to increase investment and unemployment.

A **contractionary policy** decreases the total money supply, helping to reduce demand and easing inflation.

Open market operations refer to a government buying/selling bonds.

Quantitative easing

DEFINITION   Quantitative easing is a relatively unconventional monetary policy that involves a country's central bank buying financial assets (such as government and corporate bonds) using money that it has generated electronically.

Put more simply - the central bank has essentially printed itself new money that it can spend (although in practice it is unusual for the money to actually be printed).

This has the effect of increasing the amount of cash in the economy, hopefully increasing aggregate demand. However, it can cause increased inflation and weaken a country's exchange rate – which both come with their own problems.

Economic theories

Several economists have proposed different theories about the best ways for governments to look after the economies of their countries. Different governments may follow different theories.

| **Classical theory** | This theory suggests government does nothing. It is believed that the economy will naturally move to an equilibrium point with full employment, all by itself. |

Keynesian view (demand side)	Keynes argued that governments need to manipulate the level of aggregate demand within the economy.
	It is argued that government intervention is often needed in order to move the economy closer to its ideal equilibrium point (one where there was full employment).
	Practically, this means governments should borrow money and inject it into the economy (run a budget deficit) when economic growth needs stimulating.
	Governments should increase taxes and run a budget surplus to slow the economy down if it was growing too fast and experiencing significant inflation.

> **Monetarist view (supply side)** · · ▶
>
> Monetarists returned to the classical view that there was only one equilibrium point in the economy.
>
> It is argued that the only reason that the economy does not find its equilibrium is because it will be hindered by market imperfections.
>
> The role of government is therefore to remove imperfections allowing the economy to naturally find its ideal equilibrium.
>
> Market imperfections tend to include: inflation, government spending and inflation, price fixing, minimum wage legislation, regulation of markets, abuses of monopoly power.

Unemployment

> **DEFINITION Cyclical unemployment** is due to insufficient aggregate demand.

To combat cyclical unemployment, Keynesian economists would argue the need to boost aggregate demand. Monetarists would argue the need to boost aggregate supply.

> **DEFINITION Frictional unemployment** is due to people moving from one job to another.

Frictional unemployment is not necessarily a problem. It can be reduced by better information.

> **DEFINITION Structural/ technological unemployment** is due to structural changes in industries e.g. steel production.

To combat structural/ technological unemployment, supply side policies could be implemented e.g. retraining, relocation grants.

> **DEFINITION Seasonal unemployment** is due to the seasonal nature of industries e.g. demand for fruit pickers.

Seasonal unemployment can create regional economic problems.

> **DEFINITION Real wage unemployment** is due to wages being (artificially) too high.

Real wage unemployment is a market imperfection e.g. as a result of strong unions. It can be combatted by reducing union powers and abolishing minimum wage agreements.

Inflation

As with unemployment, there are a number of different causes of inflation. Government policy will depend on which cause is dominant in the economy.

- **Demand – pull inflation**

  This occurs when demand for goods and services in the economy is growing faster than the ability of the economy to supply these goods and services. This will lead to price increases.

  Keynesian policies would focus on reducing aggregate demand through tax rises, cuts in spending and higher interest rates.

- **Cost-push inflation**

  This is where the underlying cost of the factors of production rise. This makes goods more expensive to make, forcing manufacturers to raise their prices.

- **Imported inflation**

  If the national currency weakens, the cost of imports will rise, leading to domestic inflation.

  This can be reduced by policies to strengthen the national currency.

- **Monetary inflation**

  Increasing the money supply increases the purchasing power of the economy, boosting demand for goods and services. If this expansion occurs faster than expansion in the supply of goods and services, inflation can arise.

  Monetarists would argue that this should be controlled through increased interest rates, which will reduce the growth in money supply.

- **Expectations effect**

  Many individuals and businesses will have an expectation that goods and services will increase in price each year due to inflation.

  In order to protect themselves against these rises, wages and prices will therefore be increased now.

  This may lead to an inflationary spiral, where inflation occurs because there is an expectation that it will occur.

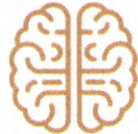

Do you understand?

1   A weakening currency could provide a boost to the aggregate demand of a country.

   True or false?

2   Inflation encourages investment in a national economy.

   True or false?

3   Which of the following are consequences of unemployment?

   (i)   There is reduced economic output.

   (ii) There is less pressure for the government to increase taxes.

   (iii) There is greater inflationary pressure in the economy.

---

1   True. A weakening currency will tend to make imports more expensive, reducing demand for them. Exports will be more competitive, increasing AD.

2   False. Inflation tends to discourage investment in a national economy in a number of ways. This includes a loss in confidence by both domestic and international investors.

3   (i) only. Unemployed people are not economically active and are not adding to the output from the economy. With reference to (ii) there is not less pressure for the government to increase taxes. During periods of unemployment, government tax receipts will be low but its expenditure (on employment and other benefits) will be high. There is therefore increased pressure on government to raise taxes to fund these obligations. With reference to (iii) there is not greater inflationary pressure in the economy. Lower levels of demand for goods and services are unlikely to put upward pressure on the price of goods and services. Equally, unemployment reduces upward pressure on wages as there is, in effect, an oversupply of labour.

1 **(a)** Here are four types of unemployment:

A   Cyclical

B   Real wage

C   Structural

D   Frictional

Required:

Identify the type of unemployment above which is associated with each of the following descriptions, by writing A, B, C or D.

(i)   **Tends to occur in industries that are highly unionised**

(ii)   **Caused by aggregate demand in the economy being too low to create employment opportunities**

(iii)   **Short-term unemployment as people move between jobs**

(iv)   **Caused by changes in the skills required by the economy.**

(b) Consider the following economics terms:

A   Deflationary gap

B   Fiscal policy

C   Monetary policy

D   Stagflation

The following sentences contain gaps which are missing a particular term from the list above.

Management of the Government's taxation and spending plans is known as _1_.

Required:

(i)   **Select the term that appropriately fills gap 1 above; i.e. select A, B, C or D.**

Poor economic growth over an extended period can sometimes lead to rises in the prices of goods and services. This is referred to as _2_.

Required:

(ii)   **Select the term that appropriately fills gap 2 above; i.e. select A, B, C or D.**

2   (a)   BVO is a small business, which manufactures and sells a number of products, including product X (a relatively low-value item). BVO has recently been considering its pricing policy for this product.

It has estimated that if it raises the current selling price (per unit) of product X from $1 to $1.50, annual demand will drop from 100,000 units to 90,000 units.

BVO is uncertain of the implications of this for its product, or what might be causing the current level of price elasticity.

Required:

Write down which FOUR of the following options could reasonably be inferred from the above information by selecting FOUR of the letters from A to H.

A   The price elasticity of demand (PED) for product X is 5

B   Product X is unit elastic

C   Product X may be a product that customers buy out of habit

D   Product X may have few, if any, substitutes

E   The price elasticity of demand (PED) for product X is 0.28

F   Product X may see a sharper fall in demand if the price rise lasts for a long period.

G   Product X has a price elasticity of demand (PED) of 0.2

H   Product X would be more profitable if the price was cut rather than raised

(b)   Consider the following micro-economics terms:

A   A shift

B   A duopoly

C   Equilibrium

D   A contraction

The following sentences contain gaps which are missing a particular term from the list above.

BVO has noted that product Y's sales have fallen in recent years due to a fall in disposable income of its major customers. This is evidence that _1_ in the demand curve for the product has occurred.

Required:

(i)   Select the term that appropriately fills gap 1 above; i.e. select A, B, C or D.

BVO sells product Z in country G. Only one other manufacturer sells a similar product in country G, meaning that the two companies dominate the market. Currently, production and sales volumes for these products has reached exactly the same levels, suggesting _2_ in the market for this product.

Required:

(ii)   Select the term that appropriately fills gap 2 above; i.e. select A, B, C or D.

8.1 SOCIAL AND DEMOGRAPHIC FACTORS

LEARNING SUMMARY

After studying this section you should be able to:

- explain the effects of social and demographic trends on business outcomes and the economy

- describe the impact of changes in social structure, values, attitudes and tastes on the organisation

- identify and explain the measures that governments may take in response to the medium and long-term impact of demographic change.

Demographic trends

DEFINITION The word **demographics** refers to the composition of the population in any given area – whether a country or an area within a country.

KEY POINT There are a number of demographic issues that businesses will need to monitor.

These include:

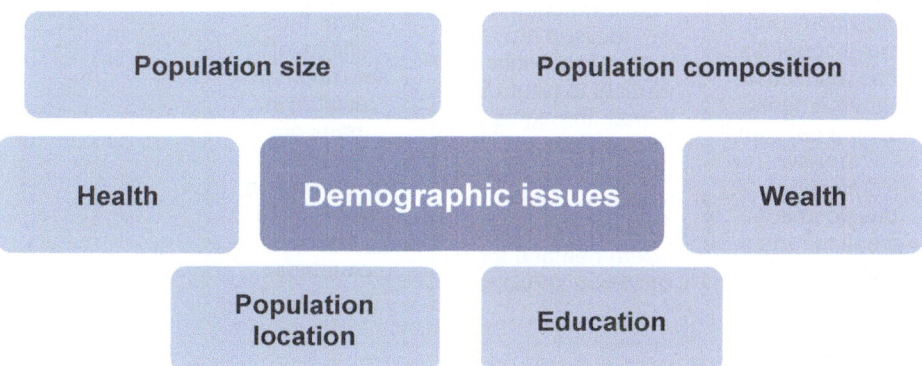

Population size

Population composition

Health

Demographic issues

Wealth

Population location

Education

Social trends

This examines how society changes over time. There are a number of key ways this change occurs, including:

Social structure

Values

Attitudes

Social trends

Tastes

Social influences

According to **Johnson and Scholes** the social influences that should be monitored include the following:

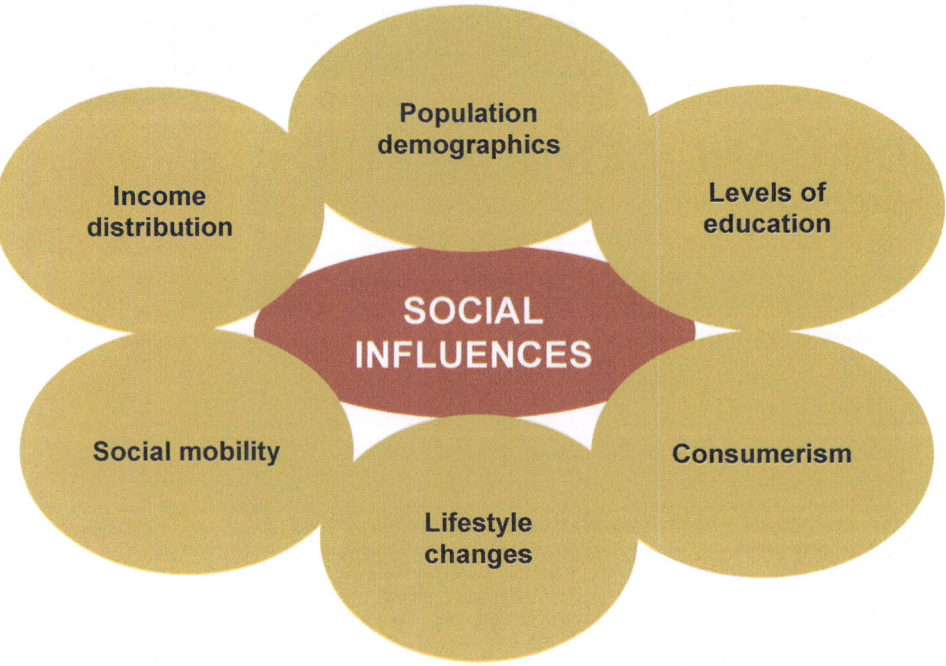

Government policy

For many firms the impact of social and demographic change is primarily through government responses to trends, for example:

Population structure	Housing	Employment	Health
e.g. governments in countries with low birth rates often introduce financial incentives to encourage women to have more children.	e.g. increasing demand for new homes in many countries has resulted in governments setting out plan for new housing developments, creating further demand for builders.	e.g. the UK government has focused on enabling single parents to return to work through a mixture of childcare vouchers and tax credits. This has created extra demand for childcare services.	e.g. concerns over the effects of smoking has resulted in bans on tobacco advertising on television in many countries.

8.2 ENVIRONMENTAL FACTORS

LEARNING SUMMARY

After studying this section you should be able to:

- list the ways in which the business can affect or be affected by its physical environment

- describe ways in which businesses can operate more efficiently and effectively to limit damage to the environment

- identify the benefits of economic sustainability to a range of stakeholders.

How can a business affect or be affected by its physical environment?

KEY POINT Before a company can decide how to look after its environment, it needs to understand the possible impacts a business and its environment may have on each other.

You could be asked to choose from a list of possible ways an organisation can reduce the amount of damage they cause to the environment.

Business effects upon the environment

- Pollution, such as production of rubbish or harmful emissions
- Wastage and resources, such as food, water or other raw materials
- Destruction of natural habitats
- Loss of plant and animal species

Environmental effects upon the business

- Changing climate may affect a number of businesses
- Lack of resources will increase the cost of raw materials
- Loss of sales – if a business has a poor environmental record, customers may no longer wish to trade with it
- Legislation – polluting companies may trigger legislation by governments. The additional compliance costs and fines may reduce profits.

Sustainability

KEY POINT Nowadays, businesses should look to be environmentally sustainable.

STAKEHOLDER	BENEFIT
Workers/ local community	Reduced waste and pollution will lead to a more pleasant, healthier environment.
Customers	Many customers prefer dealing with businesses that look after the environment as they are seen as being more ethical.
Shareholders	Reduction of waste and increased efficiency can improve business profits.
Public	Reduced pollution can lead to fewer environmental problems.

8.3 TECHNOLOGICAL FACTORS

LEARNING SUMMARY

After studying this section you should be able to:

- explain the effects of technological change on organisation structure and strategy: downsizing, delayering, outsourcing

- describe the impact of information technology and information systems development on business processes.

Introduction

Technological changes can affect a firm in many different ways, such as:

- **Organisational structures** e.g. employees working from home but still able to access files and systems at work.

- **Product developments** e.g. turntables were effectively replaced by CD players which in turn were replaced by MP3 players.

- **Production changes** e.g. computer-controlled machinery.

- **Marketing** e.g. using the internet to sell the product.

Impact on organisational structure

These changes have resulted in downsizing and delayering in firms.

> **DEFINITION Downsizing** is a term used for reducing the number of employees in an organisation without necessarily reducing the work or the output.

> **DEFINITION Delayering** is often linked to downsizing. It is the process of removing layers of management. This is usually to change the organisation from one with a rigid hierarchical framework with numerous layers of supervisory grades into a 'flatter' organisation with minimal layers of management.

> Your knowledge of these definitions can be directly tested.

Outsourcing

> **DEFINITION Outsourcing** means contracting out aspects of the work of the organisation, previously done in-house, to specialist providers.

There are four key types of outsourcing:

- **Total** – where the third-party supplier provides most or all of the organisation's IT systems and services.

- **Ad-hoc** – when the organisation needs IT support for a short period and hires in external support as needed on a temporary basis.

- **Partial** – where some IT functions are outsourced, such as maintenance or support, but others are kept in-house.

- **Project management** – similar to ad-hoc, this occurs when the creation and/or implementation of a specific IT system are outsourced to a third party supplier.

ADVANTAGES	DISADVANTAGES
Supplier may have specialist skills that the organisation lacks.	May be difficult to bring IT back in-house at a later date, as may lose staff with specialist knowledge from the organisation.
May operate on a fixed fee contract, removing uncertainty surrounding IT fees for the year.	May lead to being locked into an unfavourable contract with a poor quality supplier.
May improve business flexibility, allowing variation of the level of work the supplier performs.	Will allow third-party supplier access to the organisation's information, which may risk data security breaches.
The supplier may be more efficient at running the IT function, leading to cost savings.	By relying on a third party for its IT, the organisation will have no way to create its own, unique systems. This means it cannot obtain competitive advantage from its systems.

Do you understand?

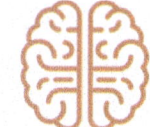

1   'The acceptable behaviours and norms that help bind a social group together' is the definition of:

(i)   Attitudes (ii) Tastes (iii) Values

2   B is a food manufacturer who is considering improving its environmental image. Which of the following would NOT help B to limit the damage it is doing to the environment?

(i)   Charging customers for using plastic carrier bags

(ii)   Improving accessibility for less able customers

(iii)   Improving sales forecasting to reduce wastage of inventory

3   Comment on how technological changes have affected the demand for holiday travel agents.

4   Downsizing is the process of reducing the number of levels of management.

True or false?

1   (iii) by definition.

2   (ii) While this would be an ethical activity for B to undertake, it would not directly reduce B's impact on the environment.

3   Demand for travel agents grew hugely when technology allowed agents to explore availability and book flights form their premises in the 1970s. More recently, the internet has allowed customers to do this from the comfort of their own homes, reducing the demand for agents. There has also been an increase in the number of online agents, such as Expedia.co.uk offering to build bespoke holidays.

4   False. Downsizing is reducing the number of employees. The definition given is that of delayering.

Exam style questions

1   Consider the following statements:

   (1)   Monitoring population growth is usually only important for public or governmental organisations.

   (2)   'Attitudes' represent an individual's personal preferences or patterns of choice.

   Which of these statements is/are correct?

   A   (1) only

   B   (2) only

   C   Both

   D   Neither

2   Outsourcing is often associated with which business processes?

   A   Allowing employees to work from home

   B   Sourcing data from outside the company

   C   Transferring call centres overseas

   D   Sending staff on foreign assignments

3   Which of the following is NOT a way in which businesses can reduce the amount of damage they cause to the environment?

   A   Rebranding of products

   B   Recycling

   C   Redesigning products to use fewer materials

   D   Careful production planning

4   Organisations should use resources in such a way that they do not compromise the needs of future generations.

   What is this a definition of?

   A   Environmentalism

   B   Sustainability

   C   Future-focus

   D   Redesign

9 Competitive factors

The following topics are covered in this chapter:

- Competitive advantage
- Porter's five forces analysis
- Generic strategies
- Porter's value chain

9.1 COMPETITIVE ADVANTAGE

LEARNING SUMMARY

After studying this section you should be able to:

- describe the activities of an organisation that affect its competitiveness.

Competitive advantage

> **DEFINITION** Part of a firm's external analysis will involve assessing the degree and sources of competition within the industry. The key issue here is whether the firm has a sustainable **competitive advantage**.

This will be analysed in three steps:

- the main competitive forces in an industry.

- the different ways a firm can achieve a competitive advantage.

- how different activities and departments within the firm contribute to its competitiveness.

9.2 PORTER'S FIVE FORCES ANALYSIS

LEARNING SUMMARY

After studying this section you should be able to:

- explain the factors or forces that influence the level of competitiveness in an industry or sector using Porter's five forces model.

> A question could describe an issue and ask you which heading of Porter's five forces model the issue would fall under.

Five forces model

- **Competitive rivalry** – will depend on the number and strength of competitors, the level of fixed costs and the rate of growth in the industry.

- **Threat of new entrants** – new entrants will bring extra capacity and intensify competition.

- **Threat of substitutes** – more substitutes makes it easier for buyers to switch to other products.

- **Power of buyers** – powerful buyers can force price cuts/quality improvements.

- **Power of suppliers** – can charge higher prices, forcing down profit margins.

9.3 GENERIC STRATEGIES

LEARNING SUMMARY

After studying this section you should be able to:

- describe and explain Porter's generic strategies.

Generic strategies

This model, developed by Porter, examines the different ways that an organisation can achieve a competitive advantage in its market.

KEY POINT Porter argued that businesses could adopt one of three strategies to gain competitive advantage. Each business can adopt the strategy that best fits their individual circumstances.

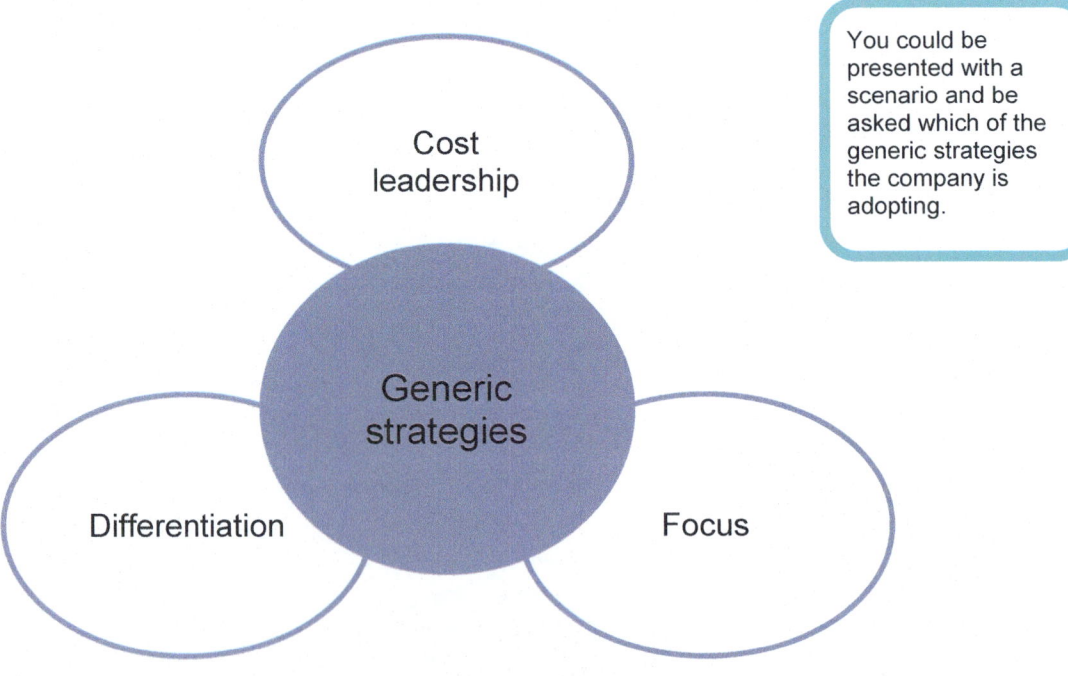

> You could be presented with a scenario and be asked which of the generic strategies the company is adopting.

- **Cost leadership** -   this involves the business making a product of similar quality to its rivals but at a lower cost. This is normally achieved through internal inefficiencies.

- **Differentiation** – this involves the business persuading customers that their product is superior to that of their rivals. It can be done by adding additional features to the product or by altering customer perception of the product through advertising or branding. Differentiation will usually allow the business to charge a premium price for its product.

- **Focus** – this involves aiming at a segment of the market, rather than the market as a whole. A particular group of consumers is identified with the same needs and the business will provide products or services that are tailored to their needs. This will typically allow the business to charge a premium for their products.

Conclusion - Porter argued that businesses needed to adopt one of the above three approaches or they would be 'stuck in the middle', which would make it difficult for them to compete successfully.

9.4   PORTER'S VALUE CHAIN

LEARNING SUMMARY

After studying this section you should be able to:

- identify the main elements within Porter's value chain and explain the meaning of a value network.

Value chain

Porter developed his value chain to determine whether and how a firm's activities contribute towards its competitive advantage.

KEY POINT The approach involves breaking the firm down into five 'primary' and four 'support' activities, and then looking at each to see if they give a cost advantage or quality advantage.

A question could ask you to choose the correct description for any of the activities within Porter's value chain.

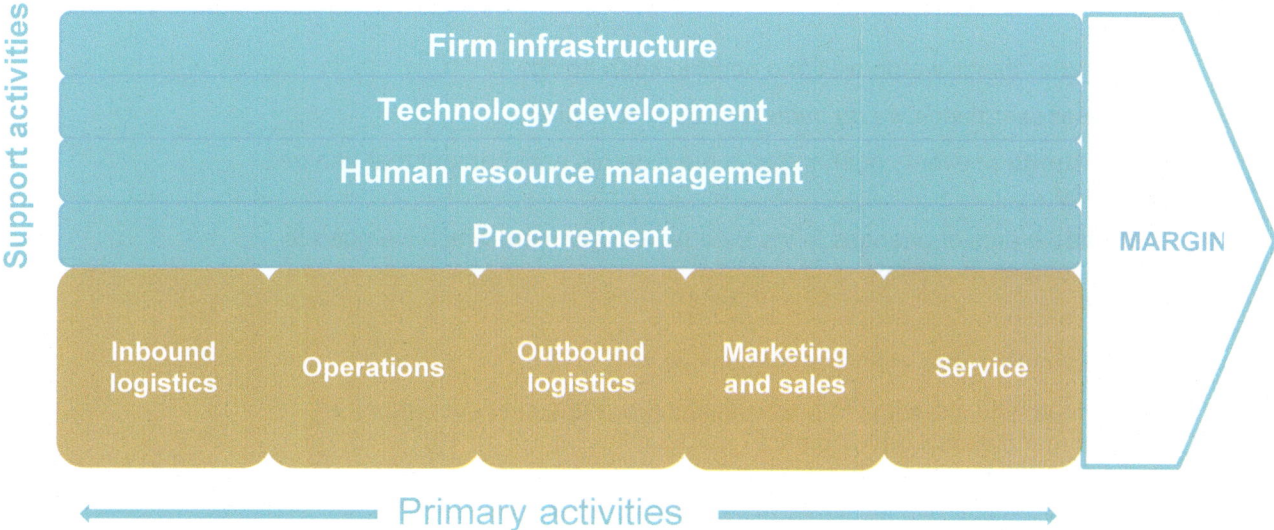

Usefulness:

- identifies activities that do not add value

- looks at relationships between activities

- helps understand an organisation's source of competitive advantage – if any!

9.5 CORPORATE APPRAISAL

LEARNING SUMMARY

After studying this section you should be able to:

- identify a business's strengths, weaknesses, opportunities and threats (SWOT) in a market and the main source of competitive advantage.

SWOT

Corporate appraisal (SWOT) provides the framework to summarise the key outputs from the external and internal analysis.

KEY POINT The strengths and weaknesses normally result from the organisation's internal factors, and the opportunities and threats relate to the external environment.

The tools and techniques used to provide the SWOT analysis will be covered in the next few chapters.

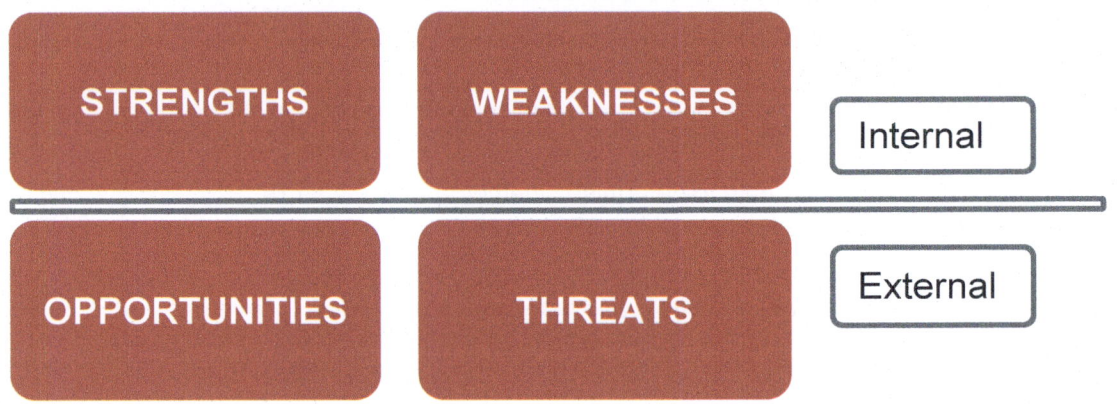

Strengths: things we do well and need to keep doing.

Weaknesses: things we do badly and need to improve.

Opportunities: events or changes in the external environment that can be exploited.

Threats: events or changes in the external environment which we need to protect ourselves against.

Once identified, management can consider:

- matching strengths to opportunities may highlight new areas for organisational development

or

- methods of removing weaknesses or dealing with the threats the organisation faces.

Do you understand?

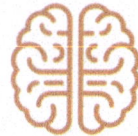

1   'Low industry profitability is a barrier to entry'.

    True or false?

2   K Co makes glass tableware. Its products are similar to those created by K's rivals, but K has managed to achieve significant economies of scale by bulk-buying its materials from one main supplier. This has enabled K to sells its products more cheaply than their competitors. Which of the following strategies has K adopted?

    (i) Cost leadership (ii) Focus (iii) Differentiation (iv) Stuck in the middle

3   Cameo Co has recently introduced a new automated inventory system that allows management to identify older inventory quickly. This will allow the company to reduce its currently high level of wastage. Which activity within Cameo's value chain will the new system improve?

    (i) Outbound logistics (ii) Inbound logistics (iii) Procurement

4   A company is attempting to analyse its competitive environment. Which of the following models would be most appropriate for it to use?

    (i) SWOT (ii) PEST (iii) Five forces (iv) Value chain

---

1   False. While low profitability may make an industry unattractive, it does not make it more difficult for firms to enter should the wish to do so.

2   (i) This would be a classic example of a cost leader.

3   (ii) Inbound logistics involves receiving, storing and handling of inventory, so a new inventory system would affect this part of the chain.

4   (iii) Five forces. PEST looks at the external environment of the company. The value chain examines the company's activities to see which contributes towards competitive advantage. Porter's value chain is specifically designed to examine the competitive nature of the company's market or industry. SWOT pulls all these models together and examines the overall position of the company.

Exam style questions

1   **(a)**   Here are four short references to activities within Porter's value chain:

A   Storing and handling inputs

B   Activities after the point of sale

C   The way the business is organised

D   Purchasing of all inputs, including materials

Required:

Identify the description above which is associated with each of the following value chain activities, by writing A, B, C, D or None.

(i)   Inbound logistics

(ii)   Procurement

(iii) Service

(iv)   Operations

(v)   Infrastructure

(b)   Below are a number of statements regarding Porter's generic strategies.

A   Focus involves offering general goods to a small segment of the market at a low price

B   Cost leadership involves manufacturing goods more efficiently than rivals

C   Businesses may become cost leaders by making their goods a lower quality than their rivals

D   A focus strategy tends to allow businesses to charge a premium price

E   Differentiation involves charging a premium for a product due to its actual or perceived benefits to the customer

F   Businesses that are stuck in the middle are trying to sell products at too high a price.

Required:

Write down which three of the above statements are correct by selecting THREE of the letters from A-F.

2   POL bottles and sells natural spring water in country H. It is the best-selling brand of bottled water in country H and has a highly recognisable brand name. POL is long-established and has a very experienced management team. Many years of high profits have enabled the company to build up significant cash reserves.

The market for bottled water has been slow-growing for many years in country H, with consumers switching to flavoured waters, which are not offered by POL. Nearby country I (which POL does not currently operate in) is seeing significant growth in this market.

One of POL's managers has recently noted an article in a popular newspaper in country H which suggested that bottled water may be harmful to health due to high levels of toxins from the plastic bottles the water is sold in. POL is one of the few bottled water manufacturers to sell its water in glass bottles, which the article suggests is safe for consumption.

One of POL's successful smaller competitors, AQA, has recently been put up for sale by its owners who wish to exit country H. POL's management team is considering making an offer for the company in order to increase their market share in country H.

(a) Below are some key issues which POL's managers have identified as part of a SWOT analysis:

A Expansion into bottled water sales in country I

B Potential health risks from plastic bottles

C Strong cash balances

D Launch of new flavoured waters in country H

E Experienced managers

F Strong brand name

G Potential purchase of AQA

H Slow growth in the bottled water market in country H

Required:

Identify the FOUR issues that are most likely to be classified as opportunities for POL, based on the above information, by selecting FOUR of the letters from A-H.

(b) In order to improve margins, POL has decided to undertake a value chain analysis of the company's existing water bottling operations. Below are four activities from the value chain model:

A Operations

B Outbound logistics

C Service

D Procurement

Required:

Identify the activity above which is associated with each of the following descriptions, by writing A, B, C or D.

(i) **POL has a small call centre dedicated to dealing with customer complaints.**

(ii) **Water is filtered through a four-stage process before being purified and bottled.**

(iii) **POL's purchasing department regularly shops around to get the lowest possible price for POL's glass bottles from suppliers.**

(iv) **Bottled water is held in large warehouses before being transported to retailers across country H.**

10 Professional ethics in accounting and business

The following topics are covered in this chapter:

- Business ethics and their importance
- Professional ethics
- Corporate codes of ethics
- Ethical threats and dilemmas

10.1 BUSINESS ETHICS AND THEIR IMPORTANCE

LEARNING SUMMARY

After studying this section you should be able to:

- define business ethics and explain the importance of ethics to the organisation and the individual.

Ethical dilemmas

DEFINITION Ethics is the system of moral principles that examines the concept of right and wrong.

An ethical dilemma involves a situation where a decision-maker has to decide what is the 'right' or 'wrong' thing to do.

KEY POINT Examples of ethical dilemmas can be found throughout all aspects of business operations.

Accounting issues:

- Creative accounting to boost or suppress reported profits.
- Directors' pay arrangements.
- Insider trading.

Production issues:

- Should the company produce certain products at all? E.g. guns, tobacco.
- Should the company test its products on animals?

Sales and marketing issues:

- Price-fixing and anti-competitive behaviour may be overt and illegal or may be more subtle.
- Is it ethical to target advertising at children? E.g. fast food or expensive toys.

Personnel/ HRM issues:

- Employees should not be favoured or discriminated against on the basis of gender, race, religion, age, disability etc.
- The contract of employment must offer a fair balance of power between employee and employer.

Approaches to ethics

KEY POINT There are several possible approaches to making ethical decisions.

You may be presented with a scenario and be asked to choose which approach has been adopted, from a list.

CONSEQUENTIALIST	PLURALIST
This approach states that the decision is right or wrong depending on the consequences or outcomes of that decision. As long as the outcome is right, then the action itself is irrelevant.	This approach involves trying to cater to the needs of all stakeholders without seriously compromising the interests of any one group.
E.g. if an individual needs to feed their family, stealing may be seen as morally acceptable if there is no other way of obtaining food.	E.g. a mining company may wish to open a new mine in order to access mineral deposits and earn its shareholders a large profit. However, local residents may be unhappy due to pollution caused by the mine. A pluralist approach would be to open the mine but ensure that enough money is spent to minimise the damage to the local environment.
This approach can be broken down into two further perspectives:	
Egoism – the action is morally correct as long as the outcome is favourable for the individual making the decision.	
Utilitarian – the action is considered to be morally correct if the outcome is favourable for the greatest number of people or 'the greater good'.	

RELATIVISM	ABSOLUTISM
This is the view that there is no universal moral code with which to judge all actions.	This approach argues that certain actions are inherently right or wrong, regardless of their context or the circumstances that they occur in.
This means that whether something can be classed as 'ethical' or not depends on the circumstances.	E.g. an absolutist would regard the taking of a human life as entirely unacceptable, regardless of the context; whether it was murder or in self-defence would be irrelevant.
What if someone stole bread to feed their starving family? Relativists may argue that different people will view this differently.	

Why business ethics are important

Benefits to individuals

- Consumer and employee expectations have evolved over recent years.
- Consumers may choose to purchase ethical items, even if they are not the cheapest.
- Employees will not blindly accept orders to act in a manner that they personally believe to be unethical.

Benefits to organisations

- Good ethics should be seen as a driver of profitability rather than a burden on business.
- An ethical framework is part of good corporate governance and suggests a well-run business.
- Investors are reassured about the company's approach to risk management.
- Employees will be motivated in the knowledge that they operate in an environment of good ethical corporate behaviour.

10.2 PROFESSIONAL ETHICS

LEARNING SUMMARY

After studying this section you should be able to:

- identify the factors that distinguish a profession from other types of occupation

- describe and demonstrate principles form the IFAC code of ethics, using examples

- explain the role of the accountant in promoting ethical behaviour.

What is a profession?

A profession, as opposed to other types of occupation, is characterised by the following factors:

- the mastering of specialised skills during a period of training.

- governance by a professional organisation.

- compliance with an ethical code.

- a process of certification before being allowed to practice.

Professional code of ethics

Both the International Federation of Accountants (IFAC) and the ACCA have developed codes of ethics for their members.

KEY POINT The ACCA Code is based on the IFAC code and takes a similar conceptual framework approach, listing an identical set of Fundamental Ethical Principles that must be followed.

PRINCIPLE	DESCRIPTION
Integrity	Members should be straightforward and honest in all professional / business relationships.
Objectivity	Members do not allow bias or conflict of interest in business judgements.
Professional competence and due care	There is a duty to maintain professional knowledge and skill at an appropriate level and to follow professional standards.
Confidentiality	Information on clients must not be disclosed without appropriate authority, or used for personal advantage.
Professional behaviour	Members must comply with relevant laws and avoid actions that would discredit the profession.

> It is common for definitions to be directly tested.

10.3 CORPORATE CODES OF ETHICS

LEARNING SUMMARY

After studying this section you should be able to:

- explain the benefits of a corporate code of ethic to the organisation and its employees.

Corporate codes of ethics

Most companies, especially if they are large, have approached the concept of business ethics by creating a set of internal policies and instructing employees to follow them.

These policies can either be broad generalisations (a corporate ethics statement) or can be specific rules (a corporate ethics code).

10.4 ETHICAL THREATS AND DILEMMAS

LEARNING SUMMARY

After studying this section you should be able to:

- identify the main threats to ethical behaviour

- outline situations at work where ethical dilemmas may be faced

- list the main safeguards against ethical threats and dilemmas

- recognise when and to whom illegal, or unethical conduct by anyone within or connected to the organisation should be reported.

Ethical threats

The IFAC Code sets out the approach that accountants should take to ethical issues:

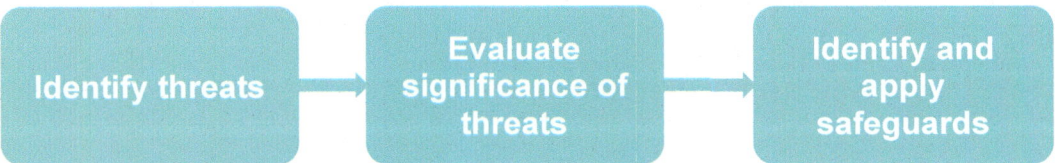

Identify threats → **Evaluate significance of threats** → **Identify and apply safeguards**

KEY POINT Safeguards are steps that the accountant can take to eliminate the threat, or reduce it to an acceptable level.

If no safeguards are available, the accountant should:

- Eliminate the interest or activities causing the threat.

- If this is not possible, decline or discontinue the engagement.

There are several **key threats** to ethical behaviour that accountants should attempt to avoid. These include:

> You may be presented with a scenario and be asked to choose which type of ethical threat is being described, from a list.

THREAT	DEFINITION	EXAMPLE
Self-interest	When a financial or other interest influences an accountant's judgement and causes a conflict of interest.	Owning shares in a client.
Self-review	When an accountant is required to re-evaluate their own previous judgement.	Auditing financial statements that have been prepared by the audit firm.
Familiarity	When an accountant becomes sympathetic to the interests of others due to a close personal relationship.	Accepting gifts or preferential treatment from clients.

Advocacy	Can be a problem if an accountant is promoting a position or opinion to the point where their subsequent objectivity is compromised.	Promoting the client's shares in a share issue.
Intimidation	When an accountant is deterred from acting objectively by actual or perceived threats.	An accountant is threatened with dismissal over a disagreement about application of an accounting principle.

Safeguards

KEY POINT The IFAC Code identifies two categories of general safeguards that may be used to eliminate or reduce the threats to independence.

Safeguards created by the profession, legislation or regulation:

- Education and training

- Continuing Professional Development requirements

- Corporate governance regulations

- Professional standards

- Monitoring of professional work including disciplinary proceedings

- External reviews

Safeguards within the work environment:

- Review procedures

- Consultations with independent third parties

- Rotation of senior staff

- Discussions with those charged with governance

- Disclosing fees and services to those charged with governance

There are six values that organisations can apply in order to create a culture that makes it easy for employees to follow their professional codes and behave ethically.

These six values can be easily remembered using the acronym HOTTER.

Honesty – the business encourages employee honesty, even when detrimental to the organisation itself.

Openness – the organisation should be willing to freely provide information to stakeholders, as needed.

Transparency – the company makes it easy for key stakeholders to review its activities.

Trust – organisations need to be trustworthy in their dealings with others and try to work in the best interests of stakeholders.

Empowerment – giving employees and other stakeholders more ability to make their own decisions.

Respect – all employees and stakeholders should be treated with dignity by the organisation, regardless of age, gender etc.

Dealing with unethical and illegal conduct

If an accountant uncovers unethical or illegal conduct within the organisation they work for, there is a series of steps that they should take to deal with the issue.

Consult with whomever is responsible for governance or ethics within the organisation

This may be a Compliance Officer, or the Board of Directors themselves

If the problem remains unsolved, the accountant should take legal advice and/ or advice from their professional body

e.g. ACCA

If the situation still cannot be resolved, the accountant should consider reporting to the relevant authorities and withdrawing from the engagement

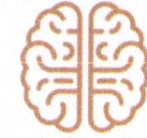

Do you understand?

1   The study of business ethics is purely concerned with legal requirements.

    True or false?

2   Paul is a manager at G Co. He has twenty employees who report to him and he has been told that he needs to reduce this number by one. Paul decides that rather than making staff redundant he will instead reduce each employee's hours by one-twentieth in order to keep everyone in the job. What approach is Paul taking to this situation?

    (i) Utilitarian (ii) Egoist (iii) Pluralist

3   Danny works in the accounts department of a large multinational company. If profits of the company are above a certain level, he will receive a large bonus. Because of this, he decides to manipulate some of the expenses, artificially increasing the profits and allowing him to get a bonus. Which of the fundamental principles has Danny NOT breached?

    (i) Confidentiality (ii) Professional behaviour (iii) Integrity (iv) Objectivity

4   Annie is an accountant who is currently helping to defend one of her clients, which is currently being prosecuted by the local government for tax evasion. Which ethical threat is Annie exposed to?

    (i) Self-interest (ii) Familiarity (iii) Intimidation (iv) Advocacy

1   False. Business ethics is partly concerned with legal requirements, but also with areas that are not covered by the law.

2   (iii) The Pluralist approach involves trying to find a solution that caters to the needs of all stakeholders – in this case all employees that report to Paul.

3   (i) There is no evidence that Danny has breached confidentiality. However, he has produced an inaccurate profit figure, compromising his integrity. He is also breaching objectivity, as he is allowing self-interest to bring bias into his work. His actions, if discovered, would also bring the profession into disrepute, meaning that he is not displaying professional behaviour.

4   (iv) Advocacy occurs when an accountant promotes a position or opinion or opinion to the point where their objectivity is lost. This may happen in court cases.

Exam style questions

1   L is an employee of Lex Co, a large multinational organisation. She has recently been accused of theft from the company. She has argued that the theft was justified as she needed the money to care for her mother, who is seriously ill.

What approach to ethics has L adopted?

A   Pluralist

B   Utilitarian

C   Absolutist

D   Relativist

2   A profession must have an ethical code to which it requires compliance.

Is this statement TRUE or FALSE?

A   True

B   False

3   **ACCA members are required to comply with five Fundamental Principles. Which of the following contains three of these principles?**

A   Integrity, Objectivity, Honesty

B   Professional competence and due care, Professional behaviour, Confidentiality

C   Social responsibility, Independence, Scepticism

D   Courtesy, Reliability, Responsibility

4   **Betty has uncovered fraudulent activity within the company she works for. Who should she alert about this matter first?**

A   Her professional accountancy body

B   The company's major shareholders

C   Her company's Compliance Officer

D   The relevant authorities

5   Helen is an ACCA member. Last year one of her clients, Cameron, asked her to value a business that he wished to purchase. She did so and informed Cameron that the business was competitively priced. Cameron subsequently bought the business for its full asking price of several million pounds. This year, Cameron has become concerned that the business has been underperforming and has asked Helen to reassess its performance and long-term prospects.

Which type of ethical threat is Helen facing?

A   Self-interest

B   Self-review

C   Advocacy

D   Intimidation

11 Governance and social responsibility in business

The following topics are covered in this chapter:

- Separation of ownership and control
- Corporate governance
- Corporate social responsibility
- Committees

11.1 SEPARATION OF OWNERSHIP AND CONTROL

LEARNING SUMMARY

After studying this section you should be able to:

- explain the concept of separation of ownership and control
- explain the agency concept.

The principle agent problem

In some, usually small, companies the owners also manage the business.

However, in larger companies shareholders usually delegate control to professional managers – the board of directors – to **run the company on their behalf**.

KEY POINT This separation of ownership and control leads to a potential conflict of interests between directors and shareholders.

DEFINITION This conflict is an example of the 'agency problem'. The principals (the shareholders) have to find ways of ensuring that their agents (the managers) act in their interests.

There are several definitions in this chapter which can be directly tested. Ensure you are comfortable with each of them.

Possible areas of conflict

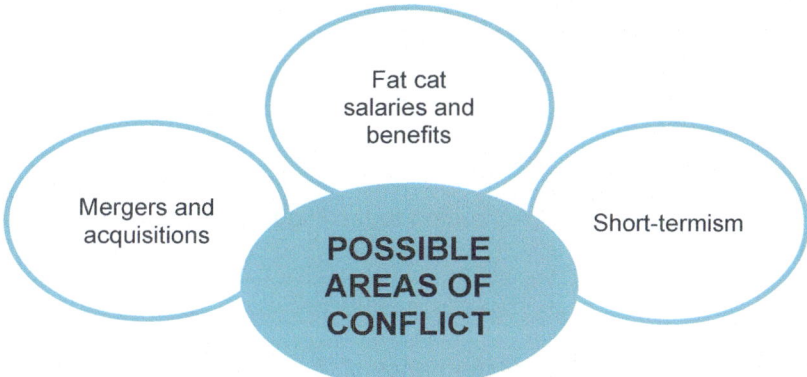

Attempts to resolve this conflict can take a number of forms:

- Corporate governance (see below)
- A review of the remuneration and bonus schemes given to directors.

11.2 CORPORATE GOVERNANCE

LEARNING SUMMARY

After studying this section you should be able to:

- define corporate governance and explain its importance in contemporary organisations

- explain the responsibility of organisations to maintain appropriate standards of corporate governance

- briefly explain the main recommendations of best practice in effective corporate governance.

Corporate governance

DEFINITION **Corporate governance** is defined as 'the systems by which companies and other organisations are directed and controlled'.

The main objectives are as follows:

- to **control** the managers/directors by increasing the amount of reporting and disclosure

- to increase the level of **confidence and transparency** in company activities for all investors (existing and potential) and thus promote growth in the company

- to increase **disclosure** to all stakeholders

- to ensure that the company is run in a **legal and ethical manner**

- to build in control at the top that will '**cascade'** down the organisation.

Types of directors

DEFINITION Those who are involved in the day-to-day running of the company are known as **executive directors.**

DEFINITION **Non-executive directors (NEDs)** are not employees of the company and have no managerial responsibilities, meaning that they do not participate in the day-to-day running of the organisation.

However, NEDs do attend board meetings and therefore have a say in the strategic decision making of the company.

Roles of NEDs

NEDs have several key roles in the organisation. According to the Higgs report (2003), these include:

- **Strategy** – NEDs should constructively challenge and contribute to the development of strategy.

- **Performance** – NEDs should scrutinise the performance of management in meeting agreed goals and objectives and monitoring senior management.

- **Risk** – NEDs should satisfy themselves that financial information is accurate and that financial controls and systems of risk management are robust.

- **People** – NEDs are responsible for determining appropriate levels of remuneration for executives and have a prime role in appointing and, where necessary, removing senior management and in succession planning.

NEDs must not:

Have been an employee of the company in the last five years	Have had a material business interest in the company for the last three years	Participate in the company's share option or pension schemes

Have close ties with the company directors or senior employees	Serve as a NED for more than nine years with the same company

If any of these apply to a NED, their independence will be seriously compromised.

Other recommendations

- **At least half the board** should be **independent NEDs** (excluding the Chairman of the Board, which is often also a NED). A smaller company should have at least two independent NEDs.

- **One of the independent NEDs** should be appointed to be the **'senior independent director'.** They are available to be contacted by shareholders who wish to raise matters outside the normal executive channels of communication.

- **Executive directors and NEDs** would typically be required to stand for **re-election by shareholders every three years**. NEDS who have been with the company for over nine years must stand for re-election on an annual basis.

Remuneration committee

DEFINITION A **remuneration committee** is a committee made up of non-executive directors which is responsible for deciding on the pay and incentives offered to executive directors.

The board of a listed company should establish a remuneration committee of at least three (or two in the case of smaller companies) independent NEDs.

The whole of Board of Directors should be responsible for deciding the level of remuneration for NEDs.

Audit committee

DEFINITION An **audit committee** consists of independent NEDs who are responsible for monitoring and reviewing the company's internal financial controls and the integrity of the financial statements.

The audit committee acts as an interface between the full board of directors and both the internal and external auditors.

Responsibilities of audit committees include:

- **Reviewing accounting policies and financial statements** as a whole to ensure they are appropriate and balanced

- **Reviewing systems of internal controls and risk management** within the organisation

- **Agreeing the work agenda for the internal audit department**, as well as reviewing the results of internal audit work

- **Making recommendations to the board**, for them to put to the shareholders, relating to the appointment and removal of the external auditors as well as their remuneration and terms of engagement

- **Liaising with the external auditors**, in particular relating to the review and monitoring of the external auditor's independence and objectivity as well as the effectiveness of the audit process

Nomination committee

DEFINITION A **nomination committee** is formed in order to ensure that the composition of the board is balanced. It monitors the process for appointment of directors to the board of directors as well as making recommendations for appointments to the board.

Public oversight boards

KEY POINT The public is a legitimate stakeholder in a large company. This means that the public has a 'right to know' how such a company is being governed as well as a right to be involved in the governance process.

The most obvious means of public oversight of corporate governance is via the publication by companies of their Annual Report and financial statements. While companies are required by law to send a copy of this information to every shareholder, many companies will also post a copy on their website.

In addition, most companies are required to submit their annual financial statements to a regulatory body (Companies House in the UK) so that any interested parties can review them.

Some countries and/or industries have set up **public oversight boards**. These organisations monitor whether organisations are complying with relevant rules and regulations and take action against those that fail to meet the required standards.

Benefits of corporate governance to the organisation

Advantages include:

- **business success** – improved controls and decision-making will aid corporate success as well as growth in revenues and profits.

- **investor confidence** – corporate governance will mean that investors are more likely to trust that the company is being well run. This will not only make it easier and cheaper for the company to raise finance, but also has a positive effect on the share price.

- **minimisation of wastage** – strong corporate governance should help to minimise waste within the organisations, as well as corruption, risks and mismanagement.

- **listing requirements** – following corporate governance guidelines, is required by many stock exchanges.

11.3 CORPORATE SOCIAL RESPONSIBILITY

LEARNING SUMMARY

After studying this section you should be able to:

- define corporate social responsibility and explain its importance in contemporary organisations

- explain the responsibility of organisations to maintain appropriate standards of corporate social responsibility

- explain how organisations take account of their social responsibility objectives through analysis of the needs of stakeholders

- identify the social and environmental responsibilities of business organisations to internal, connected and external stakeholders.

Corporate social responsibility

> **DEFINITION   Corporate social responsibility (CSR)** refers to the idea that a company should be sensitive to the needs and wants of all its stakeholders rather than just the shareholders.

It refers to an organisation's obligation to maximise its positive impacts upon stakeholders while minimising the negative impacts.

Stakeholder needs analysis

This involves an organisation undertaking research to determine:

- who its key stakeholders are, and:

- what their needs are.

A typical list is not what should be created here. Each company must sit down with a blank sheet of paper and identify the stakeholders of **their** business.

There is no better way of understanding stakeholder needs than asking them directly. Possible methods include questionnaires, focus groups and direct interviews.

The importance of CSR

ADVANTAGES	DISADVANTAGES
Attractive to customers – it enhances the company's reputation and can act as positive advertising.	Loss of business value – can be seen as management acting against their primary role of earning higher returns for investors.
Attractive to potential employees – ethical businesses can attract higher calibre staff.	Maximisation of profits can be seen as socially responsible – it benefits institutional investors (such as pension schemes) and creates more tax revenue for governments.
It can save the business money – many governments will fine or increase the taxes of businesses that cause pollution.	Increased cost of raw materials – responsibly sourced materials are likely to be more expensive.

It reduces the risk of the organisation – there will be less chance of adverse environmental reactions against the company.	Having to turn away business – an ethical company cannot be seen to be trading with unethical partners.
	Increased management time – significant management time can be taken up by a focus on CSR.

11.4 COMMITTEES

LEARNING SUMMARY

After studying this section you should be able to:

- explain the purposes of committees
- explain the types of committee used by business organisations
- list the advantages and disadvantages of committees
- explain the role of the Chair and Secretary in a committee.

The purposes of committees

> **DEFINITION** A **committee** is a group of people who are appointed to administer, discuss or make reports concerning a subject.

Purposes of committees include:

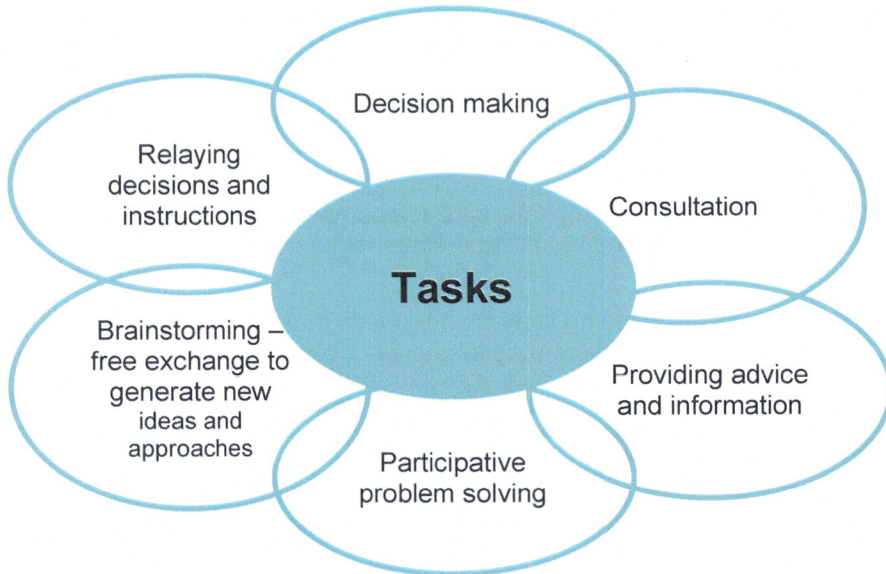

Types of committees used by business organisations

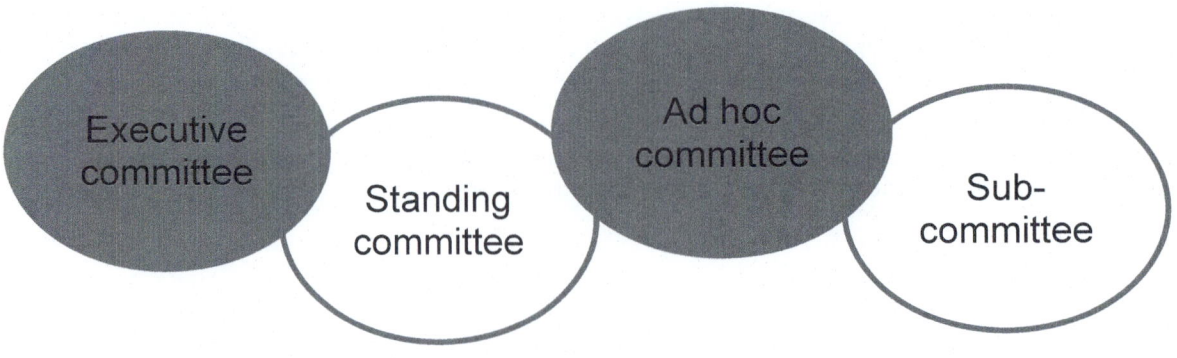

Advantages and disadvantages of committees

ADVANTAGES	DISADVANTAGES
Bring together individuals with necessary skills or knowledge for successful implementation of a given task.	Tend to be slow at making decisions. Could miss out on valuable opportunities and perhaps increase costs.
Tend to slow the decision making process down, meaning that hasty, poorly considered decisions are less likely.	Collective responsibility means that no individual is likely to be held accountable for poor performance of the committee, reducing motivation of members.
Decisions are more likely to be accepted by the organisation as they have been made by a committee with representatives from many departments.	Members of the committee may wish to further the objectives of their own departments, leading to conflict within the committee.
More people are involved in the decision making process, leading to increased motivation.	

Key roles in the committee

There are likely to be two key roles that are essential for the proper functioning of a committee.

The Chair is a crucial role that involves guiding the proceedings at committee meetings.

The Secretary undertakes all the administration relating to the committee and supports the Chair in ensuring the smooth running of the committee.

Responsibilities of the Secretary

Before the meeting:

Fixing the date and time of the meeting

Booking the venue

Preparing and issuing the agenda and other relevant documents

During the meeting:

Assisting the chairperson

Making notes

Advising the chairperson on points of procedure

After the meeting:

Preparing minutes

Acting on and communicating decisions

Dealing with correspondence

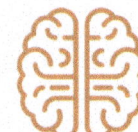

Do you understand?

1   The 'separation of ownership and control' refers to the fact that the owners of the company are always different people to the directors of the company.

    True or false?

2   Which of the following can non-executive directors accept as remuneration from the company?

    (i) shares (ii) pension payments (iii) equity options (iv) a fixed daily rate for their time

3   An advantage of using a committee rather than an individual to make a decision is that there would be increased speed in decision-making.

    True or false?

1   False. In a small company, the directors are often the sole shareholders of the company, so the agency problem does not always arise. The problem is potentially most serious in a large quoted company where there is a professional board of directors and many external shareholders.

2   (iv) NEDs should be paid fees that reflect their time commitment and the responsibilities of the role. Share options would detract from the detached judgement that they should bring.

3   False. Decisions tend to be slower when made by committees.

1   **Where there are a large number of external shareholders who play no role in the day-to-day running of a company, there is a situation that is described as:**

    A   detached corporate ownership

    B   uninvolved external ownership

    C   dividend based shareholding

    D   separation of ownership and control

2   **Corporate social responsibility refers to the idea that a company should:**

    A   play an active part in the social life of the local neighbourhood

    B   be sensitive to the needs of all stakeholders

    C   be alert to the social needs of all employees

    D   act responsibly in relation to shareholders' overall needs – not just their financial needs

3   **An audit committee should:**

    A   consist of independent non-executive directors only

    B   include at least one senior member of the internal audit team

    C   include one member from the external audit firm

    D   carry out a detailed review of critical elements of the balance sheet

4   **The most obvious means of achieving public oversight of corporate governance is via:**

    A   the company establishing a comprehensive web site

    B   publication of the Annual Report and Accounts

    C   press announcements of all significant developments

    D   shareholder access to the Annual General Meeting

5   **Which of the following would normally be included in the role of a Committee Chairman?**

    A   Making administrative arrangements

    B   Dealing with correspondence

    C   Issuing the agenda

    D   Ensuring correct procedures are followed

12 Law and regulation governing accounting

The following topics are covered in this chapter:

- Authorities to whom organisations are accountable
- Legislation governing financial statements
- Consequences of compliance failure
- International regulation of the accountancy profession

12.1 AUTHORITIES TO WHOM ORGANISATIONS ARE ACCOUNTABLE

LEARNING SUMMARY

After studying this section you should be able to:

- identify the authorities to whom organisations are accountable.

Introduction

KEY POINT Many countries have enacted legislation controlling the retention and submission of proper accounting records and financial statements. This predominantly applies to companies, as governments attempt to ensure that they are accountable for their actions.

There are usually several bodies that companies find themselves accountable to.

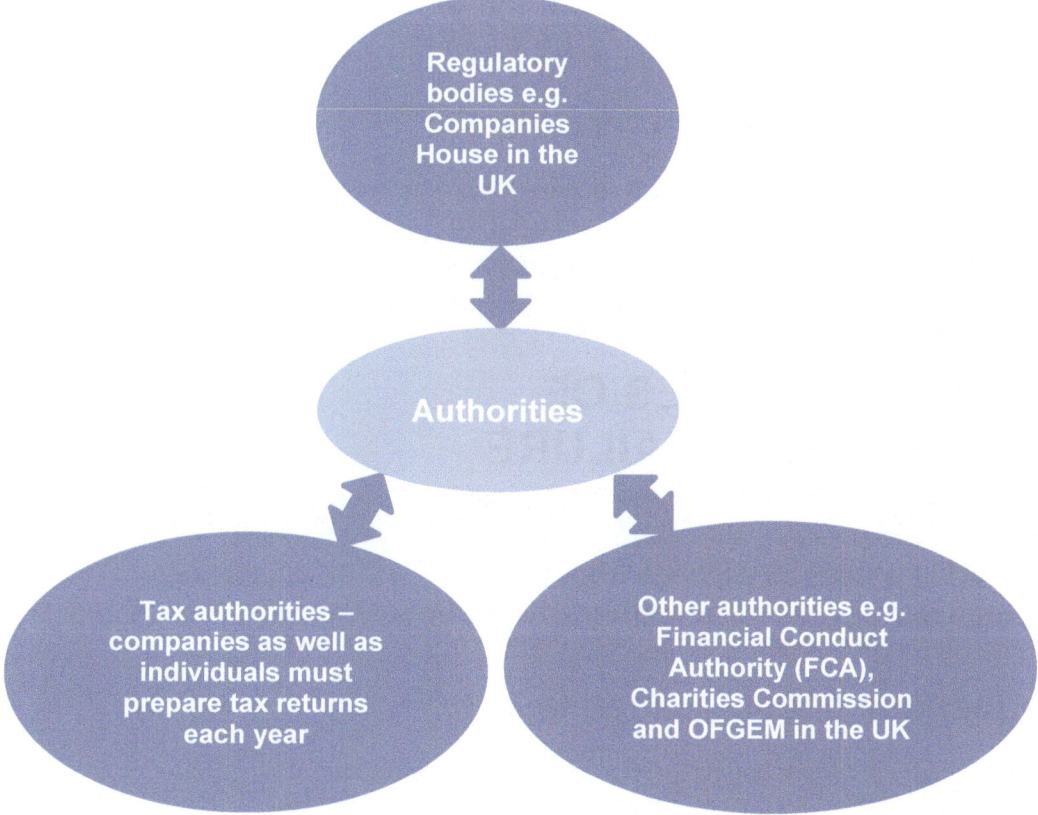

In order to satisfy the relevant authorities, most organisations have to retain their accounting records for a minimum period (usually seven years) in case the authorities wish to verify information at a future date.

12.2 LEGISLATION GOVERNING FINANCIAL STATEMENTS

LEARNING SUMMARY

After studying this section you should be able to:

- explain basic legal requirements in relation to retaining and submitting proper records and preparing and auditing financial reports.

Typical requirements for financial statements

For companies, legislation covers not only the need to prepare financial statements, but also how they should be prepared – including issues such as frequency and format.

The legislation varies between countries, but in the UK it is known as the **Companies Act 2006 (CA 2006)**.

KEY POINT The CA2006 in the UK requires that financial statements are produced that give a true and fair view of the position and performance of the company.

The term 'true and fair' is not defined in company law, but normally means that the financial statements:

- follow all appropriate accounting standards.

- contain information of sufficient quantity to satisfy the reasonable expectations of the users.

- follow generally-accepted practice.

- should not contain any material misstatement.

Companies are also required to maintain proper accounting records which are sufficient to show and explain the transactions.

You could be asked to choose from a list of reasons as to why an auditor would conclude that a set of accounts are NOT true and fair.

Responsibility for financial records

Under company legislation, directors are responsible for producing financial statements that give a true and fair view.

If the Finance Director does not have the skills to prepare the financial statements, an external accounting firm may be asked to provide assistance.

12.3 CONSEQUENCES OF COMPLIANCE FAILURE

LEARNING SUMMARY

After studying this section you should be able to:

- explain the broad consequences of failing to comply with the legal requirements for maintaining and filing accounting records.

Consequences of compliance failure

- Failure to keep proper accounting records or to prepare regular financial statements that give a true and fair view are both **criminal offences**.

- Directors can be **fined** for failure to comply.

- Should the company be listed, it may have its **shares suspended** by the stock exchange.

- There may be further problems with the tax authorities if records are found to be inaccurate. The company may be guilty of **tax evasion**, which is illegal.

- If the poor accounting records mean that the financial statements do not show a true and fair view, the company's auditors may give a qualified audit report which can **damage the company's reputation**.

12.4 INTERNATIONAL REGULATION OF THE ACCOUNTANCY PROFESSION

LEARNING SUMMARY

After studying this section you should be able to:

- explain how the international accountancy profession regulates itself through the establishment of reporting standards and their monitoring.

International regulation

KEY POINT Despite the need for companies to follow the requirements of the Companies Act (or equivalent) and the tax authorities of the country in which they operate, the accountancy profession is keen to be 'self-regulating'. This means that the profession would prefer to issue its own regulations and deal with problems itself, rather than relying on legislation.

This has led to companies not only having to follow the requirements of their country's company legislation, but also of various standard-setting bodies which were linked to their country's accountancy profession.

The role of the IFRS Foundation

The International Financial Reporting Standards Foundation (IFRS) was formed to try and harmonise accounting standards in different countries.

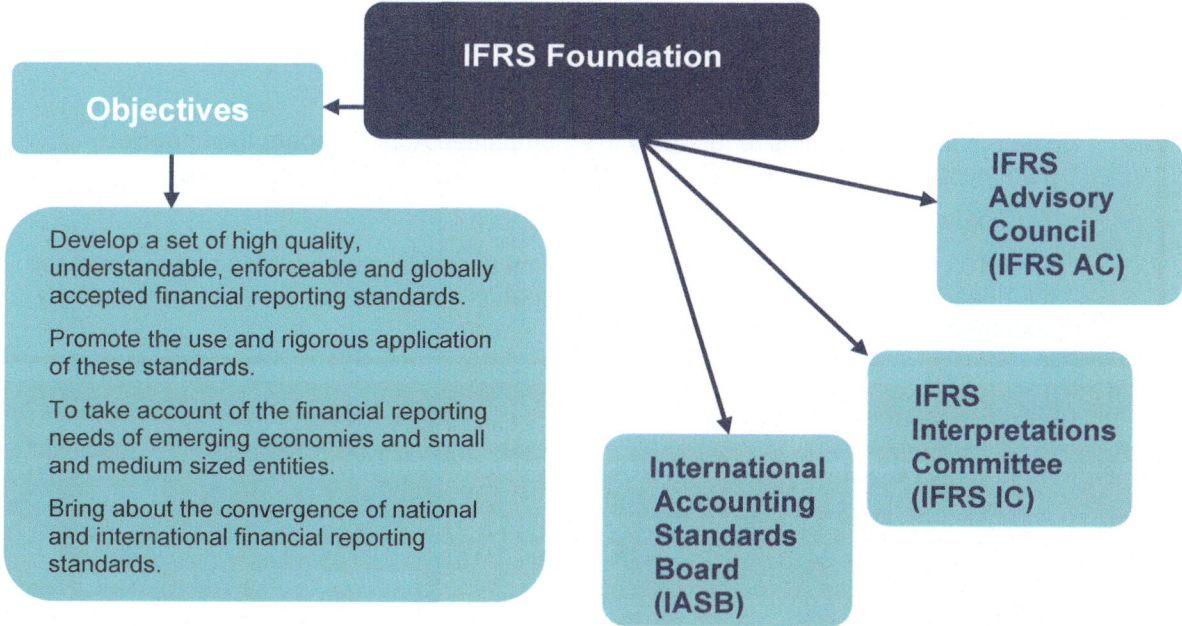

The role of the IASB

The IASB is an independent standard-setting body which is based in London. It has 14 members from nine countries.

The IASB's aims are:

- to develop a single set of high quality, understandable and enforceable global accounting standards; and

- to co-operate with national accounting standard-setters to achieve convergence in accounting standards around the world.

> Familiarise yourself with the main aims of the IFRS Foundation and the IASB.

KEY POINT Standards produced by the IASC, the forerunner to the IASB, are called International Accounting Standards (IASs). Standards produced by the IASB are called International Financial Reporting Standards (IFRSs). Collectively, these are international accounting standards.

Regulation within the UK

Accounting standards in the UK are written by the **FRC (Financial Reporting Council).**

One of its subsidiary committees – the **ASB (Accounting Standards Board)** controls the creation of UK accounting standards, known as Financial Reporting Standards (FRSs).

The FRC is then broken down into a number of other committees, including:

- **Auditing Practices Board (APB)**
- **The Professional Oversight Board**
- **The Financial Reporting Review Board**
- **The Accounting and Actuarial Disciplinary Board**

Do you understand?

1. If financial statements give a true and fair view it means there is no fraud.

   True or false?

2. The Financial Director is required by the Companies Act to prepare the financial statements.

   True or false?

3. Over 100 countries have adopted international accounting standards or have amended their national standards to comply with international standards. Give two reasons why countries would want to do this.

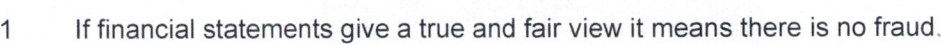

1 False. A true and fair view means that the financial statements are reasonably accurate, rather than totally accurate. If fraud is not material, then it will not cause a material misstatement.

2 False. The directors are collectively responsible for the preparation of the financial statements, not just the FD.

3 Two from the following three reasons:

(1) It is easier for multinationals, which encourages investment. A multinational will have subsidiaries in various countries, and if the subsidiaries' financial statements are prepared using international accounting standards, it will be much simpler for the holding company to prepare consolidated financial accounts for the group.

(2) It reassures investors in companies in the country. International standards are perceived as being fair and transparent, so investors will be more likely to trust the financial information given to them.

(3) It is more convenient for the national accounting standard setters, since they don't have to develop their own standards but can instead use international standards.

1 **(a)** Yoyo Co has recently prepared its most recent set of financial statements. A newly appointed finance junior has pointed out a number of issues with the financial statements, which she has argued indicate that the statements are not true and fair.

These issues include:

A   Inventory was not valued using standard generally accepted practice.

B   The financial statements used terminology that the junior felt would not be understood by the general public.

C   Information was not sufficiently detailed – liabilities were not split out into their constituent elements.

D   Yoyo's receivables balance was slightly misstated, though Yoyo acknowledged it would not affect the overall view of Yoyo's performance by users.

E   The layout of Yoyo's cash flow statement was not in accordance with the relevant accounting standard.

F   The financial statements covered 12 months – the previous set of financial statements covered 15 months.

G   The cash balance was significantly misstated, meaning that it gave a misleading view of the financial position of the company.

Required:

Write down which four of the above statements would make Yoyo's financial statements no longer true and fair by selecting FOUR of the letters from A-G.

(b) Yoyo's junior accountant has been asked to produce a briefing note to his employers that covers the roles of the main accountancy standard-setting organisations, including:

A   International Accounting Standards Board (IASB)

B   IFRS Interpretations Committee (IFRS IC)

C   IFRS Advisory Councils (IFRS AC)

D   IFRS Foundation

However, the junior accountant is unsure of which roles are undertaken by each of these bodies.

Required:

Identify which of the following statements relate to the either A (the IASB), B (the IFRS IC), C (the IFRS AC) or D (the IFRS Foundation).

(i)   Reviews widespread accounting issues and provides guidance.

(ii)   Comprised of a wide range of members affected by the work of the other two bodies.

(iii)   Development and publication of IFRSs and interpretations.

(iv)   Acts as supervisory body for the other three bodies and ensures each is properly funded.

2 **The preparation and filing of accounts by companies each year is normally required by which of the following?**

    A   Codes of corporate governance

    B   National legislation

    C   International Accounting Standards

    D   IFAC

3 **Linear Co has recently prepared its draft financial statements for the last financial year. It has been informed by its auditors that these financial statements are not 'true and fair'. Which of the following would NOT have caused this?**

    A   Linear failed to follow generally-accepted practice in the preparation of its financial statements

    B   Linear's financial statements did not set out relevant information in sufficient detail

    C   Linear failed to follow all appropriate accounting standards in the preparation of its financial statements

    D   Linear's financial statements contained minor errors

13 Accounting and finance functions within business

The following topics are covered in this chapter:
- The accounting function
- The financial accounting function
- Management accounting
- The functions of the treasury

13.1 THE ACCOUNTING FUNCTION

LEARNING SUMMARY

After studying this section you should be able to:

- identify and describe the main financial accounting functions in business.

What is accounting?

> **DEFINITION** **Accounting** is the systematic recording, reporting and analysis of financial transactions within a business.

You need to be aware of three key functions within the accounts department:
- financial accounting
- management accounting
- treasury

13.2 THE FINANCIAL ACCOUNTING FUNCTION

LEARNING SUMMARY

After studying this section you should be able to:

- explain the various business purposes for which the following financial information is required: the statement of profit or loss, the statement of cash flows, the statement of financial position, sustainability and integrated reports

- explain the contribution of the accounting function to the formulation, implementation and control of the organisation's policies, procedures and performance.

Financial accounting

> **DEFINITION** **Financial accounting** is concerned with the production of annual financial statements in accordance with the relevant accounting standards and leislation.

Statement of profit or loss details the income as well as the costs incurred in the period.

Statement of financial position shows the assets and liabilities of the business at the year end and also shows capital that the owners of the businesses have in the organisation.

Financial statements

Statement of cash flows summarises the cash receipts and payments for the year.

The normal sequence of steps in the accounting function is:

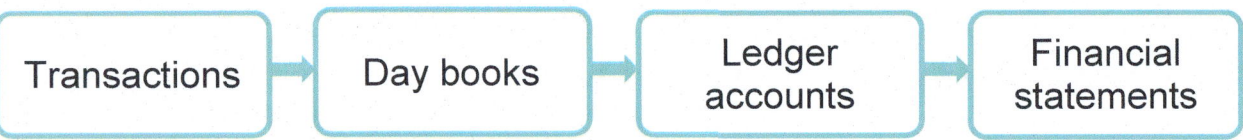

| Transactions | → | Day books | → | Ledger accounts | → | Financial statements |

Integrated reporting

Many companies adopt an integrated reporting approach which means that their financial statements cover the organisation's financial performance and position (using the three primary financial statements mentioned earlier), but also report on any other relevant information that would be of interest to the users.

For example:

- **major risks** the organisation faces and any actions they have taken to deal with these risks

- the organisation's performance regarding **ethics and corporate social responsibility**

- the organisation's performance with regard to **sustainable development.**

13.3 MANAGEMENT ACCOUNTING

LEARNING SUMMARY

After studying this section you should be able to:

- identify and describe the main management accounting and performance management functions in business

- describe the main purposes of the following types of management accounting reports: cost schedules, budgets and variance reports.

Management accounting

DEFINITION **Management accounting** is carried out to assist management in discharging their duties to plan, direct and control the operations of the business. It is concerned with the process of measuring, analysing, interpreting and communicating information to management in a form which is easy for them to understand.

KEY POINT While there are no legally required formats for management accounts, there are several key management reports that are common to many businesses.

Three of the most common are:

- cost schedules

- budgets

- variance reports.

Cost schedules

A cost schedule lists the various expenses involved in manufacturing units of a product. This is often shown as a list of the costs incurred when making a unit of each type of product we make. This may be called a **standard cost card**.

	$
Direct materials (e.g. wood and paint)	X
Direct labour (e.g. time spent cutting and painting)	X
Variable overheads (e.g. heat and light)	X
Fixed overheads (e.g. factory rent)	X
	——
Total (absorption) cost	X
	——

Budgets

Once the costs per unit have been identified, it should be possible to produce a **budget**. This shows the total planned revenues and costs for our business for the coming period.

Budgets are useful for several reasons.

A useful memory jogger is the acronym CRUMPET.

- **C**o-ordination – the budgets provides guidance for managers and ensure they are all working together for the good of the company.

- **R**esponsibility – the budget authorises managers to make expenditure, hire staff and generally follow the plans laid out in the budget.

- **U**tilisation – budgets help managers to get the best out of their business resources in the coming period.

- **M**otivation – the budget can be useful in influencing the behaviour of managers and motivating them to perform in line with business objectives.

- **P**lanning – budgets force managers to look ahead. This may help them to identify opportunities for, or threats of, the business to take effective action in advance.

- **E**valuation – budgets are often used as a basis for management appraisal.

- **T**elling – also called 'communication', budgets ensure that all members of the business understand what is expected from them during the coming period.

Variance reports

A **variance report** compares the budget to the actual results achieved for the budget period and identifies any significant differences, or variances, between the two.

Financial versus management accounting

	Financial accounting	**Management accounting**
Users	External	Internal
Purpose	Record historical financial performance and position	Assist management in planning and controlling the business to make effective decisions
Law	Required by statute (CA 06)	No legal requirements
Format/style	Must follow accounting standards and company law	Management discretion
Scope	Historical, covers business as a whole, usually gives minimum required information	Flexible, includes historical, current and future information which can focus on specific parts of the business
Information	Mostly financial	Financial and non-financial Key Performance Indicators (KPIs) (e.g. number of customers per hour)

13.4 THE FUNCTIONS OF THE TREASURY

LEARNING SUMMARY

After studying this section you should be able to:

- identify and describe the main finance and treasury functions.

The functions of the treasury

> **DEFINITION** **Treasury management** is the corporate handling of all financial matters, the generation of external and internal funds for business, the management of currencies and cash flows, and the complex strategies, policies and procedures of corporate finance.

The key roles of the treasury and finance functions include:

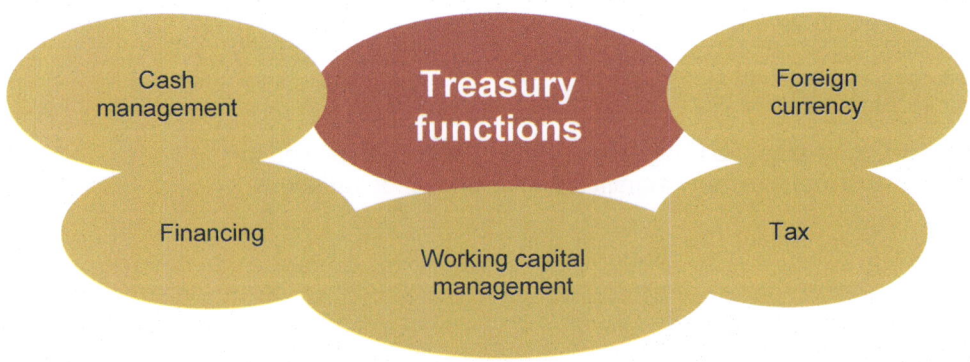

> **KEY POINT** Working capital is the capital available for conducting the day-to-day operations of an organisation, calculated as the excess of current assets over current liabilities.

Thus:

Inventory	X
Trade receivables	X
Cash	X
	——
Total current assets	X
Less: Trade payables	(X)
	——
Working capital balance	X
	——

The treasury and finance function is responsible for deciding on an appropriate level of investment in working capital for the business.

Evaluating and obtaining finance

The organisation may need additional funding to allow it to grow and invest in new projects. It therefore may need to raise finance from external sources.

There are two main types of external finance.

Debt	Equity
This involves borrowing cash from a third party and promising to repay them at a later date. Normally the company will also have to pay interest on the amount borrowed. Advantages:	This involves selling a stake in the business in order to raise cash. Advantages:
▪ interest payments allowable against tax	▪ no minimum level of dividend that must be paid to shareholders. Interest payments on debt finance must be paid each year
▪ does not change ownership of the organisation	
▪ tends to be cheaper to service than equity as it is often secured against assets of the company and takes priority over equity in the event of the business being liquidated.	▪ a bank will normally require security on the company's assets before it will offer a loan. Some companies may lack quality assets to offer, making equity more attractive as it does not require security.
▪ Job security	

The treasury and finance function will weigh up which source of finance best suits the circumstances of the business.

Determining business tax liabilities

One of the roles of the finance and treasury function is to calculate the business tax liability for the organisation and mitigate, or reduce, that liability as far as possible within the law.

> **DEFINITION** **Tax avoidance** is the legal use of the rules of the tax regime to one's own advantage, in order to reduce the amount of tax payable by means that are within the law.

> **DEFINITION** **Tax evasion** is the use of illegal means to reduce one's tax liability, for example deliberately misrepresenting the true state of your affairs to the tax authorities.

Do you understand?

1 Management accounts follow a set, pre-determined format as laid out in relevant accounting standards.

 True or false?

2 Variance analysis enables a business to identify why the actual financial results were different to those predicted by the budget.

 True or false?

3 An analyst wishes to use a company's financial statements to determine whether the business has a significant cash balance or not. Which of the following statements could the analyst use to identify this information?

 (i) Statement of profit or loss

 (ii) Statement of financial position

 (iii) Statement of cash flows

4 Which of the following is not typically prepared by the management accounting function?

 (i) Budgets (ii) Investment appraisals (iii) Business tax calculations

1 False. This describes a feature of financial accounting, rather than management accounting.
2 True.
3 (ii) and (iii). The cash balance could be determined from the statement of cash flows, which looks at cash movements in the year, or the statement of financial position, which lists the assets at the year end (of which cash is one).
4 (iii) This is the responsibility of the treasury department.

1   **In a very large company managing the total level of working
    capital would probably be the responsibility of the:**

    A   Finance director

    B   Chief accountant

    C   Treasurer

    D   Management accountant

2   Financial accountants usually produce information for the
    organisation's external stakeholders.

    Is this statement TRUE or FALSE?

    A   True

    B   False

3   David decided to record the purchases made on the 2nd of April 200X
    in tax year ending 31st of March 200X. The authorities will likely
    classify this as tax _____.

    Which of the following words correctly fill this gap?

    A   Evasion

    B   Minimisation

    C   Avoidance

    D   Suppression

4   **S is considering creating a financial accounting department
    within her business, but is unsure of what such a department
    would actually do. Which of the following would usually be
    prepared by a financial accounting department?**

    A   Cost schedules

    B   Statement of cash flows

    C   Variance analysis

    D   Tax calculations

5   **Which of the following statements regarding integrated reports
    is correct?**

    A   They involve the merging of the other financial statements to
        produce an overall view of company performance

    B   They are designed to show the organisation's profitability more
        clearly

    C   They include information on anything that is felt to be of interest
        to the users of the financial statements

    D   They include only relevant financial information for the users of
        the financial statements

14 Financial systems and procedures

The following topics are covered in this chapter:

- Overview of systems
- The purchasing, sales, payroll, cash and inventory systems
- The purpose of organisational control
- Why controls in systems are important
- Automated and manual systems

14.1 OVERVIEW OF SYSTEMS

LEARNING SUMMARY

After studying this section you should be able to:

- identify an organisation's system requirements in relation to the objectives and policies of the organisation.

Advantages of formal systems

There are several advantages to having formal, documented systems that staff must follow within the organisation. These include:

- All **transactions will be recorded in the same way**, and the required information will be recorded in the correct places.

- The 'best' practice, the most **efficient** way of recording transactions, can be adopted by everyone.

- Staff can refer to the **written procedures** if they are in doubt as to what to do.

- New staff can be **trained more quickly**.

- The auditors can **follow transactions more easily** if they are recorded in the same way.

- Transactions which have not followed the procedure, which could be **errors or frauds, may be identified** more easily.

Designing financial systems

Each system is made up of a series of procedures. The system designer will need to first consider the objectives of the system, the required outputs, and the likely inputs.

We will consider several key financial systems that operate within most organisations.

Purchasing and sales	Payroll	Cash	Working capital management

14.2 THE PURCHASING SYSTEM

LEARNING SUMMARY

After studying this section you should be able to:

- describe the purchases system within an organisation.

For each of the system types discussed in this chapter, you might be presented with a scenario and then asked to choose from a list of control measures that could help with the problem in the scenario.

Stages in the purchasing system

The main stages in the purchasing cycle and the issues to be considered are as follows:

Requisition
→ Staff decide what goods/services they wish to purchase and produce a purchase requisition.

This is authorised by the department supervisor and passed to the purchasing/ ordering department.

Ordering
→ Purchase department places order with suppliers.

Obtains several quotations to get competitive price.

Order may require authorisation, especially if large.

Goods received
→ Goods should be inspected to ensure good condition and quality is correct.

A record should be kept of all goods received.

Invoice received
→ Supplier bills company for goods/ services.

Before recording in the accounts, checks are made to ensure goods were received and price is correct.

Invoice recorded
→ Recorded in company's accounting system - manual or computerised.

Payment made
→ A cheque is produced for the amount owing.

This will be approved for payment by a senior manager who will first check that the details on the cheque agree with the invoices.

14.3 THE SALES SYSTEM

LEARNING SUMMARY

After studying this section you should be able to:

- describe the sales system within an organisation.

Stages in the sales system

The main stages in the sales cycle and the issues to be considered are as follows:

Order received	Orders may be received by post, fax, telephone, in person or electronically. A record should be made of incoming orders so checks can be made once processed.
Order processed	Check customer has a valid credit account, or has already paid in cash. Check goods are in inventory. Send order confirmation to customer.
Goods despatched	Goods sent to customer. A goods despatch note is produced, which will be signed by the customer confirming good received in good condition.
Invoicing	An invoice is sent to the customer, detailing the amount charged for the goods.
Recorded in the accounts	The invoice is coded and entered into the accounts.
Payment received	Payment received from customers. Controls should be in place to ensure no misappropriation by staff. Credit controller contacts those who are late paying.

14.4 THE PAYROLL SYSTEM

LEARNING SUMMARY

After studying this section you should be able to:

● describe the payroll system within an organisation.

Stages in the payroll system

The main stages in the payroll cycle and the issues to be considered are as follows:

Hours worked recorded	Employees record hours worked e.g. using clock cards, time cards. Hours worked usually authorised by supervisor.
Overtime recorded	Salaried employees may receive additional pay for overtime hours. If so, they will submit a timesheet with details of hours worked.
Pay rates obtained	Per hour or per month. If manual system, the pay clerk will manually look these up. If computerised, computer will do this.
Pay calculated	Hours x rate per hour, or a set monthly pay. If calculated manually, transactions should be checked.
Deductions calculated	Depending on the country, this could be tax, social security etc. Deductions are made from gross pay.
Net pay paid to employee	Usually via bank transfer. Occasionally via cash. If payment is via cash, supervision will be required to prevent theft and employees should sign to acknowledge receipt of the money.

14.5 THE CASH SYSTEM

LEARNING SUMMARY

After studying this section you should be able to:

* describe the cash system within an organisation.

Stages in the cash system

When we refer to the cash system, we are sometimes referring to the banking system, and payments into and from the bank account. We also need to consider the petty cash system.

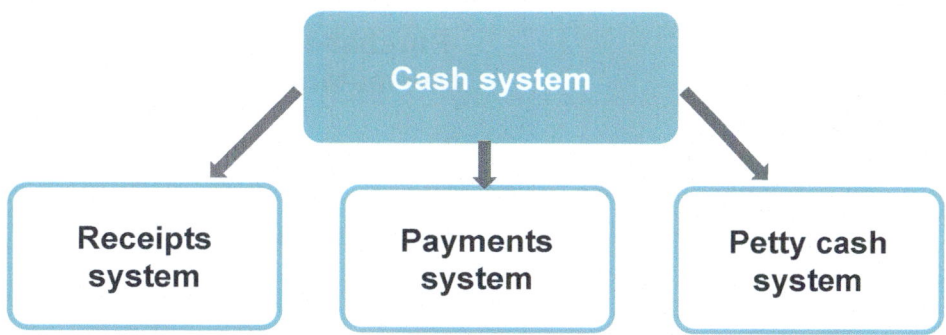

The receipts system

* Cheques are received from credit customers. These are recorded in the cash book and in the customer's personal account. The cashier then pays the cheques into the business bank account.

* Controls must be in place to ensure the cheque cannot be misappropriated before it is paid into the bank.

* Some customers may pay money directly into the company's bank account. The cashier should go through the bank statement carefully, enter details into the cash book, and ensure details are passed to the sales ledger section to deduct the amount from the customer's balance.

The payments system

* Companies pay their suppliers.

* A cheque requisition is prepared for each payment. This form details why a cheque is required. A cheque will be prepared and the invoices paid will be submitted to a senior manager for approval and to have the cheque signed.

* If the company pays its suppliers through direct bank transfer, each transfer should be approved by a senior manager before it is set up.

The petty cash system

* Companies will need to keep some cash on hand to pay for small expenses such as postage stamps, biscuits, taxi fares etc.

* A cheque will be made out to cash, to generate the initial cash for the system.

* As staff claim against the petty cash system, they complete vouchers stating what the payment is for, and attach a receipt to prove the amount.

* At regular intervals, a further cheque is made out to cash to replenish the petty cash which has been spent. The supervisor will inspect the receipts and vouchers at this point.

14.6 THE INVENTORY SYSTEM

LEARNING SUMMARY

After studying this section you should be able to:

* describe the inventory system within an organisation.

Stages in the inventory system

The main stages in the inventory cycle and the issues to be considered are as follows:

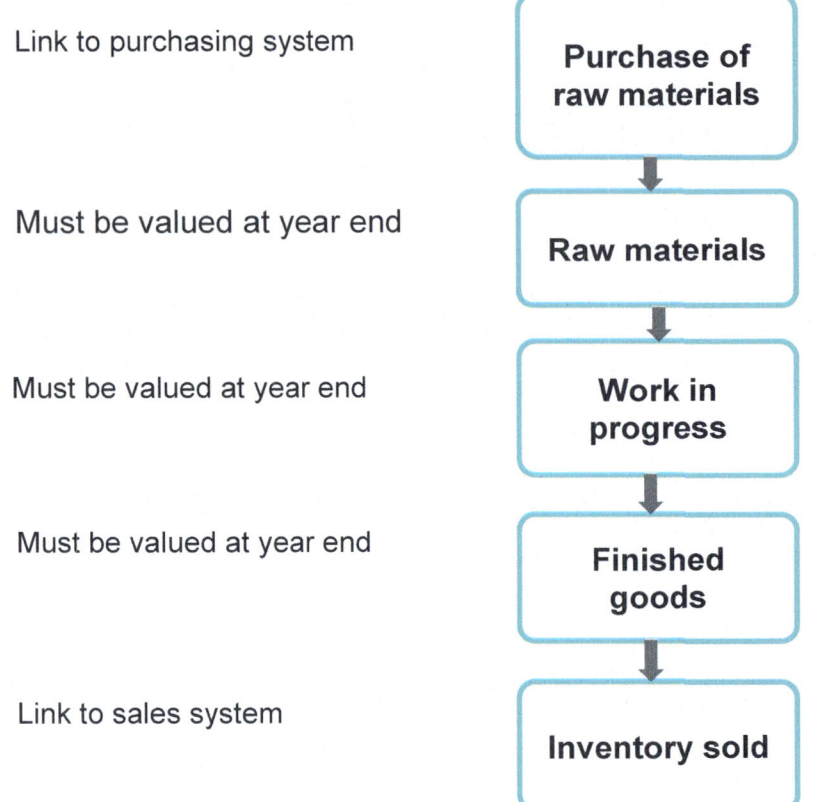

Link to purchasing system — **Purchase of raw materials**

Must be valued at year end — **Raw materials**

Must be valued at year end — **Work in progress**

Must be valued at year end — **Finished goods**

Link to sales system — **Inventory sold**

The production manager will decide on the required inventory purchases bearing in mind the items to be produced and the inventory balance on hand.

In some (automated) systems, raw materials will be ordered automatically when the balance falls to a certain level.

> **KEY POINT** At the end of the year, all inventory will be counted and valued so that the statement of financial position can be produced.

> This part of the syllabus ties in with corporate governance. The directors are required to introduce a good system of controls to safeguard the company's assets and protect the shareholders' investments.

14.7 THE PURPOSE OF ORGANISATIONAL CONTROL

LEARNING SUMMARY

After studying this section you should be able to:

- explain why appropriate controls are necessary in relation to business and IT systems and procedures.

The purpose of organisational control

Control within the organisation has several purposes:

Purpose	Why this is important
Safeguard company's assets	If assets are stolen or damaged the company will have to spend money to replace them.
Efficiency	Inefficient business practices are a waste of the company's money.
Prevent fraud	Fraud means the loss of valuable resources belonging to the company/ shareholders.
Prevent errors	Errors can lead to losses in efficiency (time spent correcting) or a loss of assets (e.g. failing to invoice the correct amount, paying for goods which have not been received).

Why controls in systems are important

System	Purpose	Key areas
Purchasing	Safeguard company's assets	ensuring that only goods that have been received are paid for ensuring goods are in good condition
	Efficiency	ensuring that the best price is negotiated before buying
	Prevent fraud	preventing purchasing staff accepting payments from suppliers to persuade them to purchase from that supplier
	Prevent errors	ensuring that the correct amount is charged to suppliers ensuring that all purchases are recorded

Sales	Safeguard company's assets	ensuring goods are only sold to customers who are likely to pay
	Efficiency	ensuring orders are processed promptly so that customers do not go elsewhere
	Prevent fraud	ensuring there is no theft of cash from customers
	Prevent errors	ensuring the correct quantity of goods is despatched and invoiced
Wages	Safeguard company's assets	ensuring that cash wages cannot be stolen
	Efficiency	ensuring that people are only paid for overtime when necessary (approved)
	Prevent fraud	ensuring there are no 'ghost' employees, people being paid but who do not work for the company ensuring employees do not claim pay for hours they have not worked
Cash	Safeguard company's assets	ensuring cash is kept safe from theft
	Efficiency	ensuring cash is banked promptly, so as to gain interest
	Prevent fraud	ensuring employees do not claim for expenses not incurred
	Prevent errors	ensuring the entries in the cash book are correct
Inventory	Safeguard company's assets	ensuring inventory is kept free from damage
	Efficiency	ensuring inventory is only produced when it can be sold quickly
	Prevent fraud	ensuring inventory cannot be stolen by employees
	Prevent errors	ensuring costs of finished goods are calculated properly

14.8 AUTOMATED SYSTEMS

LEARNING SUMMARY

After studying this section you should be able to:

• describe the features of automated systems.

Automated systems

Automated systems show the following features:

Uniform processing of transactions	Every transaction will be performed in exactly the same way.
Lack of segregation of functions	One person in the company, the IT manager, has a lot of power as he/ she can access all the data within their company.
Potential for data to be corrupted easily	An inexpert operator could accidentally corrupt data. Computer files can become corrupted on their own. Alternatively, users may input data incorrectly.
Potential for increased management supervision	Management can monitor the activities of subordinates easily. Exception reports can be used to highlight unusual transactions.

14.9 COMPARISON OF MANUAL AND AUTOMATED SYSTEMS

LEARNING SUMMARY

After studying this section you should be able to:

• discuss the advantages and disadvantages of automated and manual systems.

Comparison of manual and automated systems

Advantages of manual systems	Disadvantages of manual systems
Low capital cost	Slower at performing calculations
No computer experience required	More likely to make calculation errors
Easy to correct errors (e.g. whitening fluid)	Analysis of information is more time-consuming
Ledgers are portable	Less easy to audit
Can review transactions for logical sense while entering/ performing calculations	
Advantages of automated systems	**Disadvantages of automated systems**
Quicker	Capital cost
Can perform more complex calculations	Training cost
Fewer errors	Less easy to correct errors
More security (passwords)	Systems can crash
Easier to sort and analyse data	

Do you understand?

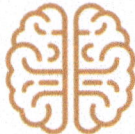

1   Which of the following is not a stage in a standard purchasing system?

    (i)   Receipt of goods (ii) Receipt of cash (iii) Placing of orders

2   Consider the following stages in the inventory control system. What order will these stages usually be performed in?

    (i)   Transfer to warehouse

    (ii)   Requisition of raw materials

    (iii)   Year-end inventory check (stock take)

    (iv)   Purchase of raw materials

3   Reduced chance of data corruption is a feature of an automated system.

    True or false?

4   The primary purposes of control within an organisation are to safeguard company assets, improve efficiency and prevent fraud and error.

    True or false?

1   (ii) The purchases system will involve making payments to suppliers, not receiving money from them.
2   (ii), (iv), (i), (iii)
3   False. It is possible for inexpert users to accidentally corrupt data on an automated system.
4   True.

1 **(a)** PDP makes and sells computer monitors. It is considering the introduction of a number of controls during the next year, including:

A   Authorisation of timesheets

B   Bank reconciliations

C   Checking creditworthiness of customers

D   Agreeing goods received notes to invoices received

Required:

Identify the control above which is associated with each of the following systems within PDP, by writing A, B, C or D.

(i)   Purchases system

(ii)   Sales system

(iii)   Cash system

(iv)   Payroll system

(b) Below are a number of statements regarding automated systems, when compared to manual systems.

A   In small businesses, automated systems will be cheaper to develop and implement than manual systems

B   Automated systems will reduce the amount of training required for new staff members

C   Automated systems ensure that transactions are processed in a uniform way

D   There is increased chance of data corruption in an automated system

E   Automated systems eliminate the risk of fraud or misstatement

F   Automated systems reduce management's ability to quickly produce reports and analyse information

G   Automated systems allow increased supervision of employees by management

H   Automation of systems may lead to a lack of segregation of functions

Required:

Write down which of the above are correct by selecting FOUR of the letters from A–H.

2   P runs a business which sells computer equipment. She is concerned that when her business pays its suppliers, the wrong amount may be paid. Which of the following control measures could help P to deal with this problem?

A   Regular purchase ledger reconciliations

B   Match the GRN to the original purchase order sent to the supplier

C   Matching of the purchase order to the requisition order

D   Prompt recording of invoices received

3   Consider the following two statements:

(1)   When petty cash is replenished, it is usual for the amount of cash to drawn to equal the value of the receipts and vouchers produced since the previous replenishment.

(2)   It would be best practice for a company that predominantly receives cheques and postal orders in payment for goods dispatched to appoint a single, designated and trusted individual to open the mail.

Which of these statements is/are correct?

A   (1) only

B   (2) only

C   Both

D   Neither

15 The relationship between accounting & other business functions

The following topics are covered in this chapter:

- Purchasing (procurement)
- Production
- Marketing
- Service provision

15.1 PURCHASING

LEARNING SUMMARY

After studying this section you should be able to:

- explain the relationship between accounting and other key functions within the business.

Questions can ask you to choose ways, from a list, in which each of the business functions covered in this chapter co-ordinate with the accounting department.

Purchasing/ procurement

The purchasing/ buying function is responsible for placing and following up orders. It co-ordinates with the accounting department as follows:

Establishing credit terms	The accounting department will work with the purchasing department to liaise with suppliers to obtain a credit account and to negotiate acceptable credit terms.
Prices	The accounting department can advise the purchasing department of the maximum price that should be paid to maintain margins.
Payment	Payments may be approved by the purchasing department but are made by the accounting department.
Data capture, e.g. orders	Order details will be input by the purchasing department and details passed to the accounting department.
Inventory	The purchasing department will consult with the inventory section of the accounting department to determine the quantity of items already in stock and therefore the quantity required.
Budgeting	The accounting department will consult with the purchasing department on likely costs in preparing budgets.

15.2 PRODUCTION

Production

The production department plans and overseas the production of goods. It co-ordinates with the accounting department as follows:

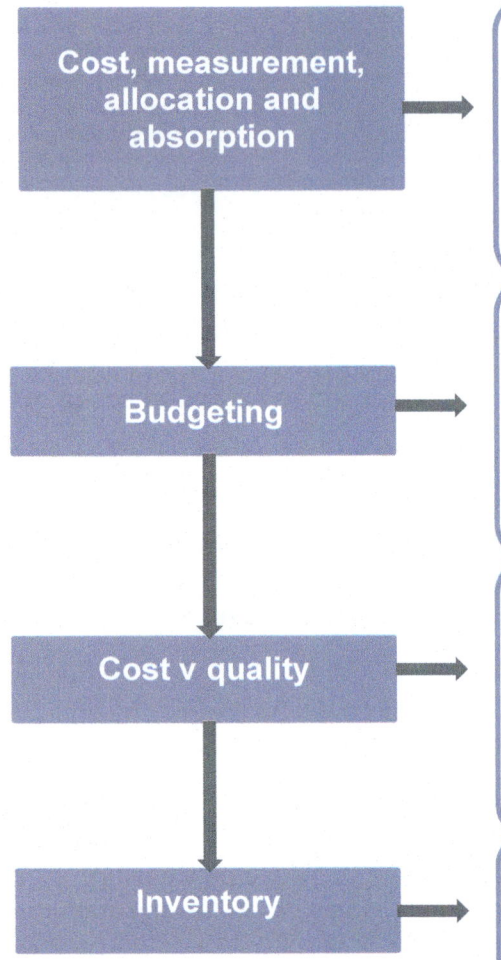

Cost, measurement, allocation and absorption	The production department measures quantities of materials and time used; the management accountant gives a monetary value to the item. Costs are then allocated and absorbed to calculate production costs based on advice given by the production department.
Budgeting	The production department will decide how many items of what type are to be produced. The cost of producing these will be determined by the accounting and production departments together, and incorporated into the overall budget.
Cost v quality	The production and accounting departments will discuss the features that can be included in products and the raw materials that should be used. They should agree which better quality materials and features justify the extra cost, and discuss how to maximise quality and profit.
Inventory	The production department will liaise with the inventory section to ensure that there are significant raw materials in inventory for the production that is planned.

5.3 MARKETING

LEARNING SUMMARY

After studying this section you should be able to:

- identify the financial issues associated with marketing.

Marketing

The marketing department co-ordinates with the accounting department as follows:

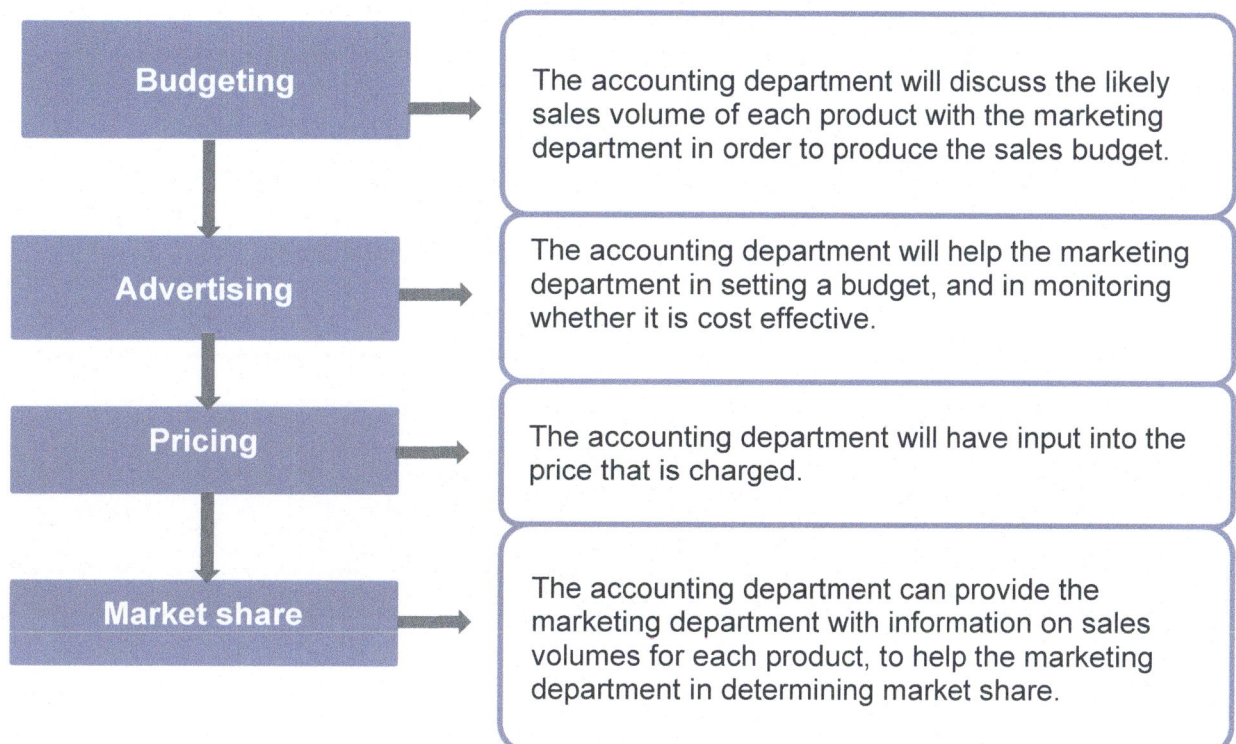

| Budgeting | The accounting department will discuss the likely sales volume of each product with the marketing department in order to produce the sales budget. |

| Advertising | The accounting department will help the marketing department in setting a budget, and in monitoring whether it is cost effective. |

| Pricing | The accounting department will have input into the price that is charged. |

| Market share | The accounting department can provide the marketing department with information on sales volumes for each product, to help the marketing department in determining market share. |

15.4 SERVICE PROVISION

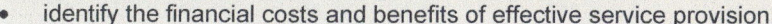

LEARNING SUMMARY

After studying this section you should be able to:

- identify the financial costs and benefits of effective service provision.

The nature of services

Companies very often provide services to customer, at the same time as the sale or afterwards.

- **Intangibility** –. Services are activities undertaken by the organisation on behalf of its customers and therefore cannot be packaged for the customer to take away with them.

- **Inseparability** – services are often created by the organisation at the same time as they are consumed by the customer e.g. a taxi driver will create the service they offer as they are carrying a passenger to their desired destination. The service cannot therefore be easily distinguished from the person or organisation providing the service.

- **Perishability** – services cannot be stored for later.

- **Variability** – each service is unique and cannot usually be repeated in exactly the same way, making offering a standardised service to customers very difficult.

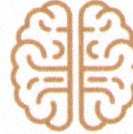

Do you understand?

1   Which of the following is an example of co-ordination between the purchasing and accounting departments?

   (i)   Establishing credit terms (ii) Allocating costs (iii) Determining sales prices

2   Which of the following NOT an example of co-ordination between the marketing and accounting department?

   (i)   Pricing (ii) Assessing market share (iii) Assessing creditworthiness

3   'Most services provided by an organisation will be created at the same time as they are consumed.' Which feature of services is being described?

   (i)   Intangibility (ii) Inseparability (iii) Perishability (iv) Variability

1   **E Co has a large marketing department. In which of the following ways would this department co-ordinate with E's accounting department?**

A   Decisions on the quantity of raw materials required

B   Establishing credit terms for customers

C   Calculating pay rises for staff

D   Decisions on the selling price of the product

2   **Which of the following is NOT a way in which an organisation's production department would co-ordinate with its accounting department?**

A   Calculating charge out rates for services provided by the organisation

B   Calculating the budgets for the number of units to be produced

C   Estimation of the costs of the raw materials required for production

D   Decisions on the quality of raw materials that the organisation can afford to use

3   **Which of the following is a feature of services provided by an organisation?**

A   Permanence

B   Innovation

C   Variability

D   Separability

4   HGF is a company that operates taxis within several cities in country U and has received a number of complaints regarding the behaviour of its drivers towards passengers. One of HGF's marketing executives has pointed out that even if the customer's journey is fast, cheap and reliable, customers will still see the service offered by HGF as poor if the driver behaves poorly.

What aspect of the nature of service provision is HGF's marketing executive referring to?

A   Intangibility

B   Perishability

C   Variability

D   Inseparability

16 **Audit and financial control**

The following topics are covered in this chapter:

- Internal controls and internal checks
- Management responsibility
- Internal and external auditing

16.1 THE MEANING OF INTERNAL CONTROL AND INTERNAL CHECK

LEARNING SUMMARY

After studying this section you should be able to:

- explain internal control and internal check.

Definitions

> **DEFINITION** **Internal control** is the process designed and effected by management to provide reasonable assurance about the achievement of the entity's objectives with regards to the reliability of financial reporting, effectiveness and efficiency of operations and compliance with applicable laws and regulations.

There are several technical terms defined in the chapter. A question may directly test your knowledge of any one of these definitions.

> **DEFINITION** **Internal check** is an element of internal control, concerned with ensuring that no single task is executed from start to finish by only one single person. Each individual's work is subject to an independent check by another person in the course of that person's duties.

16.2 THE PURPOSE OF INTERNAL CONTROL

LEARNING SUMMARY

After studying this section you should be able to:

- explain the purpose of internal control.

The purpose of internal control

The purpose of internal control is implied by the definition given earlier, to help management achieve the entity's objectives, especially in terms of ensuring:

- the orderly and efficient conduct of the business.
- the safeguarding of assets.
- the prevention and detection of fraud and error.
- the accuracy and completeness of the accounting records.
- the timely preparation of reliable financial information.

16.3 THE COMPONENTS OF INTERNAL CONTROL

The components of internal control

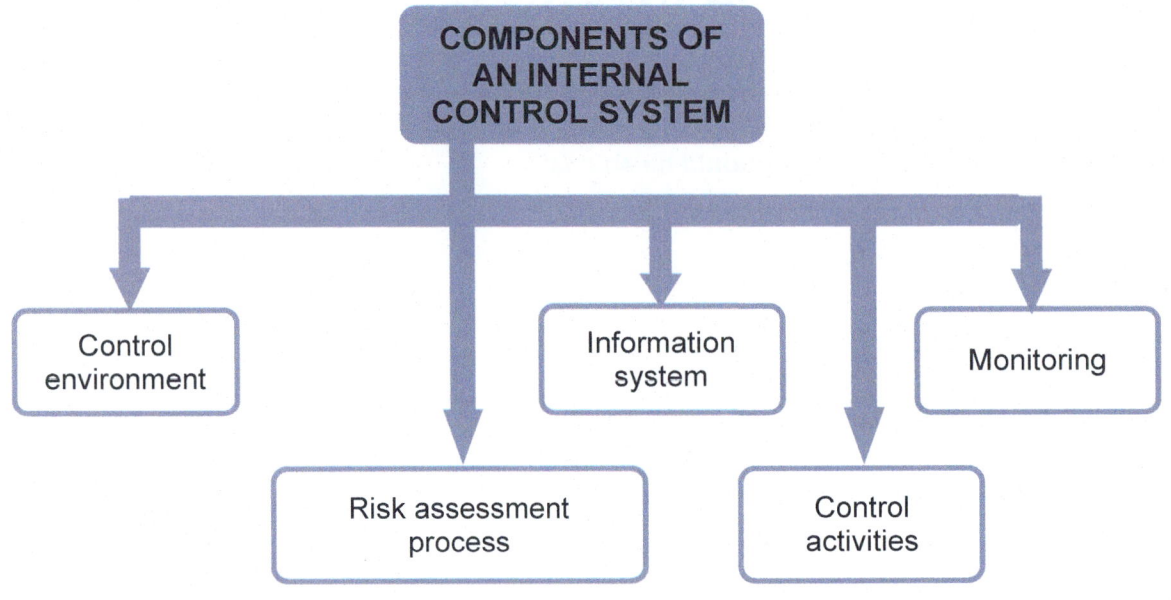

> **DEFINITION** The **control environment** is the overall attitude of management regarding internal controls and their importance. It encompasses management's philosophy e.g. a commitment to integrity and ethical values, a formal organisation structure and proper training of staff.

> **DEFINITION** The **risk assessment process** is an entity's process for identifying and responding to business risk.

> **DEFINITION** The **information system** relevant to financial reporting objectives consists of the procedures and records established to process the transactions that the entity carries out, and to maintain accountability for the related assets, liabilities and equity balances.

> **DEFINITION** **Control activities** are manual or computerised procedures that help an organisation to achieve its objectives and mitigate the business risks it faces.

There are different categories of control activities. One possibility is:

Authorisation

Involves members of staff having to obtain approval from managers or other key members of staff for various transactions. These could include expense claim forms, purchases or cash transfers.

Comparison

Involves looking at analysis and reports in order to identify management or control issues from past performance.

Computer controls

Tend to be of two separate types – general and application controls (see later). Both are designed to ensure that computer systems operate as intended.

Arithmetic controls

These check for minor errors or frauds that would not otherwise have been detected. Figures can be recalculated to check accuracy.

Maintaining a trial balance and control accounts

This will often enable the organisation to easily see if errors or frauds have occurred by way of a simple review.

Accounts reconciliation

Receivable and payables ledger reconciliations and bank reconciliations are useful tools in identifying errors and frauds and can be performed regularly.

Physical controls

These are often overlooked, but they are just as important as administrative or accounting procedures. E.g. there is no point in having an efficient inventory tracking system if there is inadequate security to prevent theft of high value items.

Segregation of duties

This splits any given transaction into three elements: authorisation, recording and maintaining custody of assets. This is a potentially effective means of preventing fraud because it will require collusion between at least two staff members.

> A question may present a scenario and ask you to choose from a list as to which type of control activity is being described in the scenario.

> The mnemonic ACCAMAPS may help you remember this list.

> **DEFINITION   Monitoring of controls** is a process to assess the quality of internal control performance over time. It involves assessing the design and operation of controls on a timely basis and taking necessary corrective actions.

Alternative analysis of internal controls

Preventative controls
prevent errors or frauds occurring

Detective controls
detect if any problems have occurred

TYPES OF CONTROL

Corrective controls
address any problems that have occurred

16.4 INFORMATION TECHNOLOGY AND INTERNAL CONTROL

LEARNING SUMMARY

After studying this section you should be able to:

- identify and describe the types of information technology and information systems used by the business for internal control

- describe general and application controls in business.

The use of IT in internal controls

For many businesses, the use of IT can be a valuable tool when setting internal controls in two main areas: financial and operational controls.

> **KEY POINT Financial controls** – this involves IT being used as a check for the financial data in the organisation.

This could include ensuring the security of financial data, such as through the use of passwords and authorisation, but it could also allow organisations to make sure that financial procedures are followed.

e.g. many businesses have IT based sales ledger facilities. The system could be set to prevent staff making sales to customers who have already reached their credit limit.

> **KEY POINT Operational controls** – this is where IT is used as a control on the day-to-day activities of the business.

e.g. a manufacturing business may have automated systems that check each unit and reject any that are defective.

The protection of IT systems and software within business

Computer controls fall into two categories: general controls and application controls.

> **DEFINITION General controls** are policies and procedures that relate to many applications and support the effective function of application controls by helping to ensure the continued proper operation of information systems.

Examples of general controls include:

- **Physical controls** – to avoid unauthorised access to computer equipment, such as security personnel, door locks and card entry systems.

- **Hardware and software configuration** – to ensure that any new IT is tested and installed correctly to minimise the risk of errors or damage to the system.

- **Logical access** – to prevent unauthorised access to the organisation's information systems. These could include password systems.

- **Disaster recovery** – to ensure the organisation will be able to continue operating despite adverse conditions.

- **Output controls** – to ensure the outputs from the system are both complete and secure.

- **Technical support** – it is important that all the users of the IT systems are competent. Training policies and technical support for workers can be a valuable control.

These controls will vary from system to system, but are often designed to ensure:

- **Completeness** – has all necessary data been input?

- **Authorisation** – is the person inputting the data authorised to do so?

- **Identification** – can the person inputting the data be uniquely identified?

- **Validity** – is the information being input by the user valid?

- **Forensic checks** – is the information being input by the user mathematically accurate?

16.5 MANAGEMENT RESPONSIBILITY

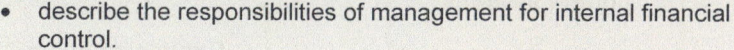

LEARNING SUMMARY

After studying this section you should be able to:

- describe the responsibilities of management for internal financial control.

Responsibility

It is the **director's (and senior management's) responsibility** to establish proper internal control arrangements within their company.

This responsibility may derive from statutory requirements or from general corporate governance arrangements.

16.6 THE MEANING OF INTERNAL AUDITING AND EXTERNAL AUDITING

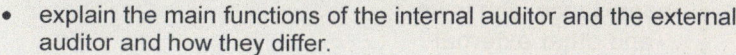

LEARNING SUMMARY

After studying this section you should be able to:

- explain the main functions of the internal auditor and the external auditor and how they differ.

Differences between internal and external audit

	External audit	Internal audit
Required by	Company law	Board of Directors/Audit Committee
Appointed by	Shareholders or Board of Directors	Board of Directors/Audit Committee

Reports to	Shareholders	Board of Directors/Audit Committee
Reports on	Whether the financial statements are • true and fair • properly prepared. Whether the directors' report is consistent with the financial statements	Adequacy of internal controls etc.
Scope of assignment	Unlimited, to fulfil statutory obligations	Prescribed by management

Roles of internal audit

The activities of internal audit generally involve the following roles:

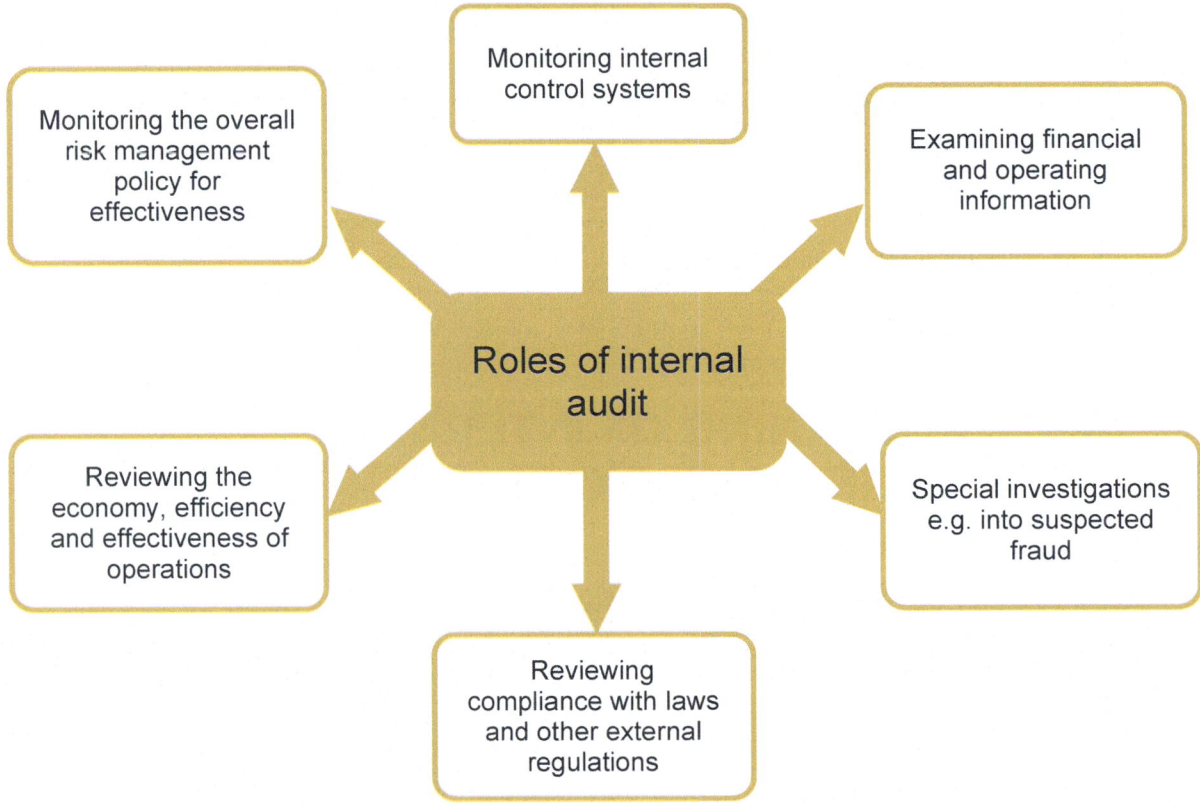

Limitations of internal audit

KEY POINT Internal auditors have an unavoidable independence problem. They are employed by the management of the company and yet are expected to give an objective opinion on matters for which management are responsible.

Internal audit will only succeed if it is properly staffed and resourced.

If internal auditors identify fraud, they may be unwilling to disclose it for fear of repercussions.

These limitations can be reduced if an **audit committee**:

- sets the work agenda for internal reports.
- receives internal audit reports.

- is able to ensure the internal audit is properly resourced.

- has a 'voice' at main board level.

The purposes of external audit

International Standards on Auditing (ISAs) state that the overall objectives of the external auditor are:

- to obtain reasonable assurance about whether the financial statements as a whole are free from material misstatement, whether due to fraud or error

- to express an opinion on whether the financial statements are prepared, in all material respects, in accordance with an applicable financial reporting framework.

ADVANTAGES	DISADVANTAGES
Disputes between management may be more easily settled e.g. a partnership which has complicated profit-sharing arrangements may require an independent examination of those accounts to ensure accurate assessment and division of those profits.	The audit fee!
Major changes in ownership may be facilitated if past accounts contain an unqualified audit report, for instance, where two sole traders merge their businesses.	The audit involves the client's staff and management giving time to providing information to the auditor.
Applications to third parties for finance may be enhanced by audited accounts.	
The audit is likely to involve an in-depth examination of the business and may enable the auditor to give constructive advice to management on improving the efficiency of the business.	

16.7 INTERNAL CONTROL AND AUDIT

Why internal controls interest the external auditor

Auditors need to gain an understanding of the systems and controls.

This enables the auditor to:

- Assess the level of control risk.

- Determine the audit approach to take

KEY POINT Reliance on internal controls will reduce the amount of substantive testing of transactions and resultant balances in the ledger accounts required.

At an early stage in their work the auditors will have to decide the extent to which they believe they can place reliance on the internal controls of the enterprise.

Why internal controls interest the internal auditor

A key objective of the internal auditor is to review the organisation's system of internal control and to provide assurance that the corporate governance requirements are being met.

Like external auditors, internal auditors have to make decisions on the extent of reliance on controls to manage risks and therefore the level of testing to be carried out.

Do you understand?

1   'A company's internal controls can be so well designed that they eliminate the risk of failing to achieve the company's objectives.'

     True or false?

2   Which of the following groups is responsible for the creation and operation of satisfactory operating controls within an organisation?

     (i)   The board of directors (ii) External auditors (iii) Internal auditors

3   Why might a bank insist on an external audit of a company's accounts before lending money to the company?

1   False. There will always be a residual risk of not achieving the company's objectives, however well the internal controls are designed. Internal controls will always have inherent limitations, such as the possibility that they will be circumvented by employees colluding together, or the possibility that they fail due to human error.

2   (i) The board of directors has ultimate responsibility for ensuring the satisfactory nature of internal controls.

3   Before a bank lends money to a company, it wants to be reasonably certain that it will get its money back, plus interest. The bank will want to make sure that the financial statements can be relied upon to give a true and fair view.

1   (a)   Below are a number of components.

A   Control environment

B   Corrective

C   Monitoring

D   Risk assessment

E   Application

F   Information systems

G   General

H   Management responsibility

Required:

Write down which FOUR of the above statements are components of internal control systems by selecting FOUR from A–H.

(b)   Below are a number of statements regarding internal and external audit.

A   It is a legal requirement for larger companies

B   The scope of work is decided by management

C   Can be undertaken by employees of the company

D   Ultimately reports to the company's shareholders

E   Reviews whether financial statements are true and fair

F   Must be undertaken by independent auditors

G   Mainly focuses on reviewing internal controls

H   Ultimately reports to management

Required:

Write down which FOUR of the above statements relate to internal audit by selecting FOUR of the letters from A-H.

2   **The key purpose of internal auditing is to:**

A   detect errors and fraud

B   evaluate the organisation's risk management processes and systems of control

C   give confidence as to the truth and fairness of the financial statements

D   express an internal opinion on the truth and fairness of the financial statements

3 Consider the following statements regarding control activities:

(1) The primary purpose of the segregation of duties between individuals within the organisation is to locate and identify frauds that employees have perpetrated.

(2) 'General' computer controls include physical controls to prevent unauthorised access to computer equipment, such as door locks and card entry systems.

Which of these options is/are correct?

A   (1) only

B   (2) only

C   Both

D   Neither

17 Fraud, fraudulent behaviour & their prevention in business

The following topics are covered in this chapter:

- The meaning and prerequisites of fraud
- Fraudulent financial reporting
- Money laundering
- Implications of fraud
- Fraudulent financial reporting
- Measures to prevent and detect fraud
- Duties of management regarding fraud

17.1 THE MEANING OF FRAUD

LEARNING SUMMARY

After studying this section you should be able to:

- explain the meaning of fraud.

The meaning of fraud

> **DEFINITION Fraud** is an intentional act involving the use of deception to obtain an unjust or illegal advantage – essentially 'theft by deception'. Fraud is a criminal offence, punishable by a fine or imprisonment.

- **Error** – refers to unintentional mistakes.

- **Irregularity** – something contrary to a particular rule or standard.

- **Misstatement** – something stated wrongly. Misstatement can arise due to fraud, irregularity or error.

17.2 THE PREREQUISITES OF FRAUD

LEARNING SUMMARY

After studying this section you should be able to:

- explain the circumstances under which fraud is likely to arise.

The prerequisites of fraud

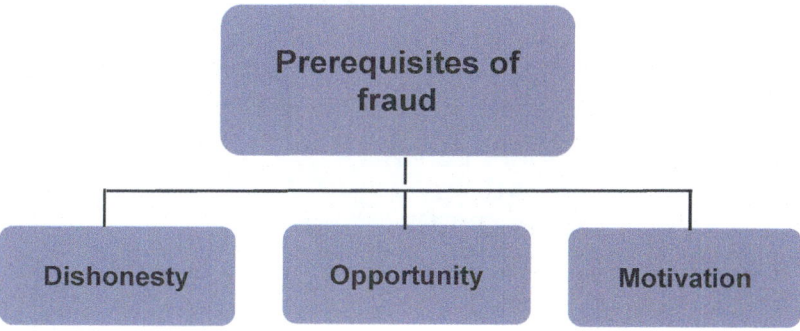

All three are usually required – for example an honest employee is unlikely to commit fraud even if they are given the opportunity and motive.

Factors that might indicate an increased risk of fraud and error include (amongst others):

- management domination by one person, or a small group of people

- unnecessarily complex corporate structure

- poor staff morale

- personnel who do not take leave/ holidays

- lavish lifestyles of employees

- inadequate segregation of duties

- lack of monitoring of control systems

- payments for services disproportionate to effort.

KEY POINT If management have established a strong system of internal control then the potential for fraud is greatly reduced.

17.3 EXAMPLES OF FRAUD IN A BUSINESS ORGANISATION

LEARNING SUMMARY

After studying this section you should be able to:

- give examples of recognised fraudulent activity in a business organisation.

Examples of fraud

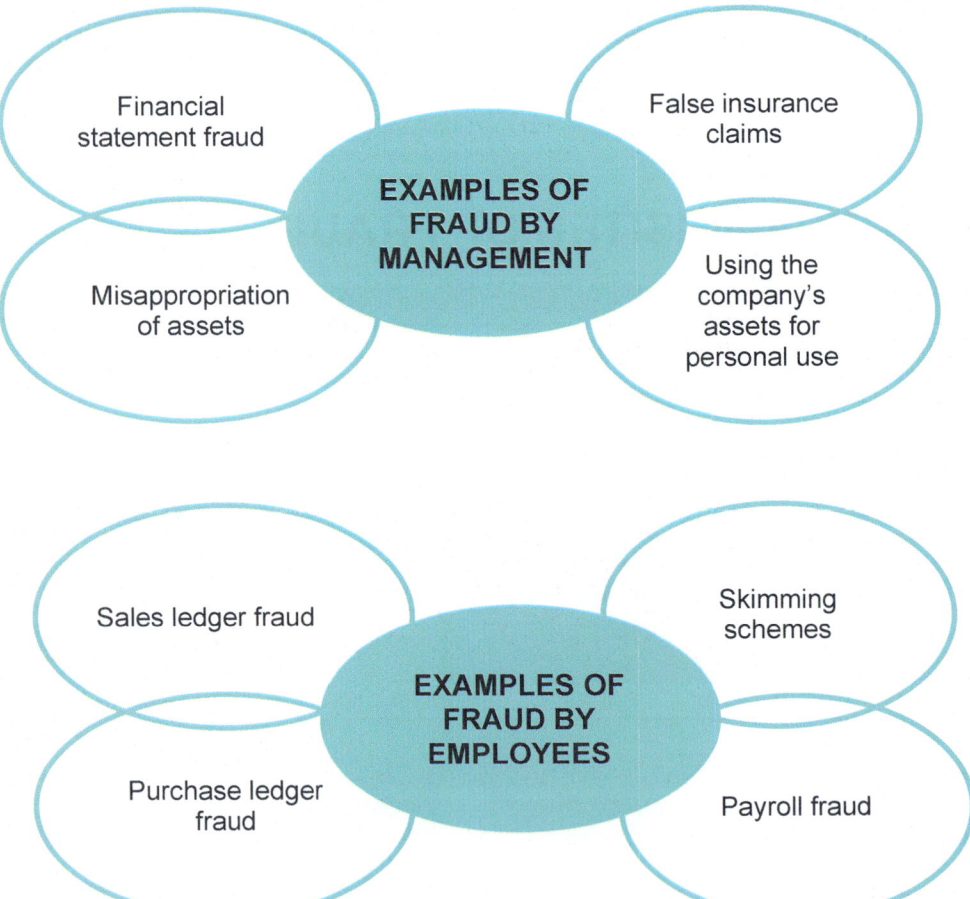

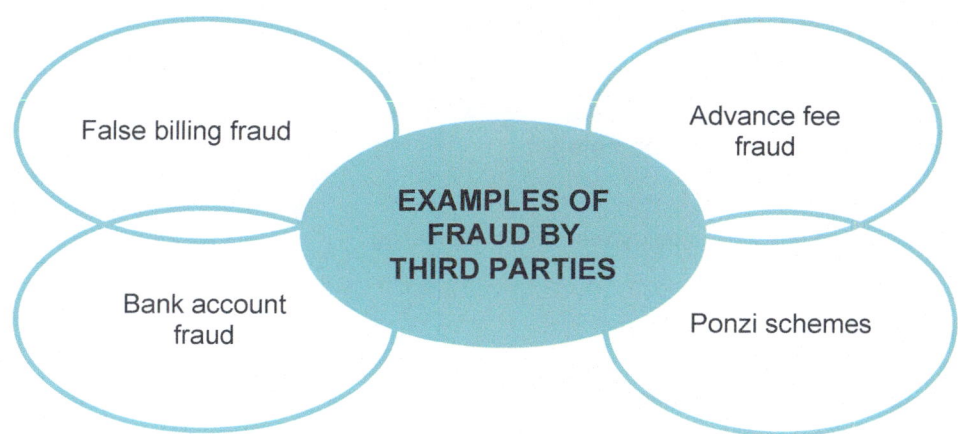

17.4 FRAUDULENT FINANCIAL REPORTING

LEARNING SUMMARY

After studying this section you should be able to:

* give examples of recognised fraudulent financial reporting and creative accounting in a business organisation.

Examples

DEFINITION Fraudulent financial reporting involves intentional misstatements in financial statements in order to deceive financial statement users.

Examples of fraudulent financial reporting include:

* recording fictitious entries in the accounting records.

* inappropriately adjusting assumptions or judgements used to estimate account balances.

* omitting, advancing or delaying recognition in the financial statements of transactions that have occurred during the year.

* concealing facts that could affect the amounts recorded in the financial statements.

* altering records related to significant and unusual transactions.

Examples of creative accounting include:

* window dressing.

* delaying or accelerating a company's expenses.

* inaccurate revaluation of company assets.

* manipulation of revenue recognition.

* off-balance sheet accounting.

> Be familiar with these real-life examples as they could appear as the basis of a scenario.

17.5 MONEY LAUNDERING

LEARNING SUMMARY

After studying this section you should be able to:

- define the term money laundering

- give examples of recognised offences under typical money laundering regulation.

Money laundering

DEFINITION **Money laundering** is the exchange of 'dirty' money and assets that have been criminally obtained for 'clean' money and assets that have no clear link to criminal activity.

Typical money laundering legislation recognises three main offences relating to money laundering.

- **Laundering** – this may involve acquiring, using or possessing criminal property, handling or being involved with criminal activity, investing the proceeds of criminal activity or transferring criminal property.

- **Failure to report** – failing to disclose proof or suspicion of money laundering can carry a maximum 5 year prison term, along with fines.

- **Tipping off** – disclosure of information which may prejudice a money laundering investigation carries a maximum 2 year prison term.

> The examiner will want to know that you are aware of your responsibilities with regards to money laundering. It is a commonly tested area of the syllabus.

Money laundering itself normally follows three distinct phases:

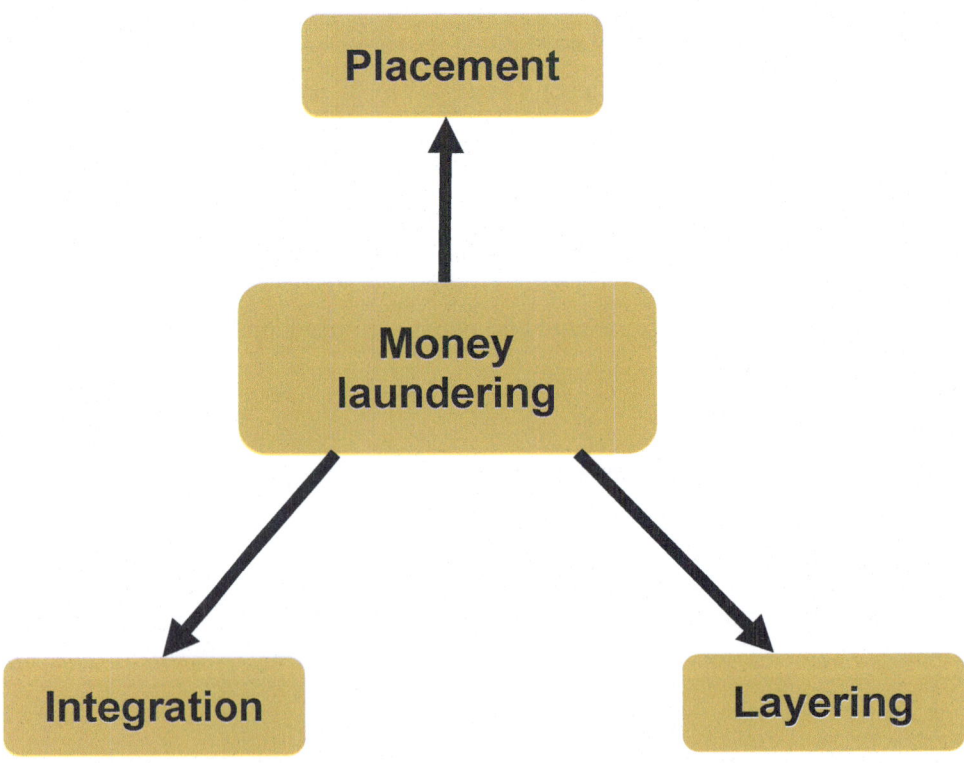

Controls and procedures required by law

The controls and procedures required by law will often include:

- Identification of large or unusual transactions.

- Scrutinising of unusual patterns of transactions.

- Taking steps to ensure all customers are identified.

- Creation of the role of Money Laundering Reporting Officer (MLRO).

Defined reporting process

It is also important that a business has a defined reporting process for any suspected money laundering. This will normally involve:

> Employees reporting suspicious activity to the MLRO

> The MLRO investigating further; and

> If there are grounds for reasonable suspicion, the MLRO should report to the relevant authorities (in the UK this would be the Serious Organised Crime Agency (SOCA))

17.6 THE POSSIBLE IMPLICATIONS OF FRAUD TO THE COMPANY

LEARNING SUMMARY

After studying this section you should be able to:

- explain the implications of fraud for the organisation.

Implications

There is a spectrum of implications of fraud, from the immaterial to the critical, including:

- Loss of shareholder confidence.

- Loss of assets.

- Financial difficulties.

- Collapse of the company.

- Fines by tax and other authorities.

17.7 MEASURES TO PREVENT AND DETECT FRAUD

LEARNING SUMMARY

After studying this section you should be able to:

• identify methods for preventing and detecting money laundering.

Measures to prevent and detect fraud

KEY POINT The principal strategy of any organisation to prevent and detect fraud is to establish an effective internal control system.

The first step of any fraud prevention system is therefore to ensure that each of the components of internal control are set up and working properly.

17.8 THE DUTIES OF MANAGEMENT IN PREVENTING AND DETECTING FRAUD

LEARNING SUMMARY

After studying this section you should be able to:

• explain the role and duties of individual managers in the fraud detection and prevention process.

> You should recall that internal control comprises five components: the control environment, the risk assessment process, the information system, control activities and monitoring of controls.

Duties of management

The duties of management can be split between:

The duties of the board of directors to maintain a sound system of internal control

The duties of the audit committee to monitor and review internal control and risk

The duties of employees generally will include fraud detection and prevention

Do you understand?

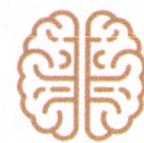

1. Suggest two reasons why the management of a company might want to undertake fraudulent financial reporting.

2. A bank employee becomes suspicious of a customer who has made several large deposits of cash into their account. He is concerned they may be laundering money. Who should he report his suspicions to?

   (i) The customer (ii) The police (iii) Immediate line manager (iv) MLRO

3. Which of the following suggests an increased risk of fraud and error in the recording of an organisation's transactions?

   (i) Simple corporate structure (ii) Employee bonus based on sales achieved

---

1. Two from the following list:
   1) Management bonuses might depend on achieving a stated profit level.
   2) Management may wish to boost the share price to please shareholders, by reporting high profits.
   3) Management may fear that their company may face a takeover threat and they will lose their jobs unless high profits are reported.
   4) There may be conditions attached to loans that have been taken out (e.g. minimum acceptable accounting ratios) and the company is in danger of breaching these conditions.

2. (iv) Money Laundering Reporting Officer. The MLRO will investigate further and decide how to proceed.

3. (ii) If employees are paid bonuses based on the level of sales they achieve, they may be tempted to invent non-existent sales in order to receive bonuses. A simple corporate structure would indicate a reduced risk of fraud.

1 **Which of the following are considered to be the three prerequisites for fraud to occur?**

(1)   Motivation

(2)   Opportunity

(3)   Authority

A   (1) and (2)

B   (2) and (3)

C   (1) and (3)

D   (1), (2) and (3)

2 **Off balance sheet accounting refers to which of the following:**

A   A focus on income and expenditure rather to the detriment of asset and liability management

B   Removal of business assets by employees for their own personal use

C   Diversion of assets from the balance sheet to a personal bank account

D   Deliberate exclusion of certain assets and liabilities from the published balance sheet

3 **Which of the following is NOT a control or procedure required by standard money laundering legislation?**

A   Identification of large or unusual transactions

B   Taking steps to ensure customers can be identified

C   Reporting of all large or unusual transactions to the relevant authorities

D   Creation of the role of Nominated Officer

4 **BNG Co has recently discovered that it has been the victim of a false-billing fraud. Which of the following controls could BNG put in place to prevent this from occurring in the future?**

A   Segregation of duties within the accounts department

B   Regular receivables ledger reconciliations

C   Authorisation of payments by management

D   Maintenance of a regular trial balance

18 Leadership, management and supervision

The following topics are covered in this chapter:

- Definitions
- Managerial authority and responsibility
- Theories of management
- Leadership

18.1 WHAT DO LEADERSHIP, MANAGEMENT AND SUPERVISION MEAN?

LEARNING SUMMARY

After studying this section you should be able to:

- define leadership, management and supervision and explain the distinction between these terms.

Definitions

DEFINITION Leadership is an interpersonal influence directed towards the achievement of a goal or goals.

DEFINITION Management is the effective use and co-ordination of business resources in order to achieve key objectives with maximum efficiency.

Note that a manager is not necessarily a leader. A manager will only be a leader if he/she is able to influence people to achieve the goals of the organisation without relying on the use of formal authority.

DEFINITION A supervisor is a person given responsibility for planning and controlling the work of a group of employees.

18.2 MANAGERIAL AUTHORITY AND RESPONSIBILITY

LEARNING SUMMARY

After studying this section you should be able to:

- explain the areas of managerial authority and responsibility.

Authority and responsibility

DEFINITION Authority is the right to give orders and the power to exact obedience.   *Fayol*

DEFINITION Responsibility is the liability of a person to be called to account for his/ her actions. Note that responsibility cannot be delegated to others.

Power

French and Raven identified five sources of power:

- **Reward power** – when one person is able to reward another person for carrying out their duties or meeting other requirements.

- **Coercive power** – when one person has the ability to punish another person for failing to carry out their orders satisfactorily.

- **Referent power** – often occurs when one person identifies with, or wishes to imitate another.

- **Expert power** – when one person is regarded by others as having special expertise or knowledge that others do not.

- **Legitimate power** – derived from being in a position of authority within the organisation.

Other sources of power may include:

- **Resource power** – based on control over key resources.

- **Negative power** – the ability to use disruptive behaviour and attitudes to prevent things from happening.

Try not to get confused between power and authority. Authority is the right to do something, while power is the ability to do something.

18.3 THEORIES OF MANAGEMENT

LEARNING SUMMARY

After studying this section you should be able to:

- explain the scientific theories of management – Fayol and Taylor

- explain the human relations school - Mayo

- explain the functions of a manager – Mintzberg and Drucker.

Classical theories of management

The classical school of management theories were developed during the Industrial Revolution of the mid-to-late 1800s and early 1900s. They are largely concerned with improving efficiency and productivity.

Fayol – the five functions of management

Fayol suggested that management of all organisations could be split into five broad areas:

Questions can easily focus on the detail of any one of the theories within this chapter. You will need to learn both the theories themselves and the terminology used within each theory.

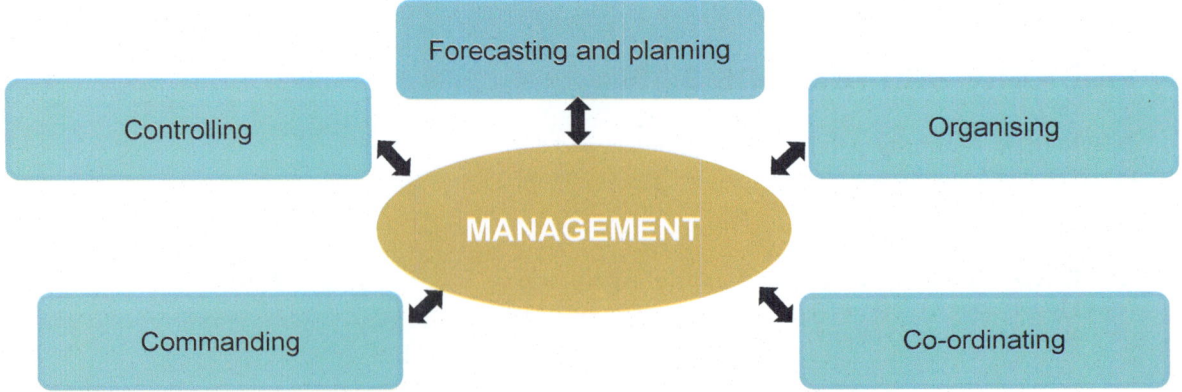

Taylor – Scientific management

Taylor believed the objective of management is to secure the maximum prosperity for both employer and employee:

To accomplish this, Taylor's scientific management consisted of four key principles:

- **Tasks should be analysed** in detail to determine the most efficient methods to use.

- **Staff member should be scientifically managed.** Only the most suitable people should be chosen, trained and developed for each job.

- **Managers should make all key decisions** and provide **detailed instructions** to workers to ensure that work was carried out in the most efficient way.

- **Work was to be divided between managers and workers**, with close co-operation between both groups to maximise efficiency.

Criticisms of the classical models

KEY POINT Whilst there are still areas where these classical theories are still relevant, most modern theorists would argue that a more progressive approach is needed where:

- it is recognised that there is not always a 'best' way of doing a particular job

- managers realise that employees can have valuable insights into a job and can make important suggestions for improvements, and

- many workers are motivated by factors other than financial rewards.

The human relations school

This model was developed by **Elton Mayo**.

Mayo argued that:

- employee behaviour depends primarily on group relations and management-worker communication, rather than working practices or physical conditions.

- wage levels were not the dominant motivating factor for most workers.

- ultimately, worker attitudes, group relationships and leadership style were the key factors that determined productivity.

Modern writers

Drucker argued that all managers perform five basic functions.

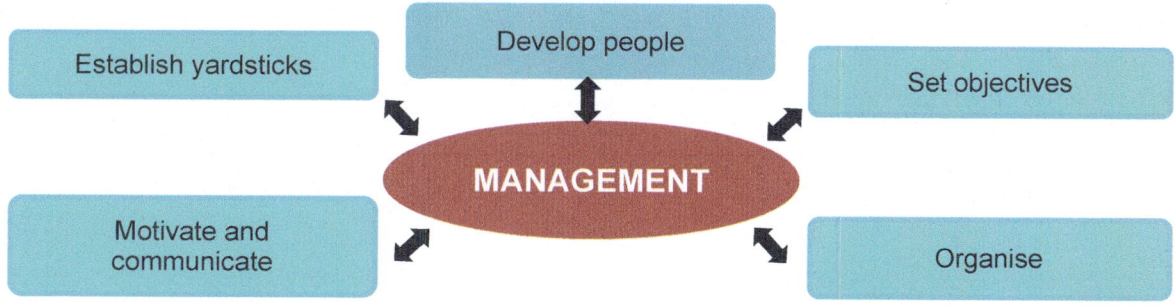

Mintzberg – the ten skills of the manager

Mintzberg identified ten skills that managers need if they are to maximise their effectiveness.

Interpersonal	Informational	Decisional
Figurehead	Monitor	Entrepreneur
Leader	Disseminator	Disturbance handler
Liaison	Spokesperson	Resource allocator
		Negotiator

18.4 LEADERSHIP

LEARNING SUMMARY

After studying this section you should be able to:

- explain the situational, functional and contingency approaches to leadership, with reference to the theories of Adair, Fiedler, Bennis, Kotter and Heifetz

- describe leadership styles and contexts using the models of Ashridge and Blake and Mouton.

Leadership

KEY POINT There are three main groups of leadership theories: trait theories, style theories and contingency theories.

Trait theories

These argue that good leaders have certain natural attributes to allow them to lead (such as cheerful personality, or fairness). Leaders are therefore born, not made.

Style theories

These argue that certain leadership approaches or 'styles' can be learnt and used by a manager, depending on the situation.

There are two main style theories you need to be aware of.

Blake and Mouton – the managerial grid

Blake and Mouton designed the managerial grid, which charts people-orientated versus task-oriented styles.

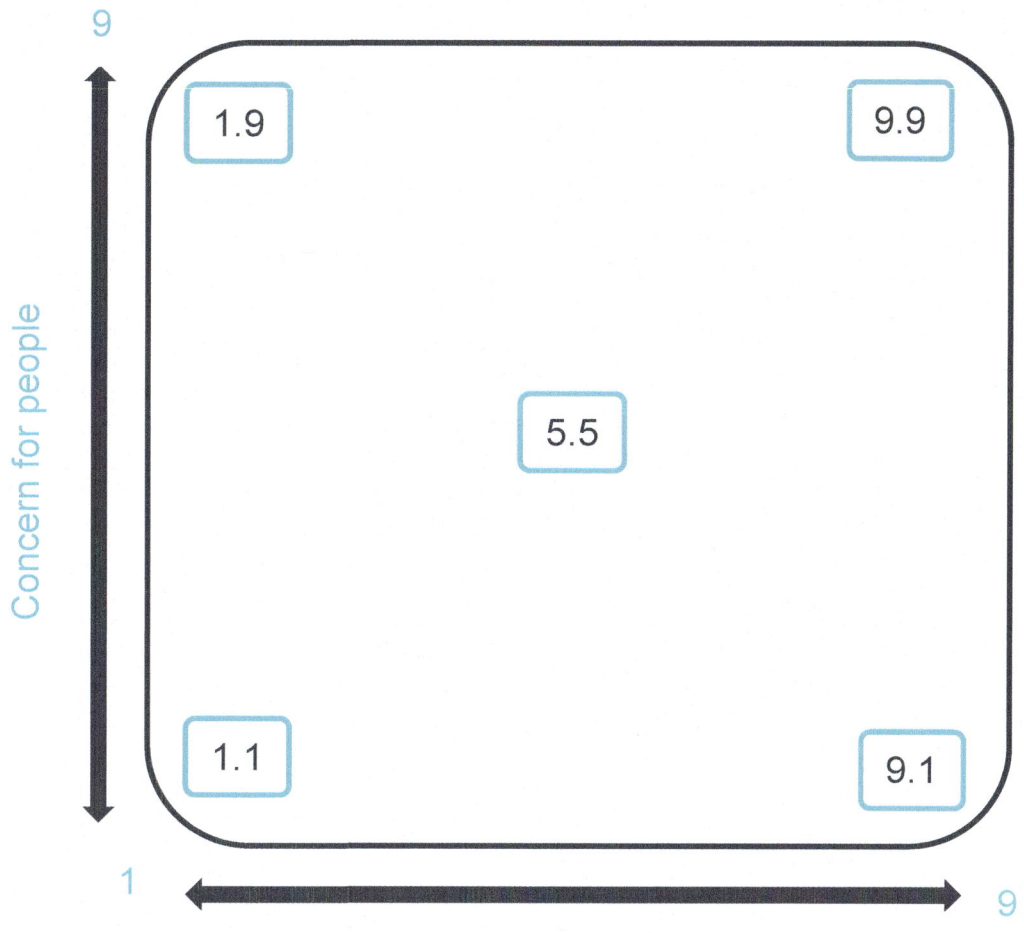

9

1.9   9.9

Concern for people

5.5

1.1   9.1

1   9

Concern for the task

- 9.9   Team management
- 9.1   Task management
- 1.9   Country club management
- 5.5   Middle of the road management
- 1.1   Management impoverished

ADVANTAGES	DISADVANTAGES
The grid shows areas where management faults can be identified and can then provide basis for training and managerial development.	The grid assumes that leadership style can be categorised into the two dimensions and that results can be plotted on the grid.
As an appraisal and management development tool to inform managers that attention to both task and people is possible and desirable.	The position of team management is accepted as the best form of leadership. This may not be practical or advisable. The concern for the task may be more important than the concern for people, and vice versa and will depend on the situation.
Managers can determine how they are viewed by their subordinates.	

Ashridge Management College

The research at **Ashridge Management College** distinguished four main management styles.

- **Tells (autocratic)** – the manager makes all the decisions and issues instructions which are to be obeyed without question.

- **Sells (persuasive)** – the manager still makes all the decisions, but believes that team members must be motivated to accept them in order to carry them out properly.

- **Consults (participative)** – the manager confers with the team and takes their views into account, although still retains the final say.

- **Joins (democratic)** – the leader and the team members make the decision together on the basis of consensus.

These suggest there is no correct style. Instead, successful leadership involves adapting to the particular circumstances in which the leader finds themselves.

Adair – Action-centred leadership

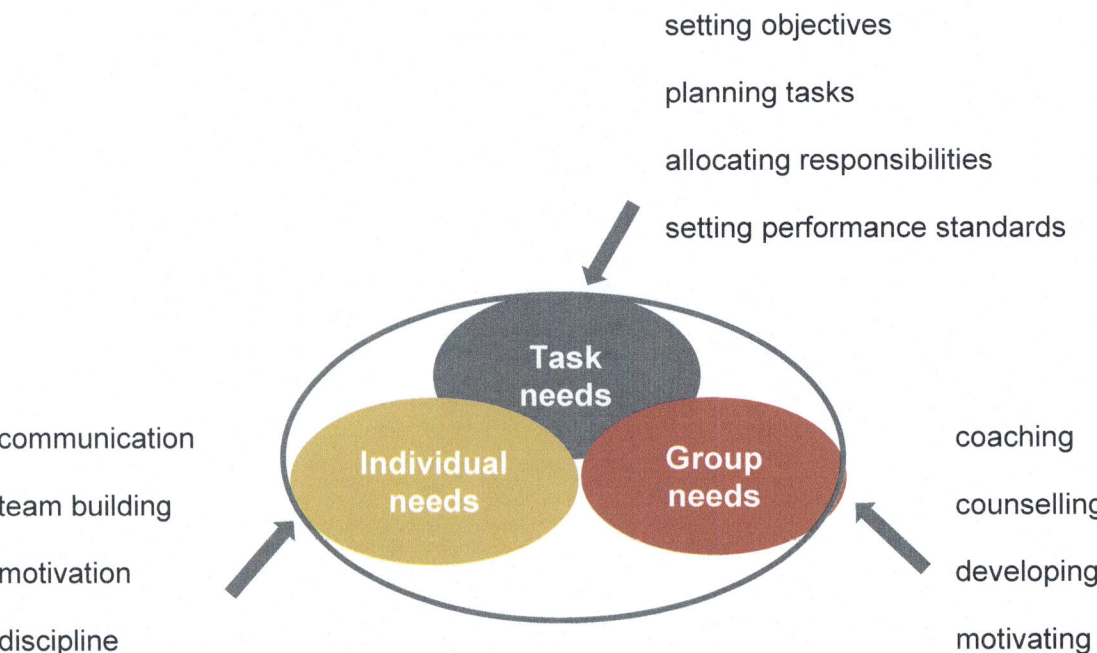

Fiedler identified two distinct styles of leadership:

- **psychologically distant managers** (PDMs)

- **psychologically close managers** (PCMs)

Fiedler suggested that the most effective style of leadership would be determined by the situation, which would be influenced by three factors:

- leader/member relations – the nature of the relationship between the leader and the group

- task structure – the extent to which the task is structured

- leader position power – the degree of formal authority/responsibility allocated to the position

Bennis – transformational leadership

Bennis argued that there were two types of leaders:

- **transactional leaders** – see the relationship with their followers in terms of a trade: they give followers the rewards they want in exchange for a service, loyalty and compliance.

- **transformational leaders** – see their role as inspiring and motivating others to work at levels beyond mere compliance. Only transformational leadership is said to be able to change team/ organisational cultures and move them in a new direction.

Kotter – managing change

Kotter set out the following change approaches to deal with resistance:

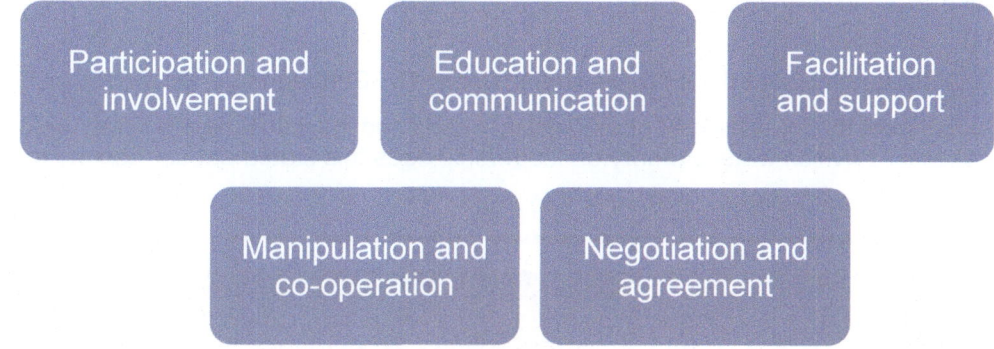

Heifetz – leadership to motivate

Heifetz argues that the main role of managers is to help people to face reality and mobilise them to make changes where necessary. A true leader does not necessarily have all the answers – instead they encourage people to tackle tough challenges themselves.

In addition, Heifetz suggested that anyone within an organisation may provide some degree of leadership in certain circumstances. This means that leaders may sometimes simply emerge, rather than being formally appointed.

Do you understand?

1   In a recent staff survey, manager G has been identified as highly focused on meeting production needs, but having little real concern for the wellbeing of the employees who report to her. According to Blake and Mouton, which key point on the managerial grid is G been placed at by the staff survey?

2   Bennis argued that effective leaders needed to display certain generic skills. Which of the following is one of those skills?

(i)   The management of self (ii) The management of finance

3   Which of the following is NOT one of the elements of management as identified by Fayol?

(i)   Control (ii) Co-ordination (iii) Commitment (iv) Command

4   Leaders need to consider task needs, group needs and individual needs if they wish to be effective. Which writer's theory on leadership does this statement correspond to?

(i)   Heifetz (ii) Fiedler (iii) Bennis (iv) Adair

1   Task management. G is focused on meeting production, but not on employee welfare. This plots her at 9.1 on the managerial grid – a task manager.

2   (i) Leaders must be able to identify their own strengths and weaknesses. The others are management of attention, meaning and trust.

3   (iii) Commitment. The five elements are planning, control, organisation, command and co-ordination.

4   (iv) Adair.

1 **(a)** According to Blake and Mouton's managerial grid, managers can be classified by their level of concern for people and concern for production.

		Concern for production	
		High	Low
Concern for people	High	A1	A2
	Low	A3	A4

In company X, the following managers have been ranked on the managerial grid.

Manager A has been classified as an 'impoverished manager'.

Manager B has been classified as a 'team manager'.

Manager C has been classified as a 'country club manager'.

Manager D has been classified as a 'task manager'.

Required:

(i) **For Manager A, select which combination of levels of concern apply from the grid above (i.e. A1).**

(ii) **For Manager B, select which combination of levels of concern apply from the grid above (i.e. A1).**

(iii) **For Manager C, select which combination of levels of concern apply from the grid above (i.e. A1).**

(iv) **For Manager D, select which combination of levels of concern apply from the grid above (i.e. A1).**

(b) Here are four short descriptions of leadership and management theories:

A   There is one best way to undertake every task

B   Interpersonal relations are a key part of determining workplace behaviour

C   Managers must control the needs of the task, individual and group.

D   Managers can be either a psychologically distant or psychologically close

Required:

Identify the description above which is associated with each of the following theories, by writing A, B, C or D.

(i) **Adair's action-centred leadership**

(ii) **Human relations school**

(iii) **Fiedler's contingency theory**

(iv) **Taylor's scientific management**

2   (a)   SAJ sells clothes and other accessories for pet dogs. It primarily sells through a small shop in an affluent area of the capital city of country P. It has been struggling to make a profit in recent years and its owner, U, is concerned about its long-term survival. SAJ has a small but dedicated workforce, which is experienced in pet retail.

U is considering a number of possible approaches to managing his staff in this period of decline:

A   He could ask the staff for ideas about how to turn the business around, though U would still have the final say on which, if any, of these ideas were used

B   He could decide on a plan to improve the profitability of the business and simply inform his staff of how this will be implemented

C   He could decide on a plan to improve profitability and explain the reasons and benefits of his proposals to his staff members

D   He could come to a mutual decision with his staff about the best way forward for the company

Required:

Identify the approach above which is associated with each of the following management styles, by writing A, B, C or D.

(i)   Joins (democratic)

(ii)   Consults (participative)

(iii)   Tells (autocratic)

(iv)   Sells (persuasive)

(b)   U has recently been reading an article on Adair's action-centred leadership model.

Consider the following statements:

A   Communication

B   Setting objectives

C   Coaching

D   Planning tasks

E   Motivating

F   Discipline

G   Setting performance standards

H   Allocating responsibilities

Required:

Identify which FOUR of the above statements are included in 'Task Needs' within Adair's action-centred leadership model by writing down FOUR letters from A-H.

The following topics are covered in this chapter:

- Recruitment and selection
- The recruitment and selection process
- Responsibility for recruitment and selection
- Equal opportunities
- Diversity

19.1 RECRUITMENT AND SELECTION

LEARNING SUMMARY

After studying this section you should be able to:

- explain the importance of effective recruitment and selection to the organisation.

Recruitment and selection

DEFINITION Recruitment involves attracting a range of suitable candidates for a given role within the organisation.

DEFINITION Selection processes are aimed at choosing the most suitable candidate for the specified position.

The importance of recruitment and selection

The consequences of poor recruitment and selection can include:

- high staff turnover.
- the high cost of advertising for vacancies.
- management time involved in selection and training.
- the expense of dismissal.
- the negative effects of high staff turnover on general morale and motivation within the organisation.
- reduced business opportunities.
- reduced quality of the organisation's products or services, leading to customer dissatisfaction.

19.2 THE RECRUITMENT AND SELECTION PROCESS

LEARNING SUMMARY

After studying this section you should be able to:

- describe the recruitment and selection process and explain the stages in this process.

The recruitment and selection process

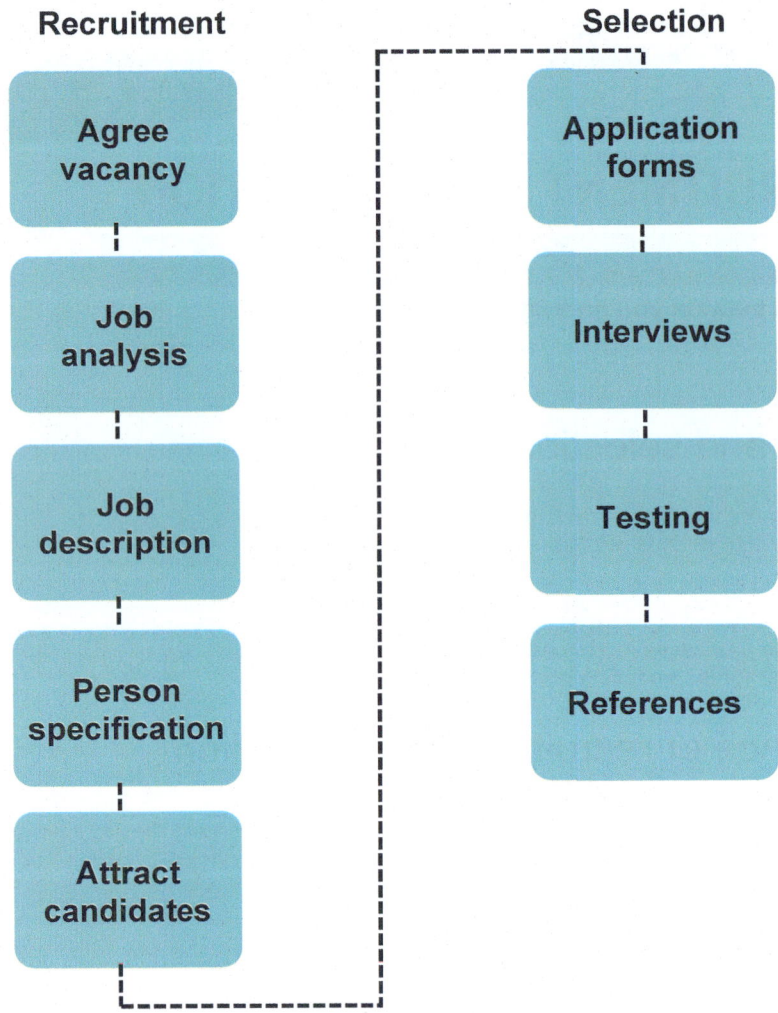

Person specification

KEY POINT Once management have a job description, they can attempt to define the key attributes and qualities that the jobholder should ideally have.

Alec Rodgers recommended that the following categories should be covered in a person specification.

- **S**pecial aptitudes
- **C**ircumstances
- **I**nterests
- **P**hysical make-up
- **D**isposition
- **A**ttainments
- **G**eneral intelligence

You may wish to use the acronym SCIPDAG to help you remember these categories.

Attracting candidates

This stage involves persuading relevant candidates to apply for the role the organisation wishes to fill.

The advantages of internal and external recruitment include:

Internal

- motivating for employees

- part of career development plan

- know the staff already

- candidate understands work

- save time and money

- no induction necessary

External

- obtain specialist skills

- inject 'new blood' into company

BUT

- may create dissatisfaction among existing employees

- may cost more (higher wages and recruitment costs)

Advertising

KEY POINT The objective of recruitment advertising is to attract the interest of suitable candidates in the vacancy that the organisation wishes to fill.

There is no correct advertising medium for a business to use. The medium chosen will typically depend on several factors, including:

- the **type of organisation**.

- the **type of job** being advertised.

- the **readership and circulation** of the medium.

- the **cost** of the advertising.

- the **frequency and duration** of the advertisements.

Selection interviews

There are various types of interview that an organisation may use, including:

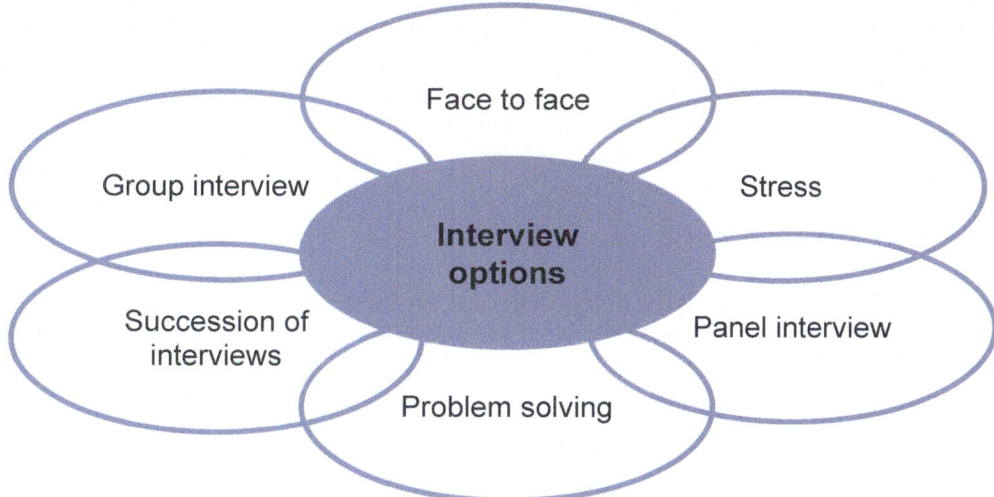

Interviews have several key advantages and disadvantages as a way of selecting candidates.

ADVANTAGES	DISADVANTAGES
places candidate at ease	too brief to get to know candidates
highly interactive	interview is an artificial situation
opportunities to use non-verbal communication	halo effect from initial impression
opportunities to assess appearance, interpersonal and communication skills	qualitative factors such as motivation, honesty or integrity are difficult to assess
opportunities to evaluate rapport between the candidate and the potential colleague/ bosses	subjectivity and bias

Selection testing

Testing can be undertaken either before or after the interview has taken place.

Two basic types of test are:

- **Proficiency and attainment** – these are used to examine the applicant's competencies, skills and abilities in areas that will be required in the job

- **Psychometric** – these are more general and test psychological factors, such as aptitude, intelligence and personality

There are a range of specific tests that you need to be aware of, including:

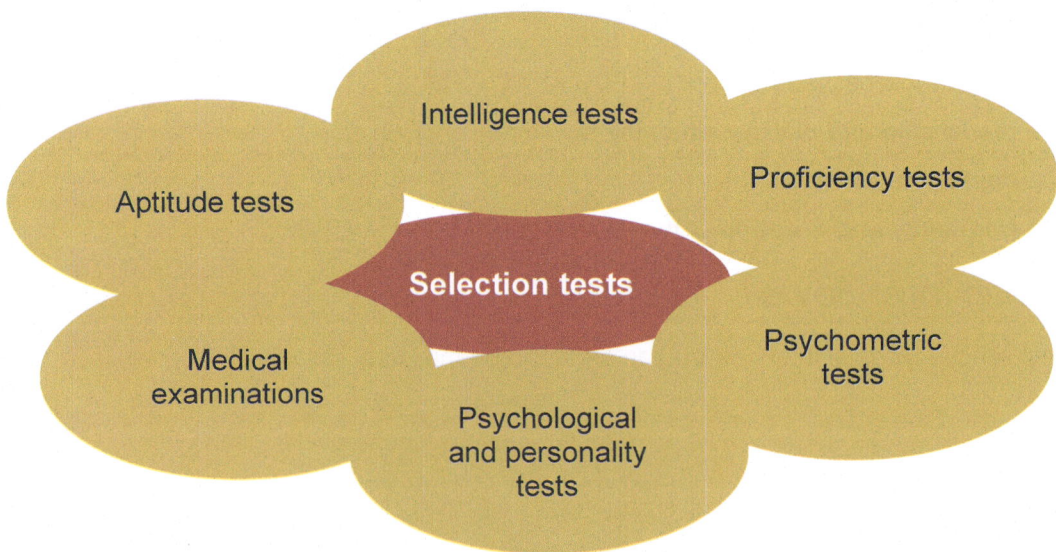

Assessment centres

Assessment centres involve candidates being observed and evaluated by trained assessors as they are given a selection of pre-programmed exercises or trials.

These exercises may include group discussions, presentations, questionnaires, simulations, games, speeches, self-appraisal, role play exercises, written tests and peer rating.

19.3 RESPONSIBILITY FOR RERUITMENT AND SELECTION

LEARNING SUMMARY

After studying this section you should be able to:

- describe the roles of those involved in the recruitment and selection processes.

Who is involved in recruitment and selection?

Senior managers/ directors

clarifying corporate objectives

designing an effective structure

providing a system for HR planning

Roles and responsibilities

Line managers in large companies

requesting more human resources

advising on requirements

having a final say on the selection

HR department

assessing staff needs

maintaining employee records

advertising for new employees

designing application forms

compliance with legislation

liaising with recruitment consultants

interviewing and selection testing

Recruitment consultants

analysing the demands of the job

helping with job analysis

designing job advertisements

Screening applications

short-listing from interview

offering list of suitable candidates

19.4 EQUAL OPPORTUNITIES

LEARNING SUMMARY

After studying this section you should be able to:

- explain the purpose and benefits of an equal opportunities policy and a diversity policy within human resource planning

- explain the practical steps that an organisation may take to ensure the effectiveness of its equal opportunities policy and its diversity policy.

Definition

Types of discrimination

There are three types of discrimination that an equal opportunities policy will attempt to prevent.

Direct discrimination occurs when an employer treats an employee less favourably than another, due to their gender, race etc.

This may be allowed by law in certain, tightly defined, circumstances

This is often illegal, unless it is necessary for the working of the business and there is no way round it

Discrimination

Indirect discrimination occurs when a working condition or rule disadvantages one group of people more than another.

Victimisation means an employer treating an employee less favourably because they have made, or tried to make, a complaint about discrimination.

The legal position

Employment legislation varies significantly from country to country, but typically prevents discrimination in various areas, including:

- selection of candidates to interview or employ.

- provision of promotion, training or other benefits.

- working conditions.

- dismissal, or other disadvantages.

Diversity and equal opportunities

The main differences between diversity and equal opportunities are:

Diversity	Equal opportunities
voluntary	government initiated
productivity driven	legally driven
qualitative	quantitative
opportunity-focused	problem-focused
inclusive	targeted
proactive	reactive

One of the goals of diversity is having a workforce that is 'representative' of the composition of the organisation's operational environment (the external community).

Benefits should include:

- increased competitive advantage.

- maximisation of the organisation's HR potential.

- increased creativity and innovation

- a broader range of skills present within the organisation.

- better customer relations and service to diverse customers.

- ability to recruit the best talent from the entire labour pool.

- improved working relations in an atmosphere of inclusion.

Do you understand?

1   If you were looking for a job, what information would you expect to find in the advertisement?

2   The economic situation in a country may have a marked effect on the ability of an organisation to attract suitable candidates.

   True or false?

3   H has been asked to attend a job interview. She has been told that she will be interviewed by the Finance Director first, followed by the Human Resources Director. What type of interview is H going to experience?

   (i)   Group (ii) Panel (iii) Succession

4   Which of the following is NOT a reason for adopting an equal opportunities policy within an organisation?

   (i)   Legal requirement (ii) Ethically correct (iii) Reduction in labour costs

1   The organisation: its main business and location.
   The job: title, main duties and responsibilities.
   Conditions: special factors affecting the job.
   Qualifications and experience, other attributes, aptitudes and knowledge required.
   Rewards: salary, benefits, opportunities for training, career development.
   Application process: how to apply, to whom and by what date.
2   True. Economic uncertainty may cause people to remain in their present job and discourage them from moving elsewhere.
3   (ii) A panel interview.
4   (iii) Equal opportunities does not mean that workers can be paid less. There should therefore be no reduction in the wages bill because of this.

1   **A document containing skills and knowledge expected of staff occupying a certain position is referred to as a:**

A   job description

B   personal specification

C   job evaluation

D   job analysis

2   Consider the following two statements:

(1)   Recruitment consultants are often particularly useful when it comes to identifying which of the short-listed candidates should get the job.

(2)   A selection interview not only aims to help choose the best person for the job but also boosts the company's image by making the candidates feel that they have been fairly treated in the selection process.

Which of these statements is/are correct?

A   (1) only

B   (2) only

C   Both

D   Neither

3   **Positive discrimination is encouraged by law when it relates to the hiring of minority groups.**

Is this statement TRUE or FALSE?

A   True

B   False

4   **Which of the following are typical differences between 'diversity' and 'equal opportunities'?**

(i)   Equal opportunities is usually voluntary, rather than being legally required.

(ii)   Diversity is normally driven by the desire to increase productivity.

(iii)   Equal opportunities is reactive, while diversity is proactive.

(iv)   Diversity tends to go further than equal opportunities and appreciates the differences in employee attitudes, personalities and beliefs.

A   (i) only

B   (i) and (ii) only

C   (ii), (iii) and (iv) only

D   (ii) and (iv) only

20 Individual, group and team behaviour

The following topics are covered in this chapter:

- Individuals
- Groups
- The contribution of individuals and teams to organisational success
- Teams

20.1 INDIVIDUALS

LEARNING SUMMARY

After studying this section you should be able to:

- describe the main characteristics of individual behaviour
- identify individual approaches to work

Characteristics of individual behaviour

Typical issues that affect individual behaviour and performance at work include:

Motivation level – relates to people's desire to perform tasks and put effort into their job.

Perception – individuals select, organise and interpret the stimuli they receive. Messages from managers are always subject to distortion, the subordinate selecting parts of the message and interpreting it in light of their own experiences, wants and needs.

Attitudes – persistent feelings and behavioural tendencies directed towards specific people, group, ideas or objects.

Personality – combination of emotional, attitudinal and behavioural responses of an individual.

Role theory

> **DEFINITION A role** is the pattern of behaviour expected by someone who occupies a particular position.

There are several key terms relating to role theory that you should be aware of.

Role behaviour

Certain types of behaviour can be associated with a particular role in an organisation e.g. a member of staff who expects to be promoted shortly may begin acting as if they have already been put in charge.

Role set

This describes the people who respond to an individual in a particular role e.g. a clerk or junior barristers would form part of a senior barrister's set.

Role signs

These are visible indications of a role e.g. styles of dress or uniforms.

Role theory also identifies several problems that these expected patterns of behaviour may cause.

Role ambiguity

This arises when an individual is unsure of what role they are to play, or others are unclear of that person's role and so hold back co-operation.

Role conflict

This occurs when individuals find a clash between different roles they have adopted.

Role incompatibility

This occurs when individuals experience expectations from outside groups about their role that are different to their own role expectation.

20.2 GROUPS

LEARNING SUMMARY

After studying this section you should be able to:

- describe the main characteristics of group behaviour
- outline the contributions of individuals and teams to organisational success.

Characteristics of groups

DEFINITION A group is any collection of individuals who perceive themselves to be a group.

Groups have the following characteristics:

- a sense of identity
- loyalty to the group
- purpose and leadership

KEY POINT There tend to be two main types of group:

Informal groups - these are groups that individuals voluntarily join to meet their social or security needs. Individual members are dependent on each other and influence each other's behaviour.

Formal groups – these are groups that are created to carry out specific tasks, communicate and solve problems. Membership is normally determined by the organisation.

Group behaviour

When dealing with other individuals within a group, people can adopt different types of behaviour:

- assertive
- aggressive
- passive behaviour

BENEFITS OF GROUPS	PROBLEMS WITH GROUPS
Increased productivity – working as part of a group can result in a better overall result than could be achieved if each person worked independently.	**Conformity** - individuals can be persuaded by group pressures to agree with decisions which are obviously wrong, and which the person must know to be wrong.
Synergy – this describes the phenomenon in which the combined activity of separate entities has a greater effect than the sum of the activities of each entity working alone – often described as a way of making 2 + 2 = 5.	**The Abilene paradox** - this is a famous case, which demonstrates that the group can end up with an outcome that none of the members wanted.
Improved focus and responsibility – each member can be given the responsibility for specific tasks, avoiding overloading one person with too much responsibility which may result in a loss of focus.	**'Risky shift' or group polarisation** - this is the tendency for groups to take decisions which are riskier than any that the individual members would take on their own.
Improved problem solving – having a group made up of members with different abilities will mean a higher likelihood of having the appropriate knowledge and skills to solve problems.	**Groupthink** - this occurs within deeply cohesive groups where the members try to minimise conflict and reach consensus without critically testing, analysing, and evaluating ideas.
Greater creativity – the idea that two (or more) heads are better than one. Group discussions can generate and evaluate ideas better than individuals working alone.	
Increased satisfaction – working as part of a group can bring social benefits and a sense of belonging to its members. In addition the group will offer support to its members and provide a facility for individual training and development needs.	
Increased motivation – members will work hard for the other members of the group. They will feel a collective responsibility and will not want to let the other members down.	
Improved information flows – there will be more effective communication through participation in group discussions.	

20.3 TEAMS

LEARNING SUMMARY

After studying this section you should be able to:

- define the purposes of a team

- identify team approaches to work

- explain the differences between a group and a team

- explain the role of the manager in building the team and developing individuals within the team. Belbin's team roles theory and Tuckman's theory of team development

- list the characteristics of effective and ineffective teams

- describe tools and techniques that can be used to build the team and improve team effectiveness.

Introduction

Teams usually:

- share a common goal.

- enjoy working together.

- are committed to achieving certain goals.

- are made up of diverse individuals.

- are loyal to their team and its project.

- have a sense of team spirit.

Belbin's team roles theory

Belbin suggested that, in order for a team to operate effectively, it needed a balance of nine different roles.

Leader (Co-ordinator)	Mature, confident. Good chairperson. Clarifies goals/delegates well.
Shaper	Challenging, dynamic. Thrives on pressure. Promotes activity.
Plant	Creative and thoughtful. Solves problems/generates ideas.
Monitor-evaluator	Strategic and discerning. Sees all options/good judge.
Team worker	Co-operative, perceptive and diplomatic. Listens/averts friction within the team.
Resource-investigator	Outgoing and enthusiastic. Explores opportunities and develops contacts.
Implementer	The Implementer or Company Worker is practical, reliable and efficient. Turns ideas into action/organises work to be done.
Completer finisher	Conscientious and anxious. Searches out errors and omissions. Delivers on time.
Specialist (expert)	Knowledgeable, self-starting and dedicated. Provides knowledge and skills in rare supply.

A question could describe an individual's personality and ask you which of Belbin's team roles is appropriate for their personality.

Tuckman's stages of group development

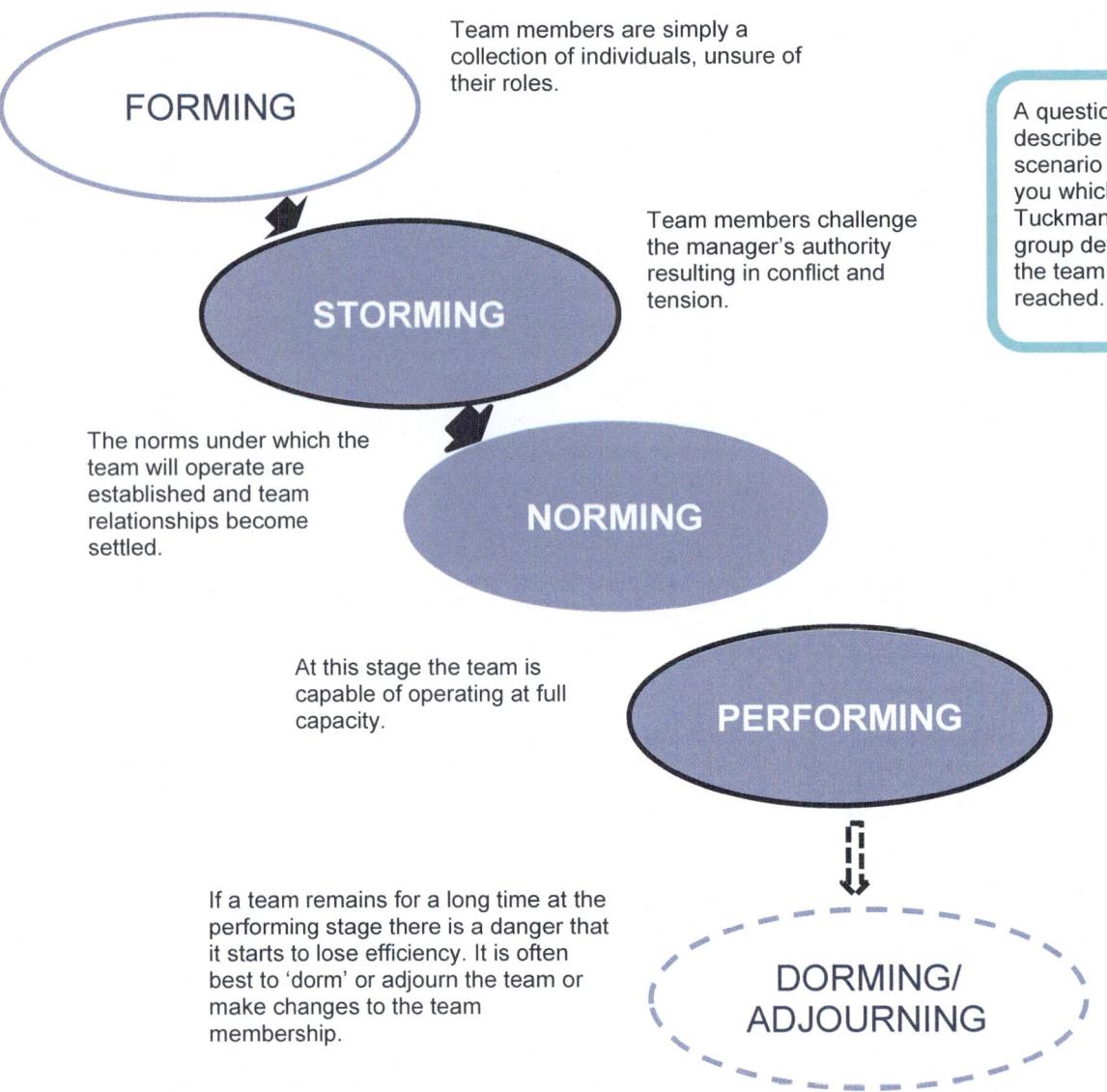

FORMING

Team members are simply a collection of individuals, unsure of their roles.

STORMING

Team members challenge the manager's authority resulting in conflict and tension.

The norms under which the team will operate are established and team relationships become settled.

NORMING

At this stage the team is capable of operating at full capacity.

PERFORMING

If a team remains for a long time at the performing stage there is a danger that it starts to lose efficiency. It is often best to 'dorm' or adjourn the team or make changes to the team membership.

DORMING/ ADJOURNING

A question could describe a team scenario and ask you which of Tuckman's stages of group development the team has reached.

Team effectiveness

Peters and Waterman define the five key aspects of successful teams as:

- The team should be relatively **small** – inevitably each member will want to represent the interests of their department, meaning that larger teams will be slower and harder to manage.

- The team should have a **limited duration**, existing only to achieve a particular task.

- Membership should be **voluntary** – a team member who does not want to be part of the group is unlikely to be a fully participating member.

- **Communication should be informal and unstructured** – there should be little documentation and no status barriers.

- The team should be **action–oriented**, meaning that the team should create a plan for action and decide what needs doing to accomplish their goals.

Building the team and improving effectiveness

Team building exercises promote:

- improved communication.

- trust building.

- social interaction.

Measuring team effectiveness

There are many possible ways of measuring team effectiveness, including:

- the degree to which the team achieved its stated objectives.

- team member satisfaction.

- efficiency.

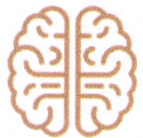

Do you understand?

1 Which of the following would describe a number of people waiting at a bus stop?

(i) A formal group (ii) An informal group (iii) Neither of the above

2 An orchestra would be considered a team.

True or false?

(ii) The customer (ii) The police (iii) Immediate line manager (iv) MLRO

3 Which of the following would be expected to be characteristics of an effective team?

(i) High labour turnover (ii) Low absenteeism (iii) High productivity

1 (iii) Neither of the above as these people do not display group attributes. They would be considered a random crowd. If they know each other or have to wait a long time, then they could develop into an informal group.

2 True. An orchestra is a team made up of talented individuals. The conductor attempts to blend them together to make an excellent team performance.

3 (ii) and (iii) High labour turnover could indicate problems inside the group, with individuals not wishing to remain members for long.

1   **Waiters in a restaurant have been told that they have to wear black suits and bow ties so that can be easily identified by customers. What aspect of role theory does this relate to?**

    A   Role behaviour

    B   Role signs

    C   Role set

    D   Role definition

2   Consider the following two statements:

    (1)   Assertive behaviour often leads to conflict within an organisation.

    (2)   Individuals usually join informal groups on a voluntary basis.

    Which of these statements is/are correct?

    A   (1) only

    B   (2) only

    C   Both

    D   Neither

3   **Match the following team roles with the appropriate personality.**

    (i)   Sarah is a very quiet person, she often reserves her opinion until being directly asked for it however she always offers unusual and creative suggestions when the team is faced with difficult problem.

    (ii)   Jim is respected by all team members for his analytical skills, though he rarely gets invited to out-of-office private parties as many find him tactless.

    (iii)   Esther is the company's HR manager, she ensures that any potential conflicts are promptly identified and resolved and the team members work harmoniously.

    A   1 – Shaper, 2 – Leader, 3 – Company worker

    B   1 – Plant, 2 – Finisher, 3 – Team worker

    C   1 – Plant, 2 – Monitor-Evaluator, 3 – Team worker

    D   1 – Resource-Investigator, 2 – Shaper, 3 – Company worker

4   **An investment bank has created a team of employees to look at potential new investments. One of the bank's senior managers has told the team that they will be assessed on their performance as a group. Which of the following is NOT a possible risk to the bank of this approach?**

    A   Lack of individual responsibility leads the group to make risky decisions

    B   Some members may put in little effort due to the lack of individual appraisal

    C   Group members may agree to poor decisions merely to 'fit in' with the group

    D   The group may have diverse backgrounds from within the bank

Motivating individuals and groups

The following topics are covered in this chapter:

- What is motivation?
- Motivation theories
- Rewards and incentives

21.1 WHAT IS MOTIVATION?

LEARNING SUMMARY

After studying this section you should be able to:

- define motivation and explain its importance to the organisation, teams and individuals.

Definition

DEFINITION In an organisation, **motivation** refers to the willingness of individuals to perform certain tasks or actions. It is the incentive or reason for them behaving in a particular way.

Having motivated staff members has a range of benefits. These include:

ORGANISATION PERSPECTIVE	INDIVIDUAL PERSPECTIVE	TEAM PERSPECTIVE
Harder working employees	Greater job satisfaction	Increased co-operation
Fewer mistakes and errors	Improves health, due to less stress	More commitment to team needs
Less waste of time and resources	Improved career prospects	Better ideas generation and evaluation
More suggestions and ideas generated	Finding the job more interesting and enjoyable	

21.2 MOTIVATION THEORIES

LEARNING SUMMARY

After studying this section you should be able to:

- explain content and process theories of motivation: Maslow, Herzberg, McGregor and Vroom.

Motivation theories

Motivation theories fall into two main groups.

CONTENT THEORIES	PROCESS THEORIES
Ask the question '**what**' are the things that motivate people? They are also referred to as '**need theories**' and assume that human beings have a set of needs or desired outcomes which can be satisfied through work.	Ask the question '**how**' are people motivated? They attempt to explain how individuals start, sustain and direct behaviour and assume that individuals are able to select their own goals and means of achieving those goals through a process of calculation.
Content theories assume that everyone responds to motivating factors in the same way and that **there is one best way to motivate everybody.**	Process theories change the emphasis from needs to the **goals and processes** by which workers are motivated.

Content theories

Maslow's hierarchy of needs

> Questions can test your knowledge of this area by asking which level of Maslow's hierarchy do certain factors relate to e.g. large pay rises, challenging work etc.

- Self-fulfilment
- Ego/Esteem
- Social/Belonging
- Safety/Security
- Basic/physiological

Criticisms of Maslow's hierarchy of needs:

- Individuals have different needs and may not necessarily reach them in the same order as each other.

- Individuals may seek to satisfy several needs at the same time.

- Not all needs are, or can be, satisfied through work.

Herzberg's two-factor theory

This model examined two sets of factors that can be used to help get the best out of workers.

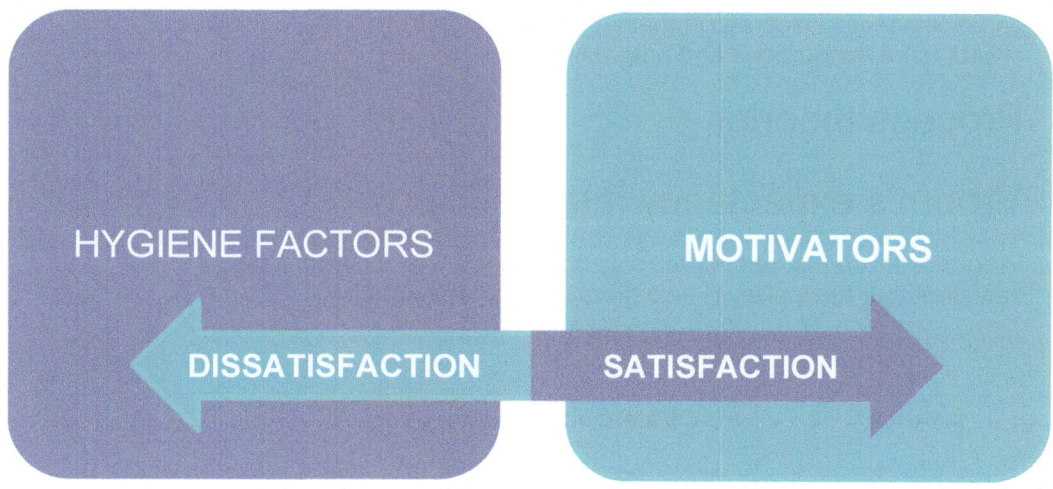

You will notice that the main motivators are to do with the value and satisfaction gained from the job itself and are largely non-financial in nature. Herzberg argued that the potential to boost employee motivation caused by increases to pay were extremely limited.

Instead, Herzberg suggested **three types of job design** that could be an effective tool for motivating employees:

- **Job enrichment (vertical job enlargement)** – this is a deliberate, planned process to improve the responsibility, challenge and creativity of a job.

- **Job enlargement (horizontal job enlargement)** – this is an attempt to widen the employee's job by giving them a larger workload. It does not involve a higher level of work.

- **Job rotation** – this is the planned rotation of staff between jobs to alleviate monotony and provide a fresh, challenging job.

McGregor's Theory X and Theory Y

KEY POINT Theory X – people dislike work and responsibility and will try to avoid both. They therefore need to be coerced.

Managers therefore need to adopt an authoritarian, repressive style with tight controls. Effectively the workforce is a problem that needs to be overcome by management.

Make sure you are happy with the aspects that motivate Theory X people and Theory Y people.

Managers who make these assumptions about their workers are more participative or democratic in their approach. Employees are viewed as assets to be encouraged and empowered.

Process theories

Vroom's expectancy theory

Vroom believed that people will only be motivated to do tasks if they are confident that the tasks will help them to reach their goals.

Vroom's theory can be stated as a formula:

Force	=	**Valence x expectancy**
where		
force	=	the strength of a person's motivation
valence	=	the strength of an individual's preference for an outcome
expectancy	=	the probability of success

21.3 REWARDS AND INCENTIVES

LEARNING SUMMARY

After studying this section you should be able to:

- explain and identify types of intrinsic and extrinsic reward

- explain how reward systems can be designed and implemented to motivate teams and individuals.

Rewards

DEFINITION A **reward** is something given, to an individual or group, in recognition of their services, efforts or achievements.

- **Intrinsic rewards** – these arise from the performance of the job itself. They include the feeling of satisfaction that comes from doing a job well, being allowed to make higher level decisions or being interested in your job.

- **Extrinsic rewards** – these are separate from (or external to) the job itself and are dependent on the decisions of others (i.e. the workers have no control over these rewards). Pay, working conditions and benefits are all examples of extrinsic rewards.

Reward systems should be carefully designed in order to ensure that they:

- are fair and consistent for all employees.

- are sufficient to attract and retain staff.

- maintain and improve levels of employee performance.

- reward progression and promotion.

- comply with legislation and regulation (i.e. minimum wage laws).

- control salary costs.

There are three main types of incentive scheme:

Performance related pay (PRP)

Piecework – reward related to the pace of work or amount of effort.

Management by objectives (MBO) – key results are identified for which rewards will be paid on top of salary.

Points system – this is an extension to MBO reward systems, where a range of rewards is available based on a point system derived from the scale of improvement made, such as the cost reduction achieved.

Commission – paid on the performance of an individual and typically paid to salaried staff in sales functions, where the commission earned is a proportion of total sales made.

Bonus schemes – usually a one off as opposed to PRP schemes which are usually a continual management policy.

Profit sharing – usually available to a wide group of employees where payments are made in the light of the overall profitability of the company. Share issues may be part of the scheme.

Do you understand?

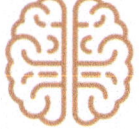

1 For each of the characteristics below, indicate whether they are due to satisfaction or motivation.

(i) Low staff turnover (ii) Fewer mistakes (iii) higher productivity

2 Which level of Maslow's hierarchy do the following factors relate to?

(i) New job title (ii) Sick pay (iii) Christmas parties (iv) Enough cash to live on

3 Highly satisfied employees always show increased levels of productivity in an organisation, compared to dissatisfied employees.

True or false?

1 (i) Satisfaction (ii) Motivation (iii) Motivation. A satisfied worker will be more content with their job and will trust their employer. Motivation is required for the employee to work harder and take more care over their work.
2 (i) Ego (ii) Safety (iii) Social (iv) Basic.
3 False. Remember that satisfaction looks at whether the worker is content with their existing job and not looking for another. It does not necessarily mean that they are working harder in their role.

1 (a) P operates a chain of hotels. The company directors are aware that the senior hotel managers may be difficult to replace, so they wish to ensure that hotel managers are adequately motivated.

P is therefore considering offering the following to its managers in order to motivate them:

A Advancement opportunities

B Compatible, friendly work group

C Safe working conditions

D Pension

E Challenging work

F Permanent job contracts

G Merit pay rises (in spite of already attractive salaries)

H High status job titles

Required:

Identify which FOUR of the above would be classified as helping to meet self-fulfilment or ego needs, according to Maslow's hierarchy of needs, by writing down FOUR letters from A-H.

(b) P is aware that motivation theories fall into two main types:

A Content theories

B Process theories

Required:

Identify which of the statements below relate to content or process theories of motivation, by writing A (content) or B (process).

(i) Assume there is one best way to motivate every employee

(ii) Attempts to explain how people are motivated, rather than examining what motivates them

(iii) Herzberg's Hygiene Factor model is an example

(iv) Vroom's expectancy theory is an example

2   UHPD is a police force based in a town in country B. It is government funded and has a number of officers, who operate a wide range of roles – from patrols on foot around the town, highway and vehicle patrols, forensic analysis and administration.

Morale in the force has been low for several years, leading to a staffing crisis due to the high levels of staff turnover. Y is the head of the UHPD and has decided to investigate ways of motivating his workforce.

Y has investigated two major models to do with motivation – Herzberg's two-factor theory and McGregor's Theory X and Theory Y.

Several key terms relating to these models are:

A   Hygiene factor

B   Job enrichment

C   Job rotation

D   Motivator

E   Theory X

F   Theory Y

The following sentences contain gaps which should contain one of the above four terms.

Y is considering the launch of a new policy that ensures that all members of staff are given an appropriate level of pay by formalising the grade boundaries of all staff. This will make pay fairer and will act as a _1_ for workers, hopefully reducing staff turnover.

Required:

(i)   Select the term that appropriately fills gap 1 above; i.e. select A-F.

Y has informed all managers within UHPD that they will be expected to delegate some responsibility down to more capable junior staff to improve UHPD's employee job design. Y referred to this in his report as _2_.

Required:

(ii)   Select the term that appropriately fills gap 2 above; i.e. select A-F.

Y has identified four managers within UHPD that have received high levels of complaints from their staff. They have adopted an authoritarian management style, assuming that employees are _3_. In fact, this is not the case and this mismatch in style has caused significant morale problems.

(iii)   Select the term that appropriately fills gap 3 above; i.e. select A-F.

Y has decided against _4_ within UHPD as he is concerned that if staff are regularly moved between departments, their overall efficiency will drop.

Required:

(iv)   Select the term that appropriately fills gap 4 above; i.e. select A-F.

22 Learning and training at work

The following topics are covered in this chapter:

- Learning
- The learning process
- Training, development and education
- The training and development process
- The role of management in the learning process

22.1 LEARNING

LEARNING SUMMARY

After studying this section you should be able to:

- explain the importance of learning and development in the workplace.

Definition

> **DEFINITION Learning** can be defined as 'the process of acquiring knowledge through experience, which leads to changes in behaviour'. It includes acquiring new skills, knowledge or attitudes, or a combination of all three.

There are three types of learning:

- **Formal** – this is undertaken deliberately and occurs when individuals 'learn' and 'study'. It is often classroom-based and highly structured.

- **Informal** – this is also usually deliberate, but is not highly structured. Examples include self-directed learning, networking, coaching and mentoring.

- **Incidental** – this is a 'by-product' of another activity. For example, attending a formal classroom course may also help a student to learn how to keep their attention focused for a long period.

The importance of learning in the workplace

Work-based learning has a number of key advantages:

- It can lead to increased competence, understanding, self-esteem and morale – leading to improved productivity.

- It may improve the level of creativity and innovation of workers in the organisation, giving an advantage over competitors.

- People who enjoy learning are more likely to be flexible in times of constant change.

- If workers are not given learning opportunities, there is a risk that they will feel undervalued and will lose motivation.

22.2 THE LEARNING PROCESS

LEARNING SUMMARY

After studying this section you should be able to:

- describe the learning process: Honey, Kolb and Mumford.

Introduction

> **KEY POINT** It is important to understand how people learn new things, as this will allow an organisation to create suitable training programmes for its employees.

Kolb: experiential learning cycle

Kolb suggested four learning stages that must be addressed:

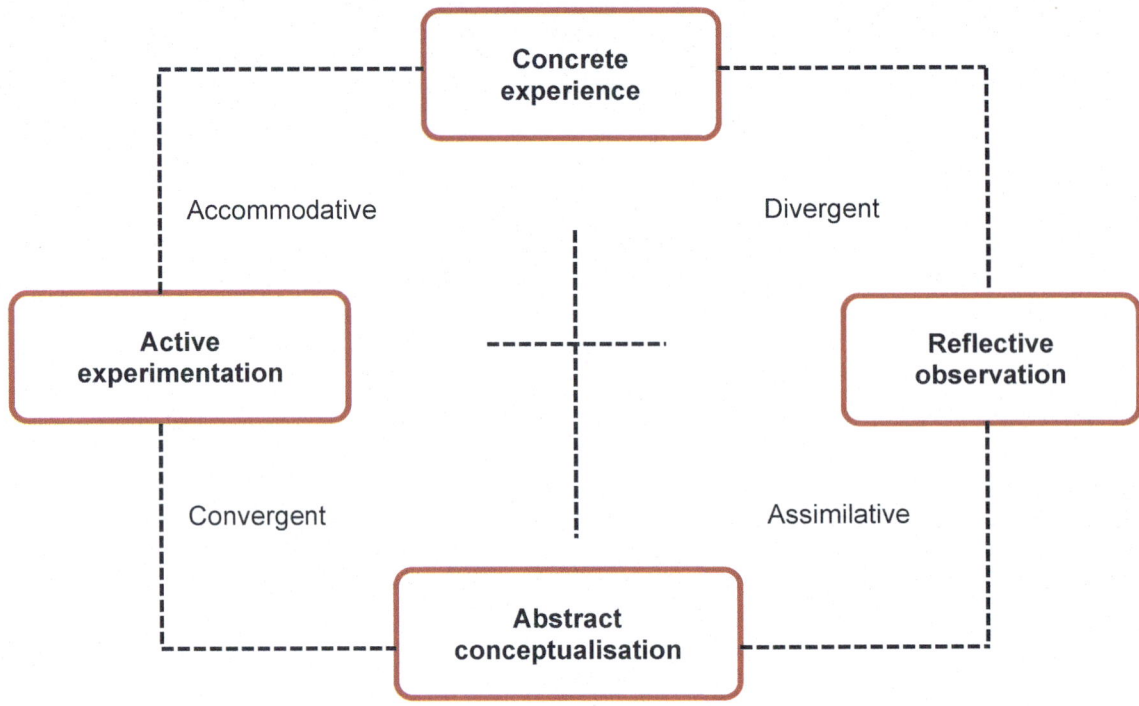

For example, if you want to learn how to use a new computer system:

- **Concrete experience** – you may decide to start using the new computer system, without any training or guidance.

- **Reflective observation** – having failed to accomplish everything you wanted, you spend some time identifying the problems you had and the tasks you were unable to perform on the new system.

- **Abstract conceptualisation** – having identified the problem areas, you go to the instruction manual and look up how to undertake these tasks.

- **Active experimentation** – once you have read the instructions relating to the areas you were uncertain about, you then go back to the computer system and try them again to see if you are now able to perform all the tasks you needed to accomplish.

Kolb identified four different learning styles (as show on the diagram above).

- **Divergent** – feeling and watching – these people prefer to watch rather than do, reflecting on what they are seeing before trying it for themselves.

- **Assimilative** – watching and thinking – these individuals take a concise, logical approach. They prefer clear explanations rather than undertaking practical examples. They then need time to think through what they have seen.

- **Convergent** – thinking and doing – prefer to apply ideas and enjoy testing ideas out in practice to see if they really work.

- **Accommodative** – doing and feeling – strong preference for concrete experiences and active experimentation (hands-on approach).

> A question may provide a scenario and ask you to choose what stage of learning the person described in the scenario is at.

Honey and Mumford: learning styles

Honey and Mumford built on Kolb's earlier work and came up with four alternative classifications of learning styles.

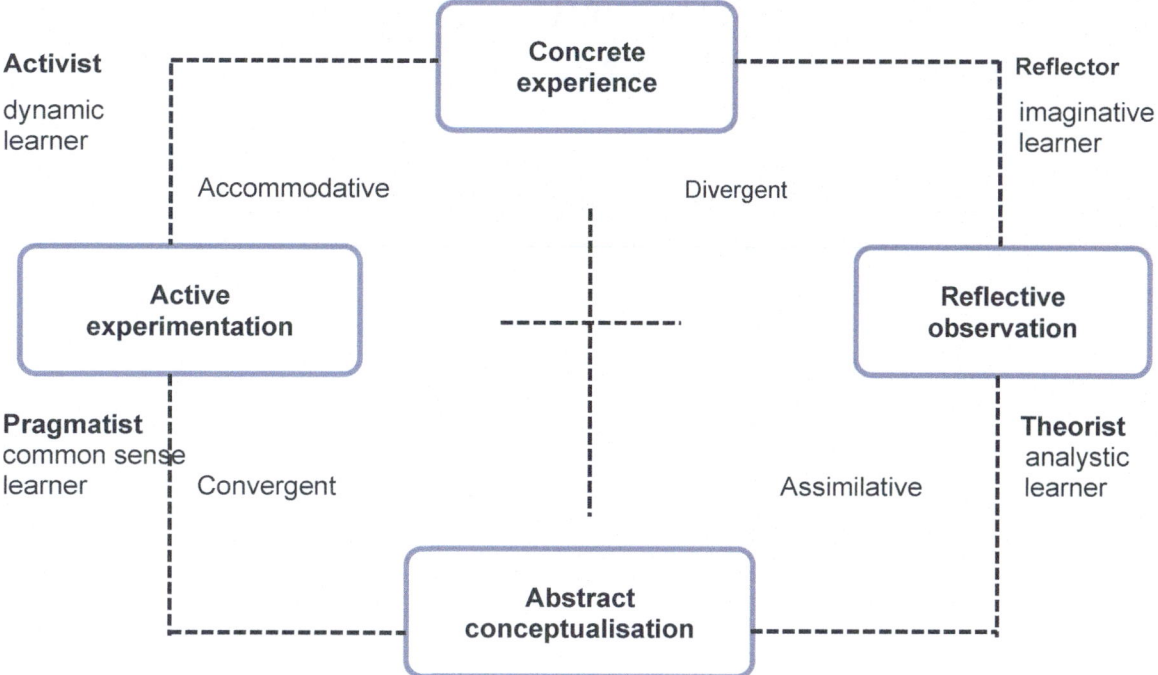

Implications of the learning models

Most individuals exhibit a clear preference for one style of learning and may struggle to switch between them.

People who have a clear learning style preference will tend to learn more effectively if learning is geared to their preference. For instance, according to **Kolb**:

- people who prefer the '**assimilating**' learning style will not be comfortable being thrown in at the deep end without notes and instructions.

- people who prefer to use an '**accommodating**' learning style are likely to become frustrated if they are forced to read lots of instructions and rules, and are unable to get hands-on experiences as soon as possible.

A feature of **Honey and Mumford's** model is that it provides suggestions about the best ways for individuals to learn. The most effective learning methods are different for each learning style.

- **Activists** – have a practical approach to training, are flexible and optimistic. They prefer practical problems, enjoy participation and challenge, are easily bored and have a dislike of theory. They must have hands-on training.

- **Theorists** – require their learning to be programmed and structured; designed to allow time for analysis; and provided by people who share the same preference for ideas and analysis.

- **Reflectors** – need an observational approach to training. They need to work at their own pace – slow, cautious and non-participative – where conclusions are carefully thought out.

> A question may provide a scenario and ask you to choose what learning style is most appropriate for the person described in the scenario.

- **Pragmatists** – need to see a direct value and link between training and real problems and aim to do things better. They enjoy learning new techniques and tasks and are good at finding improved ways of doing things.

22.3 WHAT ARE TRAINING, DEVELOPMENT AND EDUCATION?

LEARNING SUMMARY

After studying this section you should be able to:

- explain the terms 'training', 'development' and 'education' and the characteristics of each.

Definitions

> **DEFINITION Education** is defined as 'the activities which aim at developing the knowledge skills, moral values and understanding required in all aspects of life rather than a knowledge skill related to only a limited field of activity'.

Do not confuse these three definitions.

> **DEFINITION Training** is 'the planned and systematic modification of behaviour through learning events, programmes and instruction which enable individuals to achieve the level of knowledge, skills and competence to carry out their work effectively'.

> **DEFINITION Development** is 'the growth or realisation of a person's ability and potential through conscious or unconscious learning and educational experiences'.

22.4 THE TRAINING AND DEVELOPMENT PROCESS

LEARNING SUMMARY

After studying this section you should be able to:

- list the benefits of effective training and development in the workplace

- describe the training and development process: identifying needs, setting objectives, programme design, delivery and validation.

The benefits of training and development

KEY POINT Organisations should view training and development of staff as an investment.

BENEFITS TO INDIVIDUALS	BENEFITS TO THE ORGANISATION
Improved skills and (dependent on type of training) qualifications.	Increased motivation of employees, leading to higher productivity.
Increased confidence and job satisfaction.	Increased competence and confidence, meaning higher quality and few mistakes.
	Skilled workforce, leading to more innovation and a better customer experience.
	Low staff turnover, saving the organisation time and money.

Training and development as a step-by-step process

Step 1: Identification of training needs

- **Formal training needs analysis (TNA)** – this involves identification of the skills, knowledge and experience needed for a particular job and comparing to the skills, knowledge and experience of the current job-holder.

- **Performance appraisal** – Most line managers appraise their staff or carry out a performance review at least annually.

- **Observation** – there may be signs that staff require additional training, such as poor productivity or high numbers of mistakes.

- **Organisational strategy** – training and development must be linked to the overall business strategy.

Step 2: Setting objectives for training

This stage examines what the proposed training programme is supposed to accomplish. What impact do we want it to have on staff?

Objectives need to be clearly stated, measurable and specific, outlining the effect that training should have on the performance and abilities of the employee being trained.

Step 3: Programme design and delivery

TRAINING METHODS FOR INDIVIDUALS	TRAINING METHODS FOR GROUPS
formal training courses	lectures
mentoring	discussions
coaching	coaching
computer-based learning	case studies and role play
self-managed learning	business games

Step 4: Evaluation and validation of the training programme

It has been suggested that there are **five levels** at which **evaluation** can take place.

- **Reactions** of the trainees to the training

- **Learning** – new knowledge and skills required or changes in attitude

- **Job behaviour** – the extent to which training is being applied on the job

- **Organisation** – ways in which the functions of the organisation has changed

- **Ultimate value** – how the organisation as a whole has benefited

> **KEY POINT** Whatever evaluation method is used, it should be done before, during and after the event.

22.5 THE ROLE OF MANAGEMENT IN THE LEARNING PROCESS

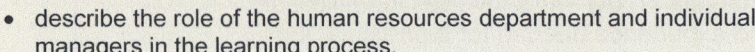

LEARNING SUMMARY

After studying this section you should be able to:

- describe the role of the human resources department and individual managers in the learning process.

Responsibility for the training and development process

There are a number of people or groups who share responsibility for training and development of employees.

The human resources (HR) department

> **KEY POINT** The HR department has overall, high-level responsibility for training and development.

This will mean that they will often need to:

- create frameworks for job appraisals and the analysis of learning gaps.

- identify when and if training is needed within the organisation.

- design career pathways for employees.

- inform employees about learning, training and development opportunities that are available to them.

Line managers

> **KEY POINT** Line managers are likely to have responsibilities for helping to apply HR department resources to their own group or department.

This may involve:

- identification of learning and training needs of the group or department they are responsible for.

- monitoring the abilities and knowledge levels of individual workers within their team.

- organising specific training programmes.

- offering informal training, such as coaching and mentoring to employees as needed.

Do you understand?

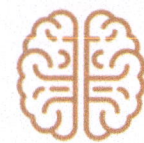

1. Peter, an employee, has recently been sent on a course by his company to help him learn about basic marketing principles. This is an example of:

   (i) Education (ii) Re-skilling (iii) Training (iv) Development

2. Andrea has been given a new role at her workplace. To prepare, she makes sure that she has read all the relevant documentation and technical summaries relating to her new role. According to Kolb, the stage of learning that Andrea is beginning at is Abstract Conceptualisation.

   True or false?

3. Emma prefers to learn by investigation, with plenty of time being provided to think about the results that she has obtained. Which of Honey and Mumford's learning styles is most appropriate for Emma?

   (i) Reflector (ii) Pragmatist (iii) Theorist (iv) Activist

1. (iii) Training. Peter is learning a new skill relating to a particular area or activity. Development is learning for growth of the individual and is not related specifically to a present or future job. Education is personal and broadly based.
2. True. Andrea is attempting to understand her new role in theory before she begins. This is an example of abstract conceptualisation.
3. (i) Reflector.

1   Consider the following three definitions:

    (1)   'The activities which aim at developing skills, values and understanding required in all aspects of life.'

    (2)   'The growth or realisation of a person's ability and potential through conscious or unconscious learning.'

    (3)   'The planned and systematic modification of behaviour through learning events, programmes and instruction.'

    Which term matches each definition?

    A   (1) – training, (2) – education, (3) – development

    B   (1) – education, (2) – training, (3) – development

    C   (1) – development, (2) – education, (3) – training

    D   (1) – education, (2) – development, (3) – training

2   A trainee accountant has been given a mentor at his firm. This mentor will be available to the student if he has any questions or needs further information about anything to do with his job.

    This would be an example of _____ learning for the trainee accountant.

    Which word correctly fills the gap in the sentence above?

    A   Incidental

    B   Formal

    C   Informal

    D   Self-managed

3   Consider the following two statements:

    (1)   J dislikes reading instruction booklets and prefers a hands-on approach to learning.

    (2)   H learns by watching others undertake a task first, before trying to imitate them.

    According to Honey and Mumford, what style of learning is being adopted by each person?

    A   J – pragmatist, H – reflector

    B   J – pragmatist, H – activist

    C   J – activist, H – pragmatist

    D   J – activist, H – reflector

4   Kolb argued that there are four stages to learning which always begins with concrete experience.

    Is this statement TRUE or FALSE?

    A   True

    B   False

23 Review and appraisal of individual performance

The following topics are covered in this chapter:

- Performance assessment
- Performance appraisal
- Training, development and education
- The training and development process
- The role of management in the learning process

23.1 PERFORMANCE ASSESSMENT

LEARNING SUMMARY

After studying this section you should be able to:

- explain the importance of performance assessment

- explain how organisations assess the performance of human resources.

What is performance assessment?

> **DEFINITION Performance assessment** is the regular and systematic review of performance and the assessment of potential with the aim of producing action programmes to develop both work and individuals.

Assessment criteria may include the following:

- Volume of work produced

- Knowledge of work

- Quality of work

- Management skills

- Personal skills

The process of performance assessment

Organisations follow four main steps when assessing performance of employees:

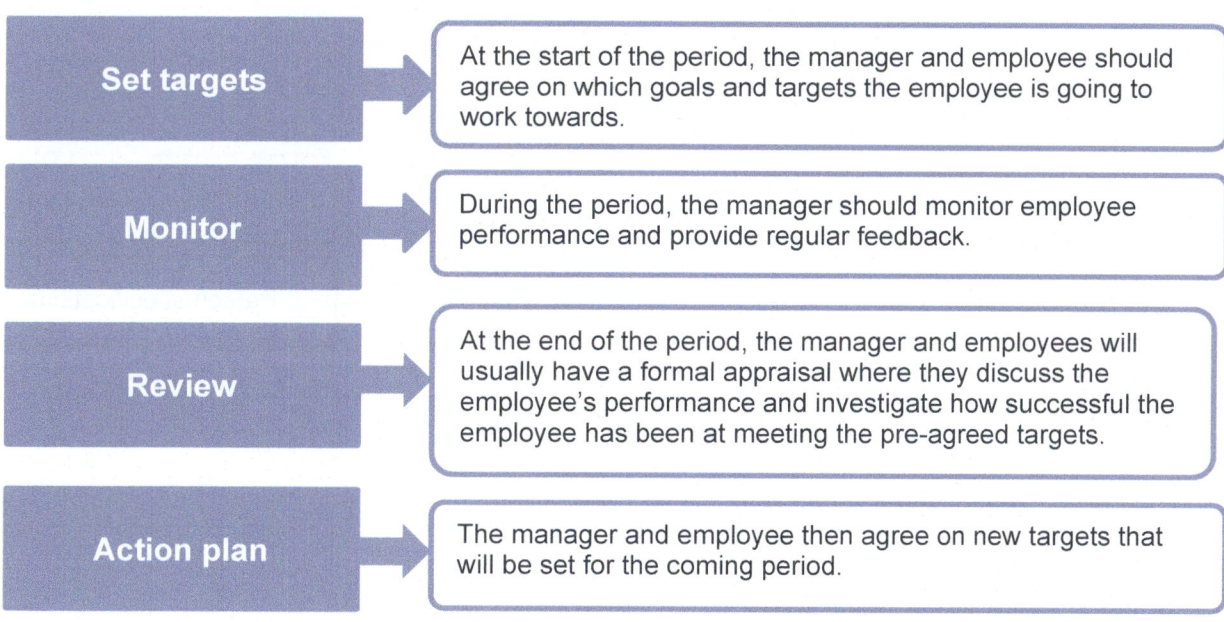

Set targets — At the start of the period, the manager and employee should agree on which goals and targets the employee is going to work towards.

Monitor — During the period, the manager should monitor employee performance and provide regular feedback.

Review — At the end of the period, the manager and employees will usually have a formal appraisal where they discuss the employee's performance and investigate how successful the employee has been at meeting the pre-agreed targets.

Action plan — The manager and employee then agree on new targets that will be set for the coming period.

23.2 PERFORMANCE APPRAISAL

LEARNING SUMMARY

After studying this section you should be able to:

- define performance appraisal and describe its process

- explain the benefits of effective appraisal

- identify the barriers to effective appraisal and how these may be overcome

- explain how the effectiveness of performance appraisal may be evaluated.

The purposes of appraisals

> **DEFINITION Appraisal** is normally a formal process by which the progress, performance, results and sometimes personality of an employee are reviewed and assessed by his or her immediate supervisor.

BENEFITS TO INDIVIDUALS	BENEFITS TO THE ORGANISATION
Providing a basis for remuneration for the coming period.	Monitoring of human resource selection processes against results.
Ensuring that work of particular merit is recognised.	Identification of the best candidates for promotion etc.
Providing a forum for the employee to voice concerns about work areas.	Identification of problems with the job that had not been previously realised.
Establishment of what is expected of the individual in the coming period and how the employee will be assessed.	Helping to formulate the training plan.
Identification of training and development needs.	Helping to formulate a human resources plan e.g. are staff over-worked?
	Improvement of communication between managers and subordinates.

The performance appraisal process

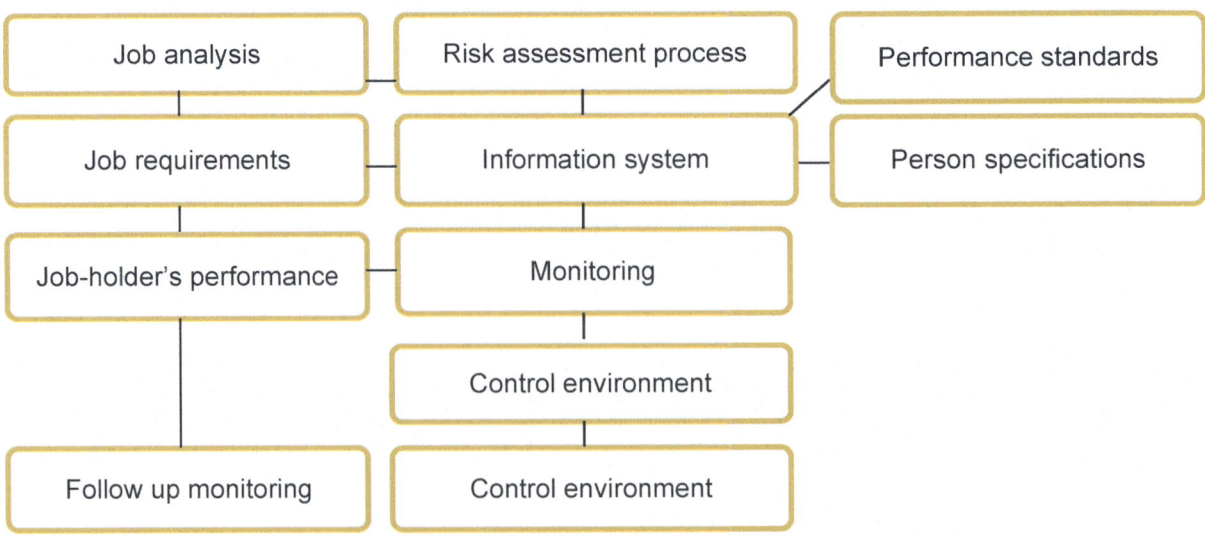

The above diagram can be explained by looking at its four main stages.

- **Identify the criteria for assessment**

This involves examining the corporate plan of the business and deciding what targets should be set for the employee in order to help the business meet its objectives. It is usually based upon job analysis, job requirements, performance standards and person specifications.

- **Production of appraisal report**

The manager will then prepare an appraisal report, detailing the appraisee's performance in the agreed criteria. In some organisations, the appraisee will also write a report and perhaps perform a self-appraisal.

- **Appraisal interview**

The manager will usually interview the appraisee, allowing an exchange of views about the appraisal reports, along with discussion and agreement on action points, training and targets for the coming period.

Maier identified three types of approach to appraisal interviews:

Tell and sell – the appraiser adopts the strategy of a salesperson, trying to persuade and convince the subordinate that the appraisal is fair and that they can and must change in certain ways. It is a one-to-one communication system.

Tell and listen – the appraiser listens to the job-holder's perception of their job and their problems, expectations and aims and does not dominate the interview.

Joint problem-solving - this represents a shift in the emphasis from the first two methods. The appraiser uses many social skills to encourage the interviewee to do a self-assessment, admit their own problems and suggest solutions, with the appraiser acting as a coach and a counsellor.

- **Follow-up/ conclusion and action plan**

This involves giving out the results of the appraisal, monitoring the progress of the action plan, carrying out agreed actions on training and development and giving regular feedback.

> A question may describe an appraisal scenario and ask you to choose what type of appraisal the person in the scenario has had.

Benefits of effective appraisal

BENEFITS TO INDIVIDUALS	BENEFITS TO THE ORGANISATION
The employee gets feedback about performance at work, and an assessment of competence.	It provides a formal system for assessing the performance and potential of employees, with a view to identifying candidates for promotion.
An appraisal interview may be used as a basis for considering pay and reward.	It provides a system for identifying ways of improving the competence of employees, in order to raise the general level of efficiency and effectiveness of the workforce.
Appraisal can be used to identify and agree measures for further training and development, to improve the employee's competence.	It is a valuable system for resource planning, and ensuring that employees are ready for promotion.
	If it is well managed, communications can be improved between managers and staff.

Barriers to effective staff appraisal

Lockett suggested that there are six main barriers to effective appraisals:

- Appraisal as confrontation
- Appraisal as judgement
- Appraisal as chat
- Appraisal as bureaucracy
- Appraisal as an annual event
- Appraisal as unfinished business

Overcoming the barriers to effective staff appraisal

Best practice for appraisals is given by the 4 Fs:

- **Firm** – managers should be willing to discuss negative as well as favourable aspects of performance.
- **Factual** – subjective aspects of performance should be avoided.
- **Fair** – all employees should be treated the same
- **Frequent** – appraisals should be held on a regular basis rather than just when a problem arises

Evaluating the effectiveness of staff appraisal

Lockett argued that the appraisal process should be monitored to ensure it has:

- Relevance
- Fairness
- Serious intent
- Co-operation
- Efficiency

Staff turnover

The causes of staff leaving fall into three categories:

- **Discharge** – as a result of an employee's unsuitability, disciplinary action or redundancy.
- **Unavoidable** – due to marriage, moving house, ill health or death.
- **Avoidable** – due to pay, working conditions, relationships with work colleagues.

Staff turnover can be calculated by dividing either the total separations (those leaving the organisation) or the total replacements by the average number in the workforce, and expressing the result as a percentage.

> Learn this formula – questions can be numerical in nature.

KEY POINT Examination of this figure may highlight vital information e.g. poor selection techniques or poor working conditions.

Do you understand?

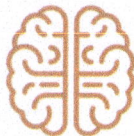

1   Feedback should typically only be provided to employees at the end of each period, when their performance over the entire period can be discussed.

   True or false?

2   Appraisals are always good for motivation.

   True or false?

3   Place the following stages of the performance appraisal process in the correct order.

   (i)   Action planning and monitoring

   (ii) Production of an appraisal report

   (iii) Identification of assessment criteria from the corporate plan

   (iv) Appraisal interview

1   False. While feedback will be provided at the end of the period, it should also be provided regularly throughout the period to help employees improve their performance.

2   False. While appraisals are often good for motivation, if they are done poorly they can actually demotivate workers.

3   (iii), (ii), (iv), (i)

1   Alex's manager has informed him of the goals that will be measured against for the coming year. At the end of the year, Alex's manager then discussed how well Alex performed against these targets in the year and what the following year's targets should be, along with how Alex would be expected to achieve these targets.

Which stage of the performance appraisal process is missing from Alex's appraisal?

A   Monitor

B   Review

C   Action plan

D   Set targets

2   **Which of the following is NOT a usual purpose of annual performance appraisal?**

A   Deciding on remuneration levels for the coming period

B   Decisions about whether to terminate an employee

C   Identification of training and development needs

D   Ensuring that work of particular merit is recognised

3   Mary is an employee having an appraisal with her manager, Sarah. Sarah informs Mary that her performance has been poor throughout the year, giving a number of incidents and scenarios to back up her statements. She concludes that she needs additional training during the following year in order to improve her performance.

What type of appraisal has Mary had?

A   Tell and sell

B   Tell and listen

C   Problem solving

D   360 degree

4   Staff turnover can be calculated by dividing _____ by _____ and expressing the result as a percentage.

(1)   The total number leaving the organisation

(2)   The total number in the workforce

(3)   The average number in the workforce

(4)   The weighted average number leaving the organisation

Which of the above options should be inserted into the gaps IN THE CORRECT ORDER to complete the calculation?

A   (1) then (2)

B   (1) then (3)

C   (4) then (2)

D   (4) then (3)

24 Personal effectiveness at work

The following topics are covered in this chapter:

- Time management
- Competency frameworks
- Coaching, mentoring and counselling
- Personal development plan
- Conflict
- Consequences of ineffectiveness

24.1 TIME MANAGEMENT

LEARNING SUMMARY

After studying this section you should be able to:

- explain the importance of effective time management

- describe the barriers to effective time management and how they may be overcome

- describe the role of information technology in improving personal effectiveness.

What is time management?

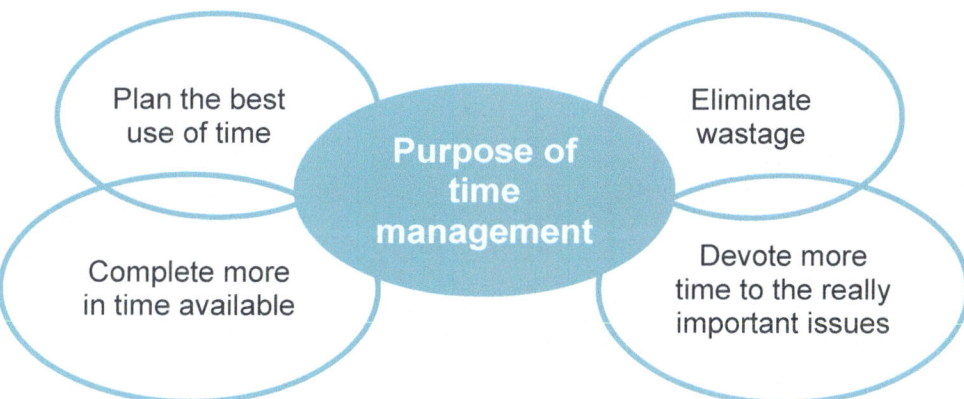

Plan the best use of time

Eliminate wastage

Purpose of time management

Complete more in time available

Devote more time to the really important issues

Time management techniques

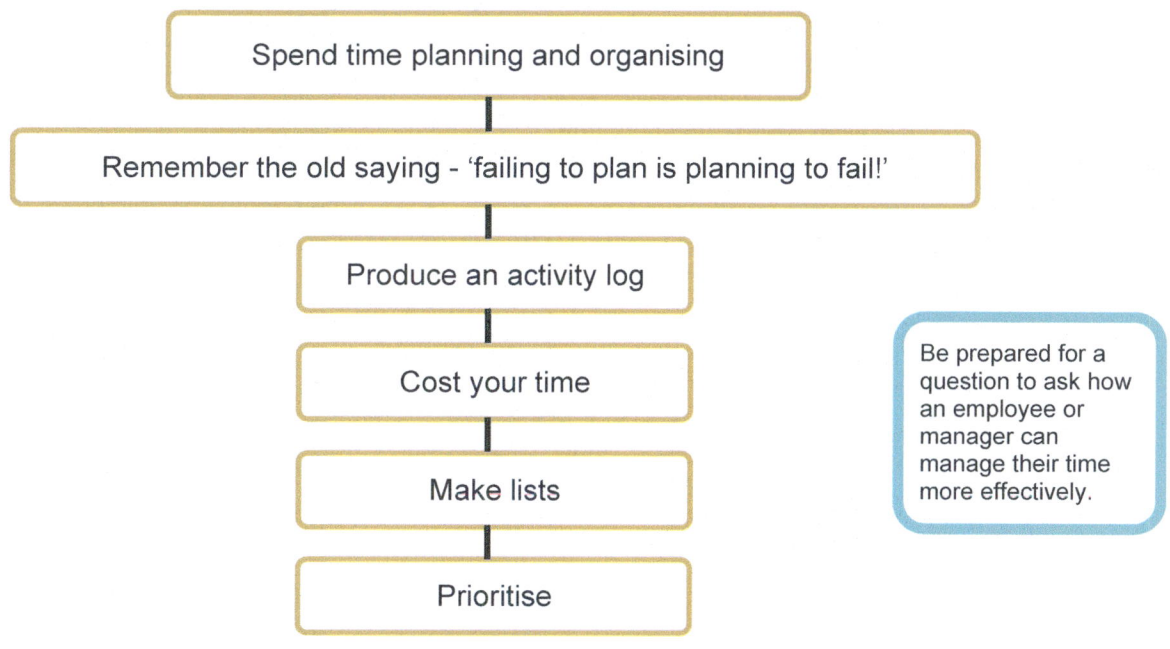

Spend time planning and organising

Remember the old saying - 'failing to plan is planning to fail!'

Produce an activity log

Cost your time

Make lists

Prioritise

Be prepared for a question to ask how an employee or manager can manage their time more effectively.

Barriers to effective time management

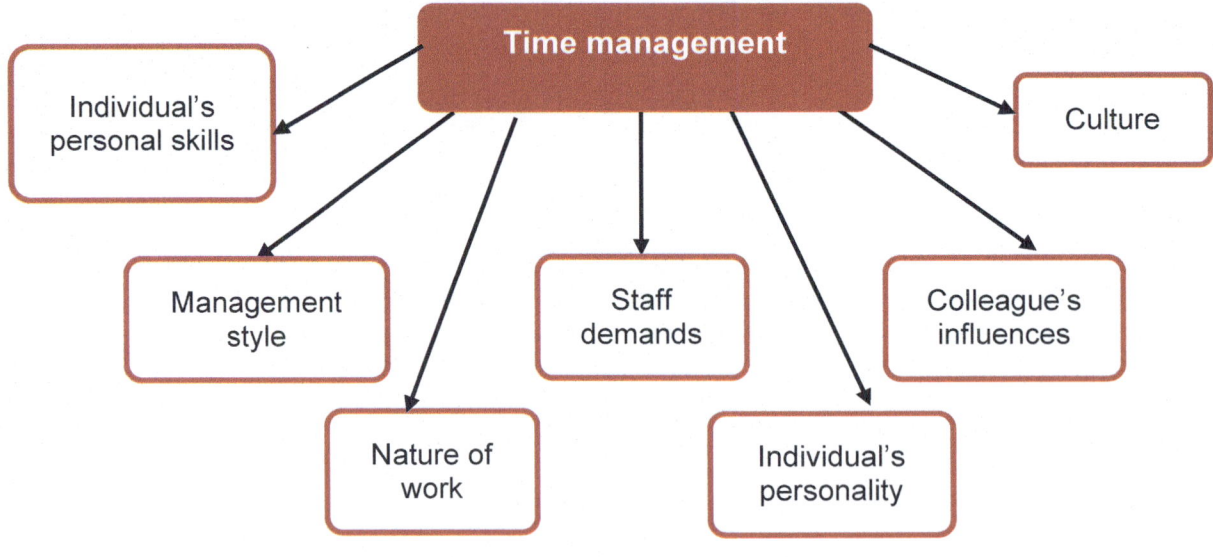

Internal

Discipline
Procrastination
Lack of motivation

External

Workload issues
Available resources

Overcome the internal barriers

- Be assertive – identify your time wasters and resolve to deal with them, learn to say NO, delegate

- Identify and make use of your personal biorhythms, or 'up' time and 'down' time

- Conquer procrastination – find out what causes you to put off doing something and remedy it

- Promise yourself a reward

Overcome the external barriers

- Do the right thing right – doing the right thing is effectiveness; doing things right is efficiency

- Urgent tasks with short-term consequences often get done to the detriment of the important tasks i.e. those with long-term, goal-related implications

- Break big jobs into little steps

- Use negotiation to improve the use of time

The role of information technology in improving personal effectiveness

There are a wide range of different IT tools that individuals and businesses may use, including:

- Email

- Video conferencing

- Electronic Data Interchange (EDI)

- Intranets

- Office automation e.g. word processors, spreadsheets, databases

- Homeworking

24.2 COMPETENCY FRAMEWORKS

LEARNING SUMMARY

After studying this section you should be able to:

- describe the features of a competency framework

- explain how a competency framework underpins professional development needs.

Competency frameworks

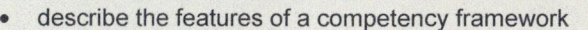
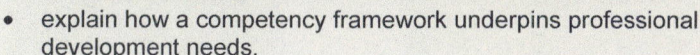

DEFINITION Competency frameworks attempt to identify all the competencies that are required by anyone taking on a particular role within the organisation.

KEY POINT A list of key competencies is produced which can be used as a benchmark to either ensure that the correct individual is chosen for the role or as a way of checking that an existing member of staff has all the up to date skills needed for their role.

Most competency frameworks cover the following categories:

- communication skills

- people management

- team skills

- customer service skills

- results-orientation

- problem-solving skills

- selecting and managing subcontractors

- recommending termination where necessary

24.3 COACHING, MENTORING AND COUNSELLING

LEARNING SUMMARY

After studying this section you should be able to:

*   explain the purpose and benefits of coaching, mentoring and counselling in promoting employee effectiveness.

Differences between mentoring, coaching and counselling

> You will need to understand the differences between these terms – they can easily be confused with one another.

Personal development

Mentoring

Help, guidance, advice and support to facilitate learning

Coaching

Focuses on achieving specific objectives

Counselling

Problem solving, helping people to help themselves

24.4 PERSONAL DEVELOPMENT PLAN

LEARNING SUMMARY

After studying this section you should be able to:

*   describe how a personal development plan should be formulated, implemented, monitored and reviewed by the individual.

Training and development

KEY POINT Development is more general than training, is more forward looking and orientated towards the individual, and is concerned with enabling the individual to fulfil his/ her potential.

Training	Development
Immediately practical	No immediate practical application
Connected to job performance	Over time it enables a person to deal with wider problems

Preparing a personal development plan

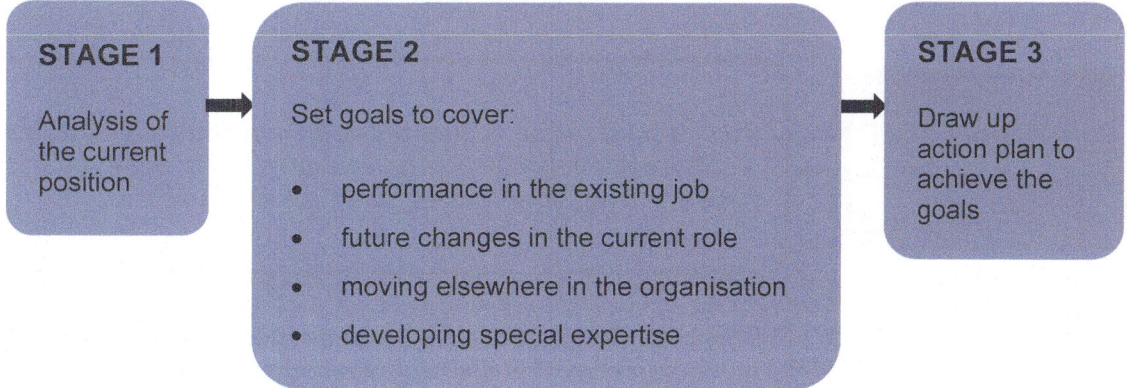

STAGE 1	STAGE 2	STAGE 3
Analysis of the current position	Set goals to cover: • performance in the existing job • future changes in the current role • moving elsewhere in the organisation • developing special expertise	Draw up action plan to achieve the goals

Goals should have the following objectives:

- **S**pecific

- **M**easurable

- **A**chievable

- **R**elevant

- **T**imely

The acronym **SMART** will help you remember the characteristics of good quality objectives.

The importance of continuous monitoring and feedback

- Feedback should be clear and frequent and this can only be achieved if there is continuous monitoring of the task.

- Feedback can also have a motivating effect by providing recognition of work done which in turn provides the incentive to sustain and improve performance levels.

- Recognition, praise and encouragement create a feeling of confidence, competence, development and progress that enhance the motivation to learn.

24.5 CONFLICT

LEARNING SUMMARY

After studying this section you should be able to:

- identify situations where conflict can arise at work

- describe how conflict can affect personal and organisational performance

- explain how conflict can be avoided

- identify ways in which conflict can be resolved or referred.

What is conflict?

DEFINITION Conflict is defined as any personal divergence of interests between groups and individuals.

Types of conflict

There are two main types of conflict:

Vertical	This is conflict that occurs between individuals and groups at different levels of the organisation's hierarchy e.g. between a junior employee and his/her manager.
Horizontal	This is conflict that occurs between individuals and groups at the same level of the organisation's hierarchy e.g. between individual directors.

How to avoid conflict

- Good communication
- Rules and procedures
- Avoiding a blame culture
- Ensuring a fair allocation of resources

Conflict management strategies

- Denial
- Suppression
- Reduction/ negotiation
- Resolution

24.6 CONSEQUENCES OF INEFFECTIVENESS AT WORK

LEARNING SUMMARY

After studying this section you should be able to:

- explain how individual or team ineffectiveness can affect organisational performance.

Consequences of ineffectiveness at work

- Poor quality work produced.
- Missing deadlines and targets.
- Lack of communication with others.
- Having a poor attitude to work.
- Failing to maintain appropriate levels of key skills.

This can have significant effects on the organisation itself, such as:

- Loss of reputation and customers, due to poor quality products and services.
- Poor productivity and motivation.
- Lack of information from staff about key issues, making it harder to make key business decisions and solve problems.

Do you understand?

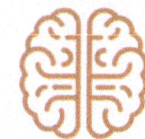

1   Which of the following would tend to act as a barrier to effective time management for an employee?

(i)   The employee's job is routine and predictable (ii) The employee needs to regularly visit employees who are located in another town

2   Everlast is a construction company. One of its new employees, Kira, is fully trained but is not as productive as some of the other workers. The management of Everlast have therefore asked a more experienced employee, Manos, to give Kira advice on how to improve her productivity.

Would Manos be classed as Kira's mentor, counsellor or coach?

3   Conflict between individuals always damages the operations of an organisation and should be avoided where possible

True or false?

4   Competency frameworks list the qualifications that a job-holder needs in order to perform effectively in a given role.

True or false?

1   (ii) Having to travel regularly is likely to waste time, making it harder to have effective time management.

2   Manos would be classified as Kira's coach. Coaching focuses on achieving a specific objective (in this case improving productivity). Mentoring is a broader process, involving the provision of general support and impartial advice. Counselling helps individuals to learn how to overcome problems or issues they are facing.

3   False. Remember that conflict is any divergence of interests between groups or individuals. It can therefore be a way of workers challenging the existing ways of working and suggesting innovations and improvements which may be beneficial to the organisation.

4   False. Competency frameworks list the skills, attributes and knowledge required in a particular role, rather than simply the qualifications.

1 **(a)** T works in a local government office. He has significant problems with time management and often feels that there are 'simply not enough hours in the day' for him to accomplish all of the tasks he has been given.

T has compiled a list of issues that he feels may be preventing him from achieving good time management in his role:

A   T's job is dynamic and very unpredictable.

B   T is assertive and willing to tell his managers if he does not have time to complete a task.

C   Many of the people that T has to meet face-to-face are located far from his office.

D   When in his office, T operates a 'closed door' policy meaning that colleagues have to formally book time to discuss issues with him.

E   The department that T works for is bureaucratic, requiring significant amounts of paperwork to be undertaken for both major and minor tasks.

F   T's department makes extensive use of IT to aid communication between employees.

G   T dislikes keeping a diary and feels he never 'has any time' to complete one.

H   T is skilled at breaking larger jobs down into smaller tasks.

Required:

Write down which FOUR of the above statements are most likely to be contributing to T's poor time management.

(b) T's recent appraisal has led to the development of a personal development plan. This process falls into three main stages:

A   Analysis of T's current position

B   Action plan

C   Goal setting

Required:

Identify the above stage which is associated with each of the following activities by writing A, B or C.

(i)   Ensuring that all objectives set for T are measurable

(ii)   Carrying out a personal SWOT analysis for T

(iii)   Set specific targets for T to work towards, along with details of how success will be measured

(iv)   Identifying that T has poor time management skills

2   Rosie has a large number of tasks waiting for her attention and has realised she needs to prioritise them. One task is high importance but Rosie has a number of weeks left before the deadline for the task.

What approach should Rosie take to dealing with this task?

A   Delegate or cancel the task

B   Ignore the task completely

C   Deal with the task now and devote plenty of time to it

D   Delegate the task for now

3   **Which of the following is NOT likely to be a goal of a personal development plan?**

A   Growth during a person's career

B   Meeting weekly sales targets

C   Developing skills and expertise

D   Realising personal aspirations

4   Two employees have recently been arguing over access to business computer systems. Their manager feels that the conflict is not serious and will sort itself out. Because of this, she has decided not to intervene.

Which conflict management strategy is the manager adopting?

A   Denial

B   Suppression

C   Reduction

D   Resolution

25 Communicating in business

The following topics are covered in this chapter:

- What is communication?
- The communication process
- Types of communication
- Effective and ineffective communication
- Communication patterns

25.1 WHAT IS COMMUNICATION?

LEARNING SUMMARY

After studying this section you should be able to:

- define communications

- identify methods of communication used in the organisation and how they are used.

What is communication?

DEFINITION Communication is the two-way interchange of information, ideas, facts and emotions by one or more persons. It establishes relationships and allows for direction and co-ordination of tasks.

In an organisation, communication takes many forms, including:

- giving or receiving information and instructions.

- exchanging ideas.

- announcing plans and strategies.

- laying down rules or procedures.

- comparing actual results against a plan.

- manuals, organisation charts and job descriptions.

25.2 THE COMMUNICATION PROCESS

LEARNING SUMMARY

After studying this section you should be able to:

- explain a simple communication model: sender, message, receiver, feedback, noise.

The process

The process of communication involves the following elements:

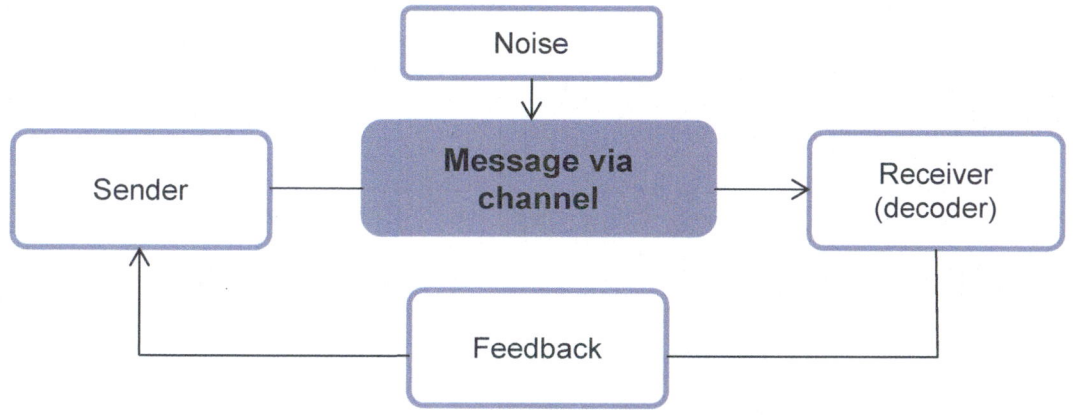

25.3 TYPES OF COMMUNICATION

LEARNING SUMMARY

After studying this section you should be able to:

- explain formal and informal communication and their importance in the workplace.

Types of communication

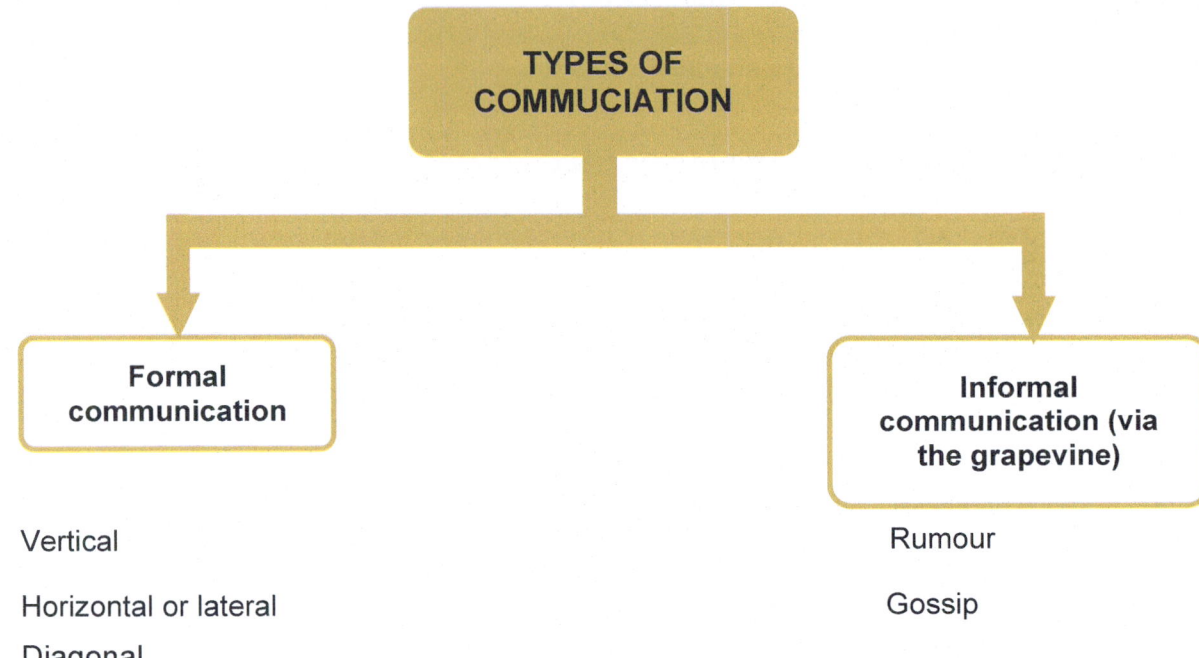

Vertical

Horizontal or lateral

Diagonal

Rumour

Gossip

25.4 EFFECTIVE AND INEFFECTIVE COMMUNICATION

LEARNING SUMMARY

After studying this section you should be able to:

- describe the attributes of effective and ineffective communication

- identify the consequences of ineffective communication

- describe the barriers to effective communication and identify practical steps that can be taken to overcome them.

Attributes of effective communication

- Timely
- Accurate and complete
- Relevant
- Directed to the right people
- Understandable
- Cost-effective

Consequences of ineffective communication

Lack of downward communication is likely to result in:

- poor awareness of corporate objectives at lower management levels.

- poor understanding of working instructions and responsibilities.

- poor morale of junior managers because they are not consulted about changes which affect them or their working conditions.

Lack of upward communication, including feedback, has the following undesirable consequences for management:

- early warning of troubled areas is not received.

- benefit of creative ability in subordinates is lost.

- participation of subordinates is limited.

- need for change is not appreciated because management is isolated from the operation areas.

- control becomes difficult.

- introduction of change is difficult.

Lack of lateral communication often leads to:

- divisions in management teams.

- lack of co-ordination.

- rivalry between sections and departments.

- lack of advice and involvement by staff specialist.

Overcoming barriers to communication

Practical ways of dealing with these problems include:

- agree and confirm priorities and deadlines for the receipt of information.

- spend sufficient time ensuring that the information is sent to all the right people.

- keep communication as simple as possible, avoiding jargon.

- confirm that the information sent has been received and understood.

- avoid inconsistent verbal/non-verbal communication, as this tends to confuse the receivers.

25.5 COMMUNICATION PATTERNS

LEARNING SUMMARY

After studying this section you should be able to:

- describe the main methods and patterns of communication.

Patterns

KEY POINT A communication pattern illustrates how individuals communicate with each other within a group or organisation.

Leavitt identified five major patterns of communication: wheel (or star), circle, all-channel, chain and 'Y'.

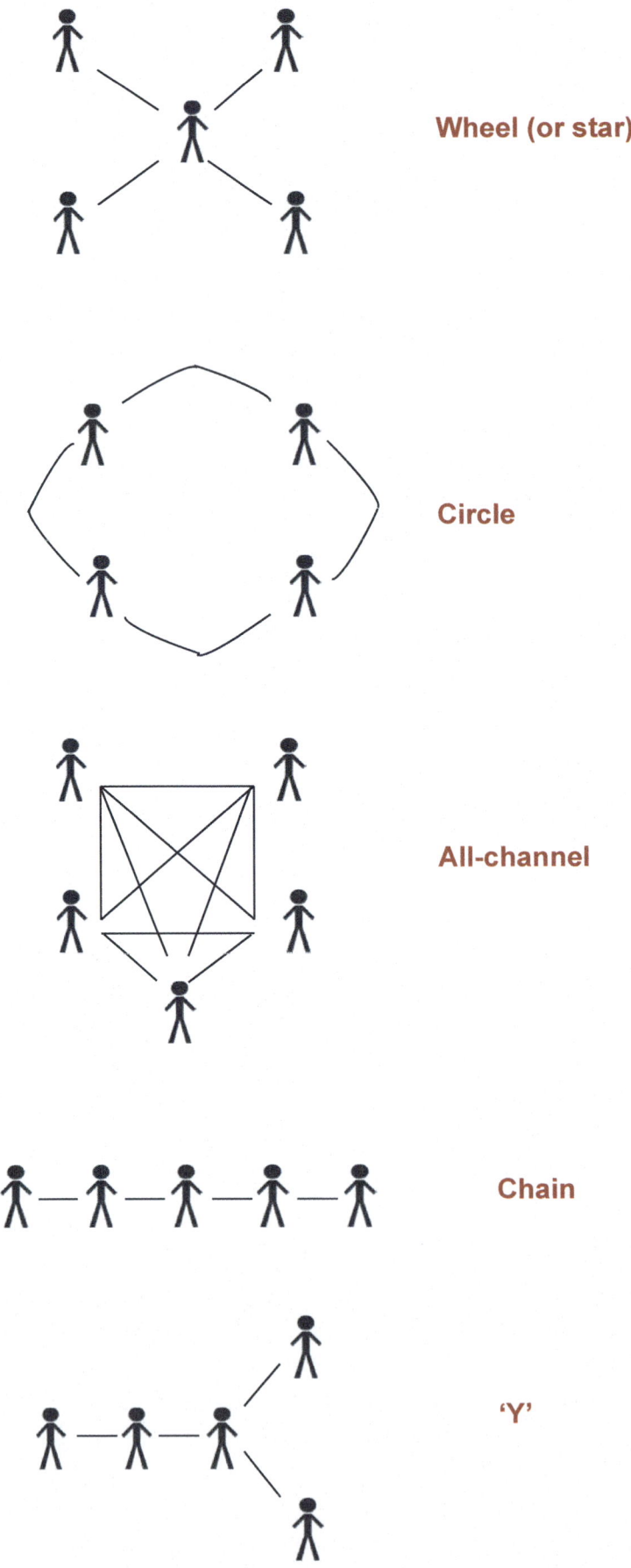

Wheel (or star)

Circle

All-channel

Chain

'Y'

These five groups can be grouped together into two main types:

- **Centralised networks** – chain, wheel and 'Y' – group members have to go through a central person in order to communicate with others. This leads to unequal access to information within the group.

- **Decentralised networks** – circle and all-channel – information flows freely between members without having to go through a central person.

Leavitt's main conclusions were that:

- The **wheel is always the fastest way to reach a conclusion**, making it ideal for problem-solving. The circle is the slowest.

- For **complex problems, the all-channel** is the most likely to reach the best decision.

- The level of **satisfaction for individuals was highest in the circle**, fairly high in the all-channel and relatively low in the other, centralised networks. The centralised networks saw high job satisfaction for the central figure, with the remaining members feeling isolated.

> You may be given a scenario and be asked to choose which communication network is most likely to facilitate the best decision in the context of the scenario.

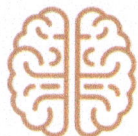

Do you understand?

1   Petra, an office junior, is asked to send a message to the head of another department. What type of communication is this?

    (i)   Diagonal (ii) Vertical

2   Which of the following patterns of communication would be best if a quick decision is needed?

    (i)   Chain (ii) Wheel (iii) All-Channel

3   Poor awareness of corporate objectives at lower levels is a likely consequence of a lack of downward communication within an organisation.

    True or false?

1   (i) Diagonal. Petra is communicating with someone who is in a different department AND at a different level of the hierarchy to her.
2   (ii) The wheel is always seen as the fastest approach to reaching a conclusion.
3   True. This will be caused by lack of downward communication , where management fail to communicate with junior staff, leading to a lack of awareness of corporate objectives among the workers.

1 Consider the following statements:

    (1) Grapevine communication network is often used by managers to pass on orders and instruction to staff.

    (2) When communicating with others, the majority of information passed on to the other person is transmitted through words rather than other means such as body language or tone of voice.

Which of these statements is/are correct?

    A   (1) only

    B   (2) only

    C   Both

    D   Neither

2 Barriers to communication consist of anything that stops information getting to its intended recipients.

Is this statement TRUE or FALSE?

    A   True

    B   False

3 **Which of the following is an example of lateral communication?**

    A   A manager explaining new operational procedures to staff

    B   A committee coming together to review health and safety issues

    C   Staff passing on to the supervisor the main points from a recent conversation with a customer

    D   During appraisal, a person receives feedback about his performance results

4 **For complex problems the network most likely to facilitate the best decision is:**

    A   circle

    B   all-channel

    C   wheel

    D   'Y'

5 Information overload usually leads to individual being unable to decide what information is relevant or not, and therefore important facts may be missed out.

Is this statement TRUE or FALSE?

    A   True

    B   False

CHAPTER 1

1   D

Organisations do not have to create a product or service in order to be classified as an organisation. For example, an orchestra may be classed as an organisation, but it does not necessarily create a product.

2   B

Partnerships and companies would both usually be profit seeking. While government departments are likely to be not-for-profit, they would be part of the public sector. Therefore only charities would be likely to be both private AND not-for-profit.

3   C

As public limited companies are able to sell their shares to the public, they will often find it easier to raise large amounts of capital for growth, if needed. This may be much harder for partnerships and sole traders. Only public companies can sell shares to the public, companies may be owned by only one shareholder and shareholders enjoy limited liability.

Co-operatives are organised solely to meet the needs of the member-owners. Non-governmental organisations (NGOs) do not have profit as a primary goal and are not linked to national governments. Charities may be examples of NGOs. Private limited companies have shareholders, not members.

4   B

Perimax is a profit-seeking organisation – given that its ten owners own 'shares', it must be a private limited company. As such, only B is likely to be appropriate from the options provided. Central government funding is usually for public sector organisations, donations would usually be the major source of funding for charities and Perimax cannot issues shares to the public as it is a private limited company.

CHAPTER 2

1   A

The features given suggest that this is an example of a professional bureaucracy – the operating core dominates.

2   A

If Rex Co wants to manage each product separately, it will need to adopt either a matrix or divisional approach, as these would allow the creation of separate divisions for each product. However, Rex Co wishes to keep its administrative costs as low as possible. As the matrix structure has high admin costs due to high numbers of managers, the company should adopt a divisional approach.

3   A

Virtual organisations exist as a network of contracts with third party suppliers and will outsource all major functions. Hollow organisations only outsource non-core functions.

4   D

Offshoring typically involves the transfer of a function to an overseas location to reduce running costs. It would not normally involve transferring existing staff members to the other country.

'Shared services' typically involves streamlining operations in order to reduce costs. It will also involve improving consistency over the way the service is undertaken and often leads to the service charging the other parts of the business to use its resources (i.e. it is run like a business).

5   B

This is a philosophy of business that permeates all areas, focusing attention on the customer.

A = a sales orientation.

6   A

Packaging, quality and design are all decisions that would fall under the 'product' part of the marketing mix.

CHAPTER 3

1   C

(1) The informal culture can either lead to improved motivation or increased inefficiency depending on its nature. This is one of the reasons managers need to be aware of the informal organisation that exists within their business.

(2) Person culture focuses on the need of the few selected individuals who occupy the prominent place.

2   B

Schein described these aspects of culture as basic assumptions and values. The other two levels are espoused values (strategies and goals, including slogans) and artefacts, which are the aspects of culture that are easy to see.

3   A

By definition. Masculinity represents stereotypical male values of competitiveness, ambition and accumulation of wealth. Femininity represents traditional female values of caring and nurturing.

4   D

The informal organisation evolves over time and is a network of relationships within an organisation that arise due to common interests or friendships. The informal organisation can either enhance or hold back the business since it often embraces both advantages (e.g. higher levels of motivation) and disadvantages (e.g. opposition to change).

CHAPTER 4

1 **B**

Only the second statement is correct. The first relates to operational level decisions. Strategic level decisions would usually require summarised, mainly external information.

Spreadsheets tend to be used to analyse data, such as lists of numbers rather than for long-term storage (which would be a function of a database application).

2 **B**

Only B is correct – the others are advantages of a manual accounting system.

3 **D**

An MIS might, for example, generate reports on total sales for each item using data from the transaction processing system.

4 **D**

The information has not been put in a user-friendly manner and cannot be easily understood by the users.

CHAPTER 5

1   **(a)**   (i)   **A**

          (ii)   **B**

          (iii) **B**

          (iv)   **A**

    (b)   (i)   **C**

          (ii)   **A**

2   (i)   **C**

    (ii)   **A**

    (iii) **B**

    (iv)   **D**

CHAPTER 6

1 **A**

B = Economic heading, C = Political heading, D = Social heading.

2 **B**

Constructive dismissal is when an employee resigns because their employer has breached the terms of their contract. The definition given in the question is that of redundancy.

3 **D**

All four are the rights of individuals with respect to information stored about them. The other three are the right to prevent processing likely to cause damage or distress, the right to take action for compensation and the right to request that the Commissioner assesses whether the legislation has been contravened.

4   D

Simple contracts can be verbal, or even implied by the actions of one of the parties. In addition, consumer legislation often also covers the provision of services.

5   A

This is known as 'intention to create legal relations'.

CHAPTER 7

1   (a)   (i)   B

         (ii)   A

         (iii) D

         (iv)   C

     (b)   (i)   B

         (ii)   D

2   (a)   **C, D, F and G are correct.**

     (b)   (i)   A

         (ii)   C

CHAPTER 8

1   D

Population growth can be important to a range of organisations in the private sector – high growth, for instance, may indicate growth in the market for the organisation's products or services.

The definition given for 'attitudes' is actually the definition of 'tastes'. Attitudes represent a person or group's like or dislike for a thing.

2   C

Outsourcing means that some of the processes previously undertaken by the company itself are now being transferred to an external supplier.

3   A

Merely rebranding a product is unlikely to reduce a company's impact on its environment. The other three, however, should all help.

4   B

This is the official definition of sustainability.

CHAPTER 9

1   (a)   (i)   A

         (ii)   D

         (iii) B

         (iv)   **None**

         (v)   C

     (b)   **B, D and E are correct.**

2   (a)   A, B, D and G are correct.

     (b)   (i)   C

            (ii)   A

            (iii) D

            (iv)   B

CHAPTER 10

1   D

L is arguing that she needed to use the money for an ethical reason, so the theft was justifiable. This would be an example of a relativist approach, where actions are justified based on their circumstances. The action is not being argued to be for the 'greater good' or for all stakeholders (presumably the theft will not be good for the shareholders of Lex!) so L is not a utilitarian or a pluralist.

2   A – True

By definition. Professions also require the mastering of specialist skills, governance by a professional organisation and a process of certification of new members.

3   B

The remaining two ethical principles are integrity and objectivity.

4   C

An accountant should first raise the issue with whoever is in charge of ethics or governance within the organisation (i.e. the Compliance Officer). If this does not solve the issue, the accountant can take legal/professional advice from their professional body. Finally, if the issue is still unresolved, the matter may be reported to the relevant authorities.

5   B

Helen recommended the purchase of the business and is now having to review the quality of that decision. This makes it difficult for her to be objective and criticise the prospects of the business.

CHAPTER 11

1   D

Reasons for the separation of ownership and control include the suggestion that specialist management can run the business better than those who own the business.

2   B

The stakeholders are all those influenced by, or those who can influence the company's decisions and actions.

3   A

An audit committee should, amongst other things, review accounting policies and financial statements as a whole to ensure that they are appropriate and balanced.

4 B

Companies are required by law to send a copy (or a summarised version) to each shareholder. Most companies will post a copy on their web site or will provide a paper- based copy free of charge to any member of the public who requests one.

5 D

Part of the Chairman's role is to maintain order, whereas A, B and C are a part of the role of Secretary.

CHAPTER 12

1 (a) A, C, E and G are correct.

  (b) (i)   **B**

     (ii)   **C**

     (iii)   **A**

     (iv)   **D**

2 B

National legislation places a requirement on companies in respect of mandatory reports to government and shareholders (and usually both). This is to ensure that limited companies adhere to certain minimum standards. In many countries an underlying purpose of this is to protect prospective and existing investors in the company, and to minimise the possibility of tax evasion.

Codes of corporate governance are now used extensively in countries that adopt a principles-based approach to corporate governance. Such codes are not underpinned by legislation and are voluntary in nature. Companies and other organisations are expected to comply with the provisions of the codes, or to explain to shareholders why they are not doing so.

International Accounting Standards seek to achieve consistency in reporting across international frontiers. They affect the content and presentation of the company accounts, but it is up to governments and their agents to decide on the requirements for preparation and filing of accounts.

3 D

Company financial statements must be free from material misstatement. They may still contain immaterial or insignificant mistakes or errors and be considered true and fair.

CHAPTER 13

1 C

The treasurer would also be responsible for debt strategy, currency management, banking forecasting and risk management.

2 A – True

Management accounting would focus on internal stakeholders.

3 A

This is tax evasion as the company is illegally reducing its tax liability. Note that it cannot be both evasion AND avoidance simultaneously.

4   B

Financial accountants would usually prepare the external financial statements, including the statement of cash flows, the income statement and the statement of financial position. A and C would normally be the responsibility of management accountants, while D would usually be undertaken by the treasury function.

5   C

Integrated reports will provide users with additional information on anything the organisation feels they would be interested in, such as the company's environmental impact or sustainability in the period.

CHAPTER 14

1   (a)   (i)   D

(ii)   C

(iii)   B

(iv)   A

(b)   C, D, G and H are correct.

2   A

Reconciliation of the purchase ledger would identify any discrepancies between the amounts that P's business believes it owes suppliers and the amount its suppliers believe it owes them. This should identify any incorrect payments that have been made. Matching the payment amount to the original invoice and ensuring that the payment is correctly authorised could also help.

3   A

The usual procedure is for the individual responsible for the petty cash to present the receipts and vouchers in order to obtain replenishment.

However, two people should open the post and list the contents.

CHAPTER 15

1   D

The accounting department can help ensure a profitable selling price is used for E's products.

2   A

Option A would most likely be a marketing or service provision crossover with the accounting department.

3   C

The four features are: intangibility, inseparability, Perishability and variability.

4   D

Inseparability looks at the fact that services cannot easily be distinguished from the person providing the service. If the taxi driver behaves badly, the customer will perceive the service itself as being poor.

CHAPTER 16

1   (a)   **A, C, D and F are correct.**

       (b)   **B, C, G and H relate to internal audit**

2   **B**

The internal audit also makes recommendations for the achievement of company objectives.

C is the role of the external auditors.

3   **B**

Segregation of roles may happen to identify frauds that have occurred in some circumstances, but its primary role is to prevent fraud as it would require collusion between multiple members of staff. Statement two is correct – general controls are designed to ensure that IT systems are operating correctly.

CHAPTER 17

1   **A**

The third prerequisite is dishonesty. An honest employee is unlikely to commit fraud even if given the opportunity and motive.

2   **D**

An example is a two-year lease of a building. Under current accounting practices you do not have to show the asset or the related obligation to pay the rental amounts on the balance sheet. However, you have the use of the asset and a contractual obligation to pay the rentals.

3   **C**

The Nominated Officer is responsible for investigating any large or unusual transactions. They would only be reported to the appropriate authorities if there were sufficient grounds for suspicion.

4   **C**

Management authorisation will increase the chances of fraudulent and inaccurate payments being made to non-existent payables.

CHAPTER 18

1   (a)   (i)   **A4**

              (ii)   **A1**

              (iii)   **A2**

              (iv)   **A3**

       (b)   (i)   **C**

              (ii)   **B**

              (iii)   **D**

              (iv)   **A**

2   (a)   (i)   **D**

              (ii)   **A**

              (iii)   **B**

              (iv)   **C**

       (b)   **B, D, G and H are correct.**

CHAPTER 19

1 B

The personal specification is focused on the attributes a candidate needs to possess in order to fulfil the job requirements. The job description is focused on duties and responsibilities of the post, whereas job evaluation considers the worth of the job to the company and therefore how much the jobholder is to be paid.

2 B

Recruitment consultants are usually involved in the early stages of the recruitment and selection process, e.g. advising on job descriptions, designing job advertisements, screening applications and assisting with short-listing of candidates for interview. They frequently conduct the first round of interviews.

Consultants are not normally involved in deciding which of the short-listed candidates should get the job.

Statement two, however, is correct. The two other key elements of an interview are to find the best person for the job and to ensure that the candidate understands what the job is and what the career prospects are. The interviewing process also impacts on the company's image.

3 B – False

Positive discrimination is typically illegal.

4 C

'Equal opportunities' is typically required by legislation. Diversity goes beyond this and is an attempt to make the organisation truly inclusive.

CHAPTER 20

1 B

Role signs are visible indications of a role, such as styles of dress. Note that 'role definition' is not a key term in role theory.

2 B

Assertive behaviour involves direct, honest and professional communication. It is aggressive behaviour that violates another person's rights and often leads to additional conflict.

3 C

The plant role is played by a creative individual; the monitor-evaluator is good at making accurate judgements, whereas the team worker looks after the atmosphere within the team.

4 D

The fact that the group has diverse backgrounds may well prove to be an advantage as they will be able to generate a wider range of ideas and bring a variety of skills to the team, improving overall effectiveness.

CHAPTER 21

1 (a) A, E, G and H are correct.

   (b) (i) A

   (ii) B

   (iii) A

   (iv) B

2 (i) A

   (ii) B

   (iii) E

   (iv) C

CHAPTER 22

1 D

By definition.

2 C

Mentoring is an example of informal learning – which is deliberate but not highly structured. Other examples of informal learning include self-directed learning and networking.

3 D

Activists prefer to learn through doing. Reflectors prefer observational learning activities.

4 B – False

While Kolb argues that there are four stages to the learning process, they form a cycle which can be started at any stage.

CHAPTER 23

1 A

Alex has had targets set, but his manager has failed to monitor his performance through the year and provide regular feedback.

2 B

The decision to terminate an employee would not normally be taken at an annual appraisal (except under unusual circumstances).

3 A

Sarah is trying to persuade Mary that the appraisal is fair and that she should agree with her recommendations. Communication is one way.

4 B

One should divide the total number of employees leaving the organisation (or the total replacements) by the average number in the workforce.

CHAPTER 24

1   (a)   A, C, E and G are correct.

     (b)   (i)   C

            (ii)   A

            (iii)   B

            (iv)   A

2   D

     This task will become more urgent over the next few weeks

3   B

     The goal of a PDP is to develop the individual themselves.

4   A

     Suppression involves the manager threatening the conflicting
     employees with punishment, reduction involves negotiating a
     settlement and resolution involves solving the problem that is the root
     cause of the conflict.

CHAPTER 25

1   D

     A grapevine network connects people who have a common interest
     and usually circulates rumours and gossip.

     Also, Research has established that only 10% of the message is
     communicated through words, the other 90% is transmitted through
     non-verbal communication.

2   B – False

     Barriers to communication also include anything that stops
     information from being understood by its recipients or being acted
     upon in the way intended.

     Barriers to communication can be caused by many things, e.g. 'noise'
     (message confused by extraneous matters); difference in education
     levels; overload (too much information); distortion of information by
     the receiver; use of technical or professional language.

3   B

     Lateral is another name for horizontal communication, within a
     committee people from different functions come together to present
     their view on an issue.

4   B

     The all-channel is the most likely process to reach the best decision.

5   A –True

     Information overload is one of the barriers to communication; it makes
     it difficult to prioritise.

Index

Index

Index

Index

Index

Index